A SENSE FOR HUMANITY

A SENSE FOR HUMANITY

The Ethical Thought of Raimond Gaita

EDITED BY CRAIG TAYLOR WITH MELINDA GRAEFE

© Copyright 2014
All rights reserved. Apart from any uses permitted by Australia's Copyright Act 1968, no part of this book may be reproduced by any process without prior written permission from the copyright owners. Inquiries should be directed to the publisher.

Monash University Publishing
Building 4, Monash University
Clayton, Victoria 3800, Australia
www.publishing.monash.edu

Monash University Publishing brings to the world publications which advance the best traditions of humane and enlightened thought.

Monash University Publishing titles pass through a rigorous process of independent peer review.

http://www.publishing.monash.edu/books/sh-9781922235459.html

Series: Philosophy

Design: Les Thomas

National Library of Australia Cataloguing-in-Publication entry:

Title:	A sense for humanity : the ethical thought of Raimond Gaita / editors, Craig Taylor with Melinda Graefe
ISBN:	9781922235459
Series:	Philosophy.
Notes:	Includes bibliographical references
Subjects:	Gaita, Raimond, 1946---Criticism and interpretation.
	Ethics.
	Philosophical anthropology.
	Philosophy.
Other Authors/ Contributors:	Taylor, Craig, 1963- editor;
	Graefe, Melinda Kathleen, 1972- editor.
Dewey Number:	170.92

Printed in Australia by Griffin Press an Accredited ISO AS/NZS 14001:2004 Environmental Management System printer.

The paper this book is printed on is certified against the Forest Stewardship Council ® Standards. Griffin Press holds FSC chain of custody certification SGS-COC-005088. FSC promotes environmentally responsible, socially beneficial and economically viable management of the world's forests.

CONTENTS

Introduction vii
Rai Gaita's Ethical Thought
Craig Taylor

The Track xvii
Nick Drake

Romulus and *After Romulus*

1. Raimond Gaita, *After Romulus*. 3
   J.M. Coetzee

2. Rai Gaita's *Mont Blanc* 8
   A New Poem Imagined
   Barry Hill

3. Sophie's Choice 28
   Alex Miller

4. *Romulus, My Father* and the Australian Literary Imaginary. 37
   Brigitta Olubas

5. The Time of Friendship. 50
   Helen Pringle

Politics, Law and Society

6. A Political Friendship 63
   Robert Manne

7. International Law's Common Humanity,
   or Are Pirates Necessary? 73
   Gerry Simpson

8. 'Even the Most Foul Criminals Are Owed Unconditional
   Respect'. 85
   The Ethical Lawyer and the Ideal of Respect
   Steven Tudor

9. On Raimond Gaita's 'Assimilationist Multiculturalism'...........99
   Geoffrey Brahm Levey

10. A Crucible of Compassion, a Harbinger of Hope...............113
    Reflections on Child Protection and the Vulnerable Child
    Dorothy Scott

Ethics

11. Moral Philosophy in the Midst of Things....................125
    Christopher Cordner

12. Moral Thought and Ethical Individuality....................141
    Craig Taylor

13. The Power of Negative Thinking............................152
    Remorse and Blame
    Miranda Fricker

   Afterword..165
   Anne Manne and Raimond Gaita in Conversation

   List of Contributors 196

   Bibliography 199

INTRODUCTION
Rai Gaita's Ethical Thought

Craig Taylor

Raimond Gaita is a moral philosopher. At the same time, he stands apart from the mainstream in moral philosophy. There are two aspects to this: one concerns Rai's distinctive conception of what moral philosophy might be, a conception that poses a challenge to the prevailing orthodoxy in moral philosophy, at least in what is termed 'contemporary analytic philosophy.' As the renowned (analytic) philosopher Alasdair MacIntyre puts the point commenting on Rai's first book, *Good and Evil: An Absolute Conception*, the book 'puts the rest of us to the question by its account of what it is to have a serious sense of good and evil and of how moral philosophy ought to proceed.' But precisely this way of articulating the challenge to moral philosophy points to the significance of Rai's ethical thought beyond the academy. For reflection on good and evil is not a narrow or technical question for moral philosophers. On the contrary, such reflection is part and parcel of our understanding of the meaning or significance of human life, of what it is to be human. At least so Rai argues, or seeks to remind us. Which brings me to the second aspect signalled above. Partly because of Rai's distinctive conception of moral philosophy, with its focus on good and evil and a range of other critical concepts that rarely feature if at all in works of moral philosophy – including sentimentality, remorse and love in its various forms – his thought has had an individual influence outside of academic philosophy. I say 'individual' for of course Rai's isn't the only public voice in philosophy; a range of other philosophers have in different ways influenced people outside their discipline including through their contributions to public ethical debates. But it strikes me that Rai's thinking and influence have been of a different order or kind than the broad run of his moral philosophical peers. Readers of *Good and Evil* will be familiar with Rai's suggestion that there are no 'moral experts' in the way that there can be experts in other fields, like climate science and medicine – and this is something that separates him from many philosophers working in what has been called 'practical ethics.' But Rai's thought and influence, what is distinctive about it, is hardly captured merely by that point and contrast. What is distinctive about it, and why it is important, is really something that, from many different directions, each of the essays here collected attempt to explore.

At this point then I need to say two things about this collection. Firstly, that it is not primarily concerned with examining Rai's contribution to contemporary moral philosophy as an academic discipline – significant though this is. Rather, while the collection includes contributions by philosophers, the aim of the collection is to survey the influence of Rai's ethical thought in the broadest sense. Here it is fair to say that the one work by Rai that has had the widest reach, and the one that will be for readers of this collection perhaps most immediately known, is Rai's renowned biography *Romulus, My Father*, and several essays in this collection, as I note below, focus on this important work. But *Romulus* is not the only of Rai's works that seeks to address a wide audience outside academic philosophy. In various other books and essays over many years Rai has added his distinctive ethical voice to a range of moral and political debates both in Australia and beyond. One notable aspect of Rai's ethical thought is the way in which it has engaged a range of thinkers in *other* academic disciplines, including Politics, Law, Literature and Social Work to name just a few, and a good number of the essays collected here are concerned with assessing the influence of Rai's thought in this respect.

The second thing I need to say about this collection concerns its origins and form – and they are connected. The collection emerges out of a conference of the same name held by Flinders University at which the contributors to this collection presented papers – in most cases earlier drafts of the essays collected here. But this was hardly a typical academic conference. By this I mean not only that it was a genuinely interdisciplinary conference (of course there are other such conferences), but also that many of the presenters have been influenced by Rai's thought not just in significant but quite often deeply personal ways. This point records an important fact about Rai's ethical thought; that for Rai ethical thought makes certain personal demands on us, specifically, that it requires that we be willing to participate in a conversation with others in which they and we might call (or recall) each other to a kind of seriousness. That seriousness is characterised in part for Rai by the fact that what one has to say in ethical matters is inseparable from the manner of its expression; thus various human failings, such as sentimentality, cynicism and even world weariness are not just obstacles to thinking well here, they are the *ways* our thought fails. The kind of call to seriousness within conversation that Rai envisages involves, he says, 'being present, in a disciplined sobriety, towards their partner' in conversation. Thus it is no

INTRODUCTION

coincidence that several of the contributors to this collection note in their essays the ways in which they have been influenced by Rai simply through *talking* with him, through conversation, one surmises, of precisely the kind that is envisaged by Rai's remark. The form of this collection then seeks to retain as much of the personal tone of the original presentations as possible, including in many instances the more personal reference to 'Rai' – who was himself present throughout the conference.

Turning to the contributions themselves, we have chosen to organise them thematically, dividing the book into three parts. The first part, entitled '*Romulus* and *After Romulus*,' includes contributions on or related to *Romulus, My Father* and Rai's more recent set of biographical essays, *After Romulus*. The second part, entitled 'Politics, Law and Society,' includes contributions on the influence of Rai's thought in disciplines related to those broad areas, while the third part, entitled 'Ethics,' includes contributions by philosophers that deal with aspects Rai's ethical thought from the perspective of philosophy, but in a way that is accessible to non-philosophers. The collection concludes with an afterword involving Anne Manne and Rai in conservation. The very first contribution to this collection, however, is a new poem for Rai written by Nick Drake entitled 'The Track'. Drake's poem tells a story of the 'rare adjacenies' that brought together the people who adapted *Romulus, My Father* from book to film. Drake recalls the mystery of what he calls the 'strange mediumship' of 'transposing life from memory to plot' and celebrates his friendship with Rai that came out of their creative collaboration, a friendship which is as enduring as the track, the film, the hills around Frogmore, the memories and resonances evoked by all of these associations.

Part one begins with an introductory piece from J.M. Coetzee, which in its original form was presented at the launch of *After Romulus* during the conference. As Coetzee notes, the core of *After Romulus* is a long essay entitled 'An Unassuageable Longing,' a tribute by Rai to his mother, Christine. As he also says, this essay is the most personal and poignant of the five essays in *After Romulus*, and a number of other contributors go on to reflect on the great personal honesty of this essay and the bravery involved in tackling such deep and painful memories. But Coetzee's brief remarks about *After Romulus* function also as a springboard to reflecting on Rai's writing more generally, though with a focus on the earlier *Romulus, My Father*. As Coetzee says, and as the reader will be able to glean from many other contributions to this collection, Rai's ethical thought is concerned with 'embodied values,' with 'truths that are tested not on the page but in the world.' And the most conspicuous embodiment of the values that would go on to inform Rai's life is of course his father, Romulus Gaita. Rai's gift as a writer involves his ability to convey those values, witnessed in his father, to us as his readers. But how, Coeztee asks, is that done? It is not simply a matter of writing from the heart. But nor, contrary to Plato, can one convey the kinds of truths we are concerned with here merely through the use of dialectic shorn of all rhetoric or artful composition. There is, as Coetzee notes, 'no zero degree of literature, no expression that comes without rhetorical (stylistic) dressing.' Rai, I am sure, would agree. As already noted, a distinctive (and at least for other philosophers challenging) aspect of Rai's philosophy is the claim that what we might convey to others is inseparable from the manner of its expression; in ethical understanding at least there is just no doing away with literature or poetry.

Barry Hill offers us what he calls a 'sketch-map' towards a poem that might 'do justice to the concerns that inhabit Rai's work.' As with Coetzee, Hill's reflections on this imagined poem emphasise again the way in which for Rai ethical thought must be embodied. Hill's own way with this idea is to explore a kind of continuity between Rai's love for philosophy and his love of mountain climbing. As Hill sees it, while in one sense by choosing philosophy over climbing as a career '[o]ne love had [for Rai] to surrender to the other,' in another sense they are still together at least imaginatively in Rai's life. Thus Hill's imagined poem must express for us how the mountain – what it requires of us, its testing of us, of our character – 'helps define what is serious in philosophy,' at least as Rai conceives of it. But the poem is about more than that. What pervades Hill's reflections on this imagined poem is Rai's raw and unflinching honesty about his own childhood experiences, and again in particular about his suffering in relation to the loss of his mother as expressed in *After Romulus*. It is then a very personal essay; it is in the end a healing poem that Hill imagines, offered by one friend out of care and concern for another.

Alex Miller's essay too is a kind of act of friendship; it is a 'personal reflection on Rai and our friendship,' at the same time as looking at the effect on him of *Romulus* and Rai's later essay on his mother in *After Romulus*. The essay's title alludes to the origin of this friendship, orchestrated by Sophie Halakas, the owner of the local fruit shop in Castlemaine where both Rai and Miller buy fruit and vegetables. While the thought of contacting Rai is at first intimidating for Miller, in the end Sophie proves more so. The friendship that ensues though is not quite as Miller expects; not so much a matter of agreeing on social and moral questions as a shared love of physical activity, of shovelling gravel and loading a ute with firewood. But it is also

INTRODUCTION

a matter Miller says 'of having been admitted to a special love of country,' the country of Rai's childhood so intimately connected with both 'his love and admiration for his father' and 'no less deeply ... his longing to reconnect the broken threads of his love for his mother.' Christine in *Romulus*, Miller notes, is the 'great absence of the story, the poignant presence of her despair and loss.' Only later, in the final essay in *After Romulus*, 'An Unassuageable Longing,' was Rai able to write about Christine; to write about her, but, as Miller wonderfully puts it, with 'the courage to find that the truth,' the truth about Christine, 'may not be available' to him.

Brigitta Olubas is concerned to ask as a literary critic: what kind of book is *Romulus*? Crucial for Rai is the fact that *Romulus* should, as he has put it 'bear witness to ... the values that defined my father's moral identity.' But it might now be asked: are not truth and literature, here the literary qualities of memoir, at odds with each other? Not so Olubas suggests; rather, 'it is the work of memoir to bring them compellingly together.' In the first part of her essay Olubas considers how this happens in the case of *Romulus* and the possible implications of this for what she calls the 'Australian literary imaginary – the domain within which we read and apprehend the literary.' While in the second part she goes on to consider in relation to this particular memoir and the essay 'An Unassuageable Longing,' another aspect of memoir more generally; that is, 'its significance as a form of writing in response to death.'

In her contribution Helen Pringle reflects on the nature of friendship, and in particular on 'friendship as a particular form of relation to time,' a kind of power over time in the sense of an 'encircling tenderness towards the world,' that we might think of as a kind of eternity. To understand the motivation for such a view of friendship, one needs to consider the starting point for Pringle's essay; Rai's claim in *Romulus* to know what friendship is through the example of the friendship between Romulus and Hora. A problem for Pringle – and for us – is that while this example posits friendship – in line with classical conceptions – as a moral relation, to various contemporary thinkers friendship is not a moral good nor does it require moral goodness. Pringle's response to it suggests that something of the classical conception may be recovered for us when we consider the lastingness of friendship as a moral relation, as apposed to friendships based merely on pleasure of advantage. So she says, the 'very duration of friendship over time grants a glimpse of the power of eternity.' This sense of eternity, and the way in which friendship may enable us to withstand the loss of friends, then 'becomes a practice of the good life and saves us from despair.'

The first essay of part two by Robert Manne also concerns friendship, though much more concretely; it is an account of Manne's long and deep friendship with Rai. Or rather of one persistent strand of that friendship in the form of a shared political vision, what Manne calls their 'political friendship.' Their political friendship might be summed up by saying that each of them had by the time they graduated from the University of Melbourne 'instinctively associated ourselves with the tradition of thought we have since come to call left-wing anti-communism.' While committed to a 'democratic but genuinely egalitarian socialism,' each recoiled from the radical attack on autonomy and the dignity of the individual that had been perpetrated by *both* the extreme right, in the form of the Nazi German state, *and* the extreme left, in the form of the Soviet Union under Stalin. Of particular significance for the shared worldview relevant to their political friendship are judgments concerning the Holocaust; judgments themselves informed for each in part through reflecting on Hannah Arendt's essay *Eichmann in Jerusalem*, about the trial in Jerusalem of Adolf Eichmann, one of the chief agents of the Holocaust, and the idea she introduces of a crime against humanity. Manne's essay then is a unique window on the origins and evolution of Rai's moral and political thought.

As Gerry Simpson notes in his contribution, the idea mentioned above of a crime against humanity occupies an 'equivocal place in the history of international law.' Taking as his starting point Rai's reflection on Eichmann and the Nuremberg Trials, Simpson's essay considers two ways in which the idea of humanity has been deployed in international law. On the one hand humanity as it is used in justifying humanitarian interventions against groups and individuals *excluded* from humanity; Cicero's pirates or 'enemies of mankind.' On the other hand, that idea of humanity, articulated by Rai in his essay 'A Common Humanity' and in other places, through which we might identify a kind of harm, as Simpson puts it, 'to our collective flourishing.' A kind of harm that gets its clearest expression in the attempt of the Nazi's to abolish the very concept of humanity through their programme to systematically destroy the Jewish people.

Steven Tudor's essay too concerns Rai's reflections on Eichmann, as mediated by the essay by Arendt, though not in relation to international law but in relation to an idea Rai takes to be internal to our system of criminal justice; that 'no criminals are so foul that they may be denied justice.' In the context of Arendt's essay this idea is manifest by the attitude of the presiding judge, Justice Landau, at Eichmann's trial. While the prosecutor wanted to turn this event into a show trial, Landau resisted this; even Eichmann is owed

INTRODUCTION

justice for his own sake as a human being. This idea, which Rai has described as 'one of the sublime features of our legal system,' is for him, as Tudor notes, an instance of the broader principle that all human beings, even the foulest criminals, are owed unconditional respect. Tudor's essay is an investigation of what this sublime aspect of the law might mean for individual lawyers; how might this aspect of the law be manifest in the practice and ethics of those who are charged with maintaining the institution of the criminal law?

The remaining two essays of part two are concerned not so much with the relevance of Rai's thought to law as to social policy. Geoffrey Levey's essay examines Rai's contribution to recent debates about Australian multi-culturalism; what Rai has described as his 'assimilationist multiculturalism.' Levey accepts that Rai's position provides a 'compelling answer' to those conservatives who worry that Australian multiculturalism threatens the role the Anglo-Celtic inheritance of Australia quite properly plays in helping to define the nation, at the same time as he accepts that leftist attempts to define the nation merely 'in terms of civic values and observing the rights and obligations of citizenship,' are neither desirable or even possible. Nevertheless, Levey suggests that Rai's account of what Australian multiculturalism stands for is 'overly modest and conservative.' Thus according to Levey, while Rai, drawing on his own migrant experience, focuses on the historical goodwill and forbearance of the Anglo-Celtic majority in extending liberties and opportunities to migrants, multiculturalism policy in Australia in fact refers to the *right* of all Australians, including new migrants, not only to the same liberties and opportunities as the dominant culture but more specifically 'to observe one's own cultural background within the law.' Thus the real frame for multicultural policy in Australia is not one of tolerance by the dominant culture but of the rights of those outside of it.

Dorothy Scott begins her essay by noting how *Romulus* resonated with her experience as a social worker with women who had suffered serious mental illness following childbirth. While in that context Scott had focussed on 'nurturing the mother-child relationship and the mother's capacity to respond to the needs of her child,' she had, in line with orthodox thinking, envisaged the work of child protection as ultimately a question of human rights. Rai, she goes on to say, challenged her on this orthodoxy by asking why child protection is a matter of human rights and why *ultimately* so. Her essay is her answer to Rai's challenge. While child protection is partly a matter of human rights it is, Scott now thinks, ultimately about 'compassion and responding to the child as an emotional being.' But by 'emotional being' Scott does not have in mind some theoretical perspective; rather she means the 'lived experience of the individual child,' the inner world as she otherwise puts it of a particular vulnerable child. Part of the power of *Romulus* for Scott then is Rai's gift for illuminating for the reader the inner life of the boy that he was. As Scott concludes, one thing for child protection workers to recognise about the inner world of vulnerable children, children for example whose parents suffer severe substance abuse or mental illness, is the need as Rai has put it for such children not only to be loved but *'to love their parents without shame.'*

The three essays that comprise part three are all by philosophers. While the aspect of Rai's ethical thought discussed by each varies, collectively they go some way to providing an account of what is distinctive in Rai's work in moral philosophy for interested readers outside of academic philosophy. Chris Cordner focuses on the way in which examples or, as this may be more helpfully put, narratives feature in Rai's work. Of course, and as Cordner notes, many philosophers use examples in their work, but predominantly just to illustrate some thesis that is 'already determined.' In Rai's work, by contrast, examples or narratives do not merely illustrate some moral thesis, something already clearly understood. On the contrary, for Rai the moral significance of the narrative, what *is* to be understood, 'emerges only in one's responsiveness to it.' The picture of moral thought or reflection suggested here provides a challenge to a still dominant view of moral philosophy as a kind of disinterested rational inquiry according to which moral understanding is only properly achieved by abstracting from our everyday lives and the particular narratives through which we make sense of them.

Craig Taylor notes what he takes to be two characteristic features of Rai's ethical thought; firstly, the importance for Rai that we be 'present' in what we say on moral matters, and secondly, that as Rai has put it, the meaning of what we say may not be 'extractable from the manner of its disclosure.' As Taylor says in his gloss on this second characteristic, Rai's suggestion is that in moral matters we sometimes understand what another has to say to us through being moved by what they say in specific ways. But, and here is the first characteristic, for Rai that power to move another depends on our being present in what we say to them. Taylor's essay then examines this important idea in Rai's work; as Taylor sees it, being present in Rai's sense in what we say to another is for one's particular life, what one has made of it, to reveal something of the 'moral contours of human life and the ethical possibilities that that may indicate.' Here, again, we can see how Rai's work challenges the dominant picture of moral thought and understanding noted above.

INTRODUCTION

Miranda Fricker in her contribution starts by noting in a similar vein the way in which Rai has exposed the inability of moral theorising to adequately account for our sense of the moral significance of our actions in an important range of cases. Further, Fricker along with Rai holds that one important reason for this failure is the conception of morality that is so often assumed here; one that holds that moral responsibility is exclusively about praise and blame. Against this conception, as Fricker notes, Rai has defended a conception of morality in which moral responsibility is not tied to the idea of being praise- or blame-worthy, indeed one in which one need not find fault in another at all. Fricker shares with Rai a desire to loosen the connection between moral responsibility and praise and blame, however she also thinks that there remains an important role for blame in our moral relations with others. Like Rai, Fricker accepts that blame can involve a kind of objectionable 'finger pointing,' nevertheless she thinks there is room, and that Rai should leave room, for what she calls 'communicative blame,' a style of blame that continues to hold the wrongdoer welcome as a partner in conversation in which they might respond to the charge against them.

As a final contribution to the collection Rai agreed to answer a series of questions from Anne Manne, who also participated in the conference from which the collection arises. Manne's questions are both detailed and highly perceptive. As Rai tells us at the outset, they were extraordinarily challenging for him to answer. The three questions and answers presented here deal with some of the most significant moral ideas and themes that have informed, that are in different ways threaded through, all of Rai's work: of the influence of Plato and the idea of truthfulness as a 'spiritual demeanour not to falsify;' of all that is involved in seeing the full humanity of another, and in the case of the most seriously afflicted the difficulty of that, and the wondrousness of the kind of saintly love that is able to reveal it; and related to all this how our understanding of what is at issue is played out in what Rai has called 'the realm of meaning.' But what is most distinctive in this conversation is Manne's pressing Rai on his relation to psychology. Rai's answer to this question takes us to the origins of his decision to turn from the study of psychology to philosophy as an undergraduate and to the reasons for his resistance, inchoate at first, to various forms of psychological and philosophical reductionism.

There are a number of people I would like to thank for their help in producing this collection. Firstly, I thank my co-editor Melinda Graefe. The contributions to this collection are extraordinarily diverse, ranging over numerous academic disciplines and writing forms. Melinda's expertise as a literary scholar and poetry editor, so very different to my own expertise as a philosopher, has been invaluable in meeting the unique editorial challenges that this work presented. Secondly, I thank the Faculty of Education, Humanities and Law at Flinders University – and in particular the Executive Dean of Faculty, Richard Maltby – for the generous grant that made both the original conference and this collection possible. I would also like to thank Molly Murn for proofreading several contributions to this collection. Finally, and here I believe I speak for my contributors as well, I would like to thank Rai for what he has variously offered us, in friendship, conversation, and through the moral depth and honesty of his thought and writing.

THE TRACK

Nick Drake

Rai, you took me twice to where this started;
both of us with jet lag, I recall;

first, at high noon, we walked along the track
in your book, in my head, now real at last;

but where the house had been, an empire of Scotch thistles
a metre high had conquered the old place –

you found a door handle, a last survival
of a home not much bothered by doors, and held it up

smiling for my camera; and anyway,
the door was gone, the walls disappeared,

the temporary box of the farmhouse,
plank floors, kerosene stove, tables, lamp

no more; only the summer heat crackled on
like an old radio approximately tuned

to a desolate wavelength – or so it seemed to me.
Buzzing flies. Corrugated air …

So you bought me back in the evening, the light
transforming and transcending – and then I got it,

the beauty of the land, pure distances,
Romulus strolling down the hill of wheat,

his hand brushing the surface, Christina
there again at the end of day … the three of you

walking the track together before dark –
or so I'd figure it, as if we might

A SENSE FOR HUMANITY

have passed them on our way back to the ute –
as if the doors between the years had fallen

open, and our voices lightly carried
in small exchanges on the ghostly track …

How then to figure the strange mediumship
of what happened next? The film house reproduced

forty years and fifty yards away;
the script, the set, the actors and the action

surrounded by the trailers, the generator,
the lighting rig, the winter fields, the cold?

A butane canister and metal rod
perforated like a flute conjured up

the shimmer of summer heat along the track.
A huge lamp called the *Sun* stood for the sun

blazing on a grey day; the cockatoo
fled into the trees, would not come down

to do its scene, like the original Jack;
another Orloff ran along the track;

Romulus and Hora and Christina
in character, take after take, scenes from your life

to the book, to the script, to these performances –
and a marvellous boy to play you as a boy –

the pity, and the sorrow, and the joy
seen through his eyes; seen on his calm face.

Such rare adjacencies that brought us all
together in the struggle of the story –

the exigencies of transposing life from memory
to plot, condensing summers and winters,

THE TRACK

journeys to and fro, discovering a beginning,
shaping acts, puzzling out an ending ...

rollie smoke, Eskimo pies, and silences ...
and what was lost along the way, and who

the cruel absolute of narrative
could not accommodate – as we strove

to shape lost time, to let lost time shape us ...
And then one baking February afternoon

you took me to the Maryborough graveyard;
I stood by my shadow, paying my respects

to your mother and father, Hora and Mitru; and that light
blazing down on me was necessary –

A different light transmutes these images,
24 frames per second, in the dark

as we sit together at a matinee,
in the velvet cave of the quiet cinema;

a large old-fashioned light bulb, its scribbled
filament incandescent against the dark

swings in slow motion, like a wand, revealing
a working man's closed hand cupping something:

darkness, then another swing of the light:
a boy's face wondering, watching his father –

darkness again: then the pendulum of light
reveals this time the face of Romulus

passing the lightbulb back and forth
over something held in the palm of his hand:

frozen bees. Darkness ... another swing of light;
'Papi, papi ... nothing's happening ...'

A SENSE FOR HUMANITY

'Just wait, Raimond. They think it's the sun ...'
Romulus cups the mystery in both hands,

shakes it like dice, offers it to Rai
who blows on them for luck; then Romulus

opens the door, a rectangle of strong light,
and casts a handful of bees free into the air ...

Rai, dear friend, sooner rather than later,
when the evening light comes to pass, let's walk

the track again together; both houses gone now;
just the wheat fields gold and silver, and the hills

unchanging in their time; let's walk the track
with Yael and Edward in our present tense;

let's walk the track in the beauty of that light,
talking in the company of our long shadows

past where your mother stands with her small suitcase,
returning to the place where she tries to belong –

and now a boy comes running up to meet her –
Raimond Gaita, from Frogmore, Victoria.

Romulus and *After Romulus*

Chapter 1

RAIMOND GAITA, *AFTER ROMULUS*

J.M. Coetzee

Romulus, My Father reads like one of those books that miraculously write themselves, that use their author simply as a medium to be born into the world. Producing a sequel to it, after a gap of thirteen years, was always going to be a hard task. Would the second book not emerge from the womb a pale copy of its handsome, admired older brother? The very name *After Romulus* suggests an afterthought.

At the core of *After Romulus* lies the tribute that Raimond Gaita had not been able to write when he was writing the tribute to his father – had not been able to write because, as we learn, he had not at that time been able to master the feelings that memories of his mother summoned up, or, to put it in more writerly terms, had not been able to find the voice in which to speak that tribute.

The tribute emerges, after these many years, in the form of a long essay called 'An Unassuageable Longing,' the most personal and most poignant of the five essays making up the book. Along with another piece, entitled 'A Summer-Coloured Humanism' and devoted to the later lives of personages we meet with in *Romulus, My Father*, it is given a narrative form. Of the remaining essays, two are denser in texture, more recognisably philosophical in their concerns, though not difficult or abstruse – Gaita's writing, including his academic writing, has always been a model of clarity. All the pieces making up the book address moral issues of the kind that must form part of any examined life, issues to which the young Raimond Gaita was introduced by his father and his father's friend Hora back in the 1950s.

One of the characteristics of Gaita as a philosopher is his concern for embodied values, for ethical truths that are tested not on the page but in the world. It is not because he preaches certain values but because he embodies them that the unlettered blacksmith Romulus Gaita comes to serve as a lifelong moral compass to his son and, via his son, to us his readers.

Because of his concern with embodied truth, Gaita strikes one as a thinker of a rather Christian stamp, even though, in *After Romulus*, he explicitly refrains from invoking the Christian theological tradition and what that tradition has to say about embodied truth, the word made flesh. Indeed, his two good men, Romulus and Hora, strike one as virtuous pagans more than followers of Christ.

Gaita also clearly owes a great deal to Greece – to Greek literature even more than to Greek systematic philosophy. The confluence in him of Greek and Christian traditions is attested by his fellow-feeling with Simone Weil, who brings together Judaeo-Christian mysticism and a tragic, Greek sense of life. In Romulus the father these traditions sometimes come into conflict: for instance, an archaic ideal of male honour demands that he repudiate the wife who has betrayed him, whereas the goodness of his soul – a goodness that was simply not part of the archaic Greek repertoire – leads him to pity her and help her.

The historical Romulus Gaita was born an ethnic Romanian in a village that now falls into the autonomous province of Vojvodina, part of modern-day Serbia. In Vojvodina Romulus learned the blacksmith's trade before, in 1939, taking the momentous step of leaving home and going to Germany to seek his fortune. In Germany he was soon drafted into a forced labour brigade. After the war he married a German girl, became a father, and with his new family emigrated to Australia.

Where did Romulus Gaita acquire his unshakeable sense of what is right and what is wrong, his intuitions of what constitutes good for a human being and what does not? In Vojvodina? Are folk in the remoter Balkan countryside in touch with elemental values in a way that more advanced, more civilised Europeans have ceased to be? *Romulus, My Father* does not pose this question directly; but other Balkan people from Romulus's homeland appear in the book, and in respect of morality they are as mixed a bag as people from anywhere else in the world. Some, like Hora, are on a par with Romulus. Others, like the family of his betrothed bride Lydia, are decidedly not.

Romulus and Hora adhere to, or represent, a vision of what human priorities ought to be, and thus a vision of what we can call a noble life. Romulus's code of nobility strikes me as Greek. Furthermore, insofar as it is less an ideal code than a way of living in the world, it strikes me as pre-Platonic and indeed pre-philosophical. I would call it Homeric; and the fact that unlettered men like Romulus and Hora were following a Homeric code in the twentieth century suggests that the code they lived by had been passed from generation to generation for millennia.

CHAPTER 1

Nonetheless, Romulus and Hora also strike one as lonely men, poignantly lonely, particularly in the Australian phase of their lives. They stand for manual skills and honest workmanship of a kind that during their lifetime was being eclipsed by shoddy factory production accompanied by disdain for manual labour. At a more abstract level they are being consigned to history by individualism, instrumentalised social relations, and moral relativity – in a word, by modernity. Hence the ambivalence with which they are regarded by their Australian-born country neighbours, who are in their own way also on the cusp of a changing world. Gaita subjects this ambivalence to a fine analysis: it turns out to be a peculiarly Australian mix of suspicion and respect, of cultural condescension and egalitarian engagement.

* * *

Raimond Gaita is admired as a writer, and with good reason. One of the things commonly said about him is that he goes straight to the heart of the matter. This is exactly what Gaita himself says about his father. One of the lessons his father teaches him, not by precept but by example, is to brush aside the inessential. The language of *Romulus, My Father* enacts the swift passage of the arrow-like intellect as it pierces through what is unimportant and strikes its target. (A second telling metaphor from the book is the unerring aim of the blacksmith Romulus as he hammers the molten metal on his anvil.)

In the swift, direct address of his writing, his unerring aim, Gaita reminds one above all of Leo Tolstoy. What is true of Gaita's prose is true of Tolstoy's too, particularly in Tolstoy's later work. I quote from 'The Death of Ivan Ilyich:'

> From that moment began a three-day ceaseless howling, which was so terrible that it was impossible to hear it without horror even through two closed doors ... [Ivan Ilyich] realized that he was lost, that there was no return, that the end had come, the final end ...
>
> 'Oh! Ohh! Oh!' he howled in various intonations. He began by howling, 'I won't!' and so went on howling on the letter O.
>
> For all three days ... he was thrashing about in that black sack into which an invisible, invincible force was pushing him. He struggled as one condemned to death struggles in the executioner's hands, knowing he cannot save himself ... (Tolstoy 2009, 89–90).

Russian literary criticism of the early twentieth century was haunted by the question, *How did Tolstoy do it? How can one learn to write like that?* The energies of the Russian Formalist critics, Viktor Shklovsky in particular, were deployed to the task of cracking the secret of Tolstoyan style, of breaking it down into its component elements of immediacy of address, swiftness of rhythm, reinvigoration of metaphor, alienation of viewpoint, simplification of syntax. Practise each of these component elements individually like the individual lines in a fugue, the Formalists in effect said, then practise bringing them together, and perhaps you will find yourself beginning to write like Tolstoy, with the accent of truth.

There is something wrong-headed and indeed wrong with this approach to Tolstoy, but pinning down what is wrong with it is not as simple as it might seem. If Tolstoy's account of the psychological and spiritual development of a man dying of cancer strikes us as true, it is not because we have been through what Ivan Ilyich undergoes and can confirm that he represents the process correctly. A more cautious judgment would be that Tolstoy represents the process plausibly, convincingly. Alternatively one might say that he seems to represent the process truthfully.

The project of learning to write like Tolstoy, of discovering a method that will allow one to write with the accents of truth, is closely related to a question that preoccupied students of political and legal oratory in classical times: Is there a method of composition that will allow one to present falsehood in such a way that it will seem to be true; or alternatively, is there a course of study in the procedures of rhetoric that will immunise one against the falsehoods of oratory?

Clearly it is not enough to advise the writer to write from the heart, that the truth will always bear the accent of truth, whereas falsehood will be accompanied by some overtone or other that will betray its falsity. Everyday experience of the law court teaches us that even the most judicious of observers can be taken in by lies voiced with an air of sincere conviction, for who can reliably distinguish between conviction and an air of conviction? Furthermore, we have all met people who deeply and sincerely hold beliefs whose truth value is at most, to put it delicately, relative to the subject holding them. As long as we cannot draw a line between truth and sincere belief, we will be trapped in a vicious circle: a piece of writing convinces us of its truth because its author is convinced of the truth of what he writes.

Plato was all too well aware of the power of rhetoric and its dubious relations with truth. To Plato, rhetoric is a set of practices (he is not prepared to call it an art) to which he is reluctant to accord a place in the life of the

CHAPTER 1

mind. He clearly approves of the laconic Spartan who asserts that 'there is no genuine art of speaking without a grasp of truth, and there never will be,' *basta* (see *Phaedrus* 260e, 278c–d). Against rhetoric he sets dialectic, the medium of properly philosophical thinking. In a step that may seem strange to persons living in the print era, he associates rhetoric with composition and hence with the written word, while dialectic belongs with speech. Briefly, he argues that we get to the truth not by formulating our truth-claims as artfully and persuasively as we can but by subjecting our truth-claims to the cut and thrust of dialectic (*Phaedrus* 265d-266c). He is clearly suspicious of the push toward marmoreal finality, even to immortality, that is implicit in the highly wrought text.

Yet there is no escaping rhetoric, no zero degree of literature, no expression that comes without rhetorical (stylistic) dressing. Plato's very dialogues are works of high literary art, all the more persuasive because of their artistry. The same might be said of Gaita's memoirs of his childhood. They speak to the heart; very likely they come from the heart; but we would be imprudent to conclude that the vehicle that carries them from one heart to another can be ignored.

Chapter 2

RAI GAITA'S *MONT BLANC*
A New Poem Imagined

Barry Hill

The battle with the Alps: as useful as work and as uplifting as religion.

From the membership card of the Italian Alpine Club

That's what bothers me most. I can't endure seeing my suffering being reduced – being generalized – (à la Kierkegaard): it's as if it were being stolen from me.

Roland Barthes, *Mourning Diary*

In my first thirty years of life
I roamed hundreds and thousands of miles ...
Today I'm back at Cold Mountain:
I'll sleep by the creek and purify my ears.

Han-Shan, *Cold Mountain Poems* (translated by Gary Snyder)

CHAPTER 2

I

Here is a poem I dedicated to my good friend Rai Gaita. It was written after he took me to the site of his old house, the day before the premier viewing of *Romulus, My Father* in Castlemaine. It's called 'Reading on the Darkening Plain.'

In the dusk of the plains
he held his hands together palms up
each open hand the page of the book –
'I would read until there was no more light.'

Then he'd leave the veranda
go inside to light the lamp
breathe the fumes of kerosene
that singey smell that was weak heat

and light for the reading and waiting.
Eventually, across the plains, he heard
the crackling of the motorbike.
The father's head down over the handlebars

the son's still over the last page
on the road to truth … Then the soup.
Night closed in. The dog warmed him.
Outside, the moon, mother of clouds, drifted.

Now, a father, a husband
he dwells on the plains once more
reading among boulders –
books as solid as deeds, good as stone.

The house is beautifully lit
inside and out. A wood fire roars.
Under the moonless sky of the stone country
one word virtuously contests the other –

the other word, the lunar one,
sails in under the bedclothes,
reconnecting the sentences of the day.
The latest book cracks along its spine.[1]

---

[1] Hill 2008, 87.

A sorrowful poem, manifestly: Rai's sorrow, and that of the beautiful bare place, as we stood in the dusk that afternoon, and the sorrow that belongs to the film and to the book that led to it, the book itself, having come from Rai's eulogy to his father, which was interlaced, we now all know, with a complicated yearning and unresolved grief for his mother.

I was happy to have written a poem that could stand without saying too much. It's one of those poems that rests with the mood of things, and therefore not the kind of poem that could possibly do justice to the concerns that inhabit Rai's work. All I can try to offer – in the interests of love and clarity, those ancient mistresses of philosophers and poets – is a sketch-map towards such a poem. A rough sketch, necessarily, 'only a few hints,' as Whitman wrote in 'When I Read the Book' – 'a few diffused faint clews and indirections.'[2]

The intimation of the poem has been with me for some time, for reasons I should explain, not the least of which is the poetic qualities of Rai's work, as he has told me more than once he would have liked to have been a poet. Suffice to say the poem would seek to explore notions of philosophical embodiment – intellectual, moral, spiritual – a poem that bridges memoir and philosophical discourse, and which conveys what is not quite sayable otherwise because it has a music of its own.

But first let me say a few things about my sense of affinity with the physicality of Rai's lifework.

For one thing, the men in it are men like my father and my uncles. They are strong, talking, working men. They sit in singlets, smoking slowly. They roll their own. They use the same tobacco – Havelock in the green tin. It is impossible for a boy to be around them without soaking up their physical ease in the world, and picking up the respect they have for skilled manual work, for know-how, for modest work as well as modest enough talk. They are, even when they have good wives, men who can be imagined without women. They can from time to time speak chauvinistically. But this is not to say that they can actually do without women. With women they are decorous, watchful, secretly needful, and maybe, when their pride and sense of security is acutely threatened, explosive.

The physicality of Rai's Chekhovian scenes goes further. There is the landscape, obviously, and his romantic sense of its connection with the soul-states of the men and women who find themselves in it, or on it, or not of it. A similar landscape was a presence to me growing up on the lava plains

---

[2] Whitman 1973, 8.

CHAPTER 2

on the suburban edge of Melbourne, with its dryness and hard ground and hard light. When my mother left my father I stood on that ground under a clear night sky, hating my father for his stupidity. There he was sitting at the kitchen table, smoking, trying to tell me this and that about women in mid-life. It was his fault that she'd gone and why the hell did he not know it! That night I left him there and went to a party. I can still remember the electricity in my body, the bolts of grief that gave me such strength. I can remember the kitchen and the backyard of that place where I stalked about drinking Barossa Pearl and trying to pick a fight. I was fourteen. When I was about forty, the same power came back into my body when my wife and I found ourselves dealing with the Family Court over the custody of our kids. I took up karate. I know that decision kept me and possibly other people safe. When you are full of grief you need something hard, physically hard, to contend with. It's either that or lay down and die.

With regard to his own anguish as a boy Rai has until recently been strikingly reticent. He wrote his first memoir in the classic mode, letting the tragic events speak, almost, for themselves. The mode deepened our horror, aroused our anguish on his behalf, obliging us to imagine the details of the boy's experience, especially with regard to his experience of maternal love, its sexual complexity and waywardness. Rai's classic mode also suited his emotional need to continue to embrace his mother indirectly, to forgive her, if forgiveness was needed, in the light of his father's compassion for her. This narrative instinct also served to block, potentially, the readers who would judge her harshly.

That was the first book. In the second book, *After Romulus*, Rai is more declared about the felt experience of his own suffering. He makes a case for his mercurial mother under the heading of what he calls her 'romanticism.' He draws us into some aspects of how he was implicated in her physical presence. Eros enters, who had been absent in the first book, creating what I have always felt to be a blurry puritanical atmosphere. The new realism is sharp in the excruciating chapter called 'An Unassuageable Longing,' where he mentions being, in one poignantly intimate section, 'excited, frightened, resentful' (and then in another refrain, 'disturbed, anxious, hostile'). Overall, he says, the best way for us to understand his state of survival during the 'tragic' events of his early life is to think of the gruelling and deadly fight between George Foreman and Muhammad Ali. Foreman, with his terrifying strength, pounded Ali for nine rounds. Ali faced up to him in the first round and came out of that afraid for his life. He survived the fight by taking untold punishment until Foreman tired: then a few telling blows by Ali brought him down. And once he had grown up, Rai tells us, he realised that he had instinctively adopted a psychological and spiritual version of what Ali had done: 'when I was pounded by one traumatically painful event after another, I lay against the ropes.' 'In characteristic fashion,' Rai goes on, 'Ali made light of his achievement, calling his enforced strategy of lying against the ropes "rope a dope." For me it has become a morally and spiritually emblematic way of dealing with fear and suffering.'[3]

After the Family Court period of my life, I wrote a Buddhistic novel called *The Best Picture*. Its epigraph is from Wittgenstein: 'the human body is the best picture of the human soul.' There is a page that applies the idea of truth tables to the method of self-cancellation practiced in Buddhism. On the page, it was something of a conceit, but I was by then sick of trying to *think everything* through, of working things out in the head. Ideas, as such, can drive you mad; and anyway, they issue from speakers who have lives lived in bodies, with hearts that beat, more or less. This brings me to another affinity with Rai's work. It goes without saying that he is the most refined of thinkers, subtle, quiet and deeply thorough – Wittgensteinian, in some ways, but with a feeling tone that has always reminded me of G.E. Moore. We could ague about this, nuancing Rai's place in British philosophy that all too often was conducted by men in the most disembodied ways. The best, however, were always more than the inane talking heads, the *Jumpers* of Stoppard's play of that name. Wittgenstein, who was to be haunted by the suicides of two brothers, could find himself utterly desperately physical: he wrote parts of the *Tractatus* in the trenches; he left elevated cogitations at Cambridge to reach children in a village school; he went off to live stoically in the ice and snow of a fiord. Moore bound his ethics into the primal bonds of friendship, a kind of creaturely position, socially speaking.

What I want to stress is that sooner or later Rai's ideas come to rest in examples that are physical in that they involve what people *enact*. We are familiar with his golden examples of goodness, which essentially pertain to our capacity for exercising compassion without condescension. In *After Romulus*, Rai indicates, explicitly for the first time, how his experiences as a young man shaped his ethical philosophizing, its style and content, thereafter.[4] At the age of sixteen, with his childhood traumas still resounding, he took a job in a mental asylum. He tells of the nun whose unqualified love towards the patients filled him with wonder. He tells of the handful of psychiatrists

---

[3] Gaita 2011, 220-21.
[4] Gaita 2011, 49.

CHAPTER 2

who acted in the light of what they called the inalienable dignity of human beings, even those who had lost their minds. In due course, Rai would replicate and amplify examples of the good enacted in concentration camps or among the destitute of Calcutta, each case involving a meditation, on his part, on how one might deliver goodness to those who have been *abandoned* (a word he seems not to use, but which the poem will have to flesh out), or who in their hearts had something essentially sacred violated; namely, the expectation that, as Simone Weil puts it, passionately cited by Rai, 'good and not evil would not be done' to them.

Overall, good deeds are appraised less in terms of what their agents valued at the time than worthy of witness because they were a wonder to behold and seemed to embody a mystery at their heart. Of course, Rai knows the Christian teachings on love; he was after all educated at a Catholic boarding school. He notes that the West's history of saints has done much for the language of love, but because he insists on a secular account, the wonder remains a double mystery, you might say. To this continuously mysterious sphere, where love knows no bounds, as it were, he names what he calls morality as *renunciation*. By contrast, apparently, he also names another and more naturalistic notion of morality as *assertion*.[5] Here we meet the cardinal and sometimes heroic virtues of integrity, courage, nobility, and honour as they are harnessed by the concept of character. This notion of character, which is as enduring as a boulder, is no mere construct of the intellect either. As with the ethics of renunciation, it emerges as a code palpably installed in Rai as a boy sympathetically immersed in the life-stream of his father. Thus, to encounter Rai's ethics is to meet a position tenaciously held, a life affirmed and defended and which, in its golden instances, remains mysterious. As well dispossess the philosopher of these ideas as wrestle a bone from a dog. A philosopher's dog, obviously, a benighted creature deserving of admission to a higher place, a heaven, of sorts, whatever Gaita would like to call it.

I'm calling him Gaita now, the better to assert some creative distance. The poem has to work out the personal from the impersonal. And vice versa.

> *Come –*
> *this is the way*
> *of dealing with what's sacred*
> *and violated....*

---

[5] Gaita 2011, 70.

And then there is the enduring physicality of the man. At regular intervals, it seems to me, he illustrates this while doing philosophy, almost as if he must interrupt the flow of abstraction. There is, for one thing, his skillful mending of old cars and the driving of them recklessly. For another, and crucially, there is the instructive and expressive business of his rock climbing. In Victoria, Tasmania, and New Zealand, where, as he told us in *The Philosopher's Dog*, he experienced something he describes as a vision: 'Through a break in the clouds, across the valley, I saw a mountain of dramatic nobility, trailing a snow plume. Her name was Mount Christina. Moved almost to tears by her beauty, I resolved I would become a mountaineer.'[6]

Astonishingly, no mention is made of the fact that the mountain shares the name of Gaita's mother.

But there it was: the purely wondrous thing, inviting renunciation, *and* worthy of the assertion of heroic virtues.

Gaita went to England to do his doctorate, where he went climbing in Scotland and the Alps. Eventually he realised he'd have to make a choice between mountaineering and philosophy. He could not be fully serious in both professions. One love had to surrender to the other.

Yes, there is an extraordinary sweetness about this choice. And even more so if you feel they need not be apart, that they have long been together – of necessity. The mind-heart leaps. Instantly the philosophy becomes heroicised, just as the mountaineering takes on an intellectual, if not positively literary aspect – which in Europe it has long had. But with Gaita the choice was not an idle one, no mere abstraction. For years he had been mountain climbing, and the passion for that arduous activity had been coterminous with his mental work. The hard climbing did not come before the 'hard thinking' – to use one of his favourite phrases. For his definitive years in philosophy they climbed together. Not only that: they are still together, imaginatively. Much is still both absolute and precarious, as it is both classic and romantic.

Something of the new poem now looks us in the face. With regard to philosophy, the mountain helps define what is serious. The imagined poem itself must give expression to diligence and risk, to the stamina and self-exposure of extended philosophizing. Paul Klee once described drawing as taking an idea for a walk. Philosophy done with courage is taking an idea up onto a rock face. It can't not be a test of character, and, of necessity, an anguished one for a young man who has to contend with his father's

---

[6] Gaita 2002, 142.

CHAPTER 2

'*madness*' and his mother's '*badness*.' The poem will hurl these categories like lightning bolts at a cliff: the young man takes himself into the mountains because he has to find a place to put a sorrow that is grief-riddled with remorse. He must do something with it, he knows not what – perhaps a sky-burial for his mother, or for himself. Perhaps an assault on the mountain? There is test after test, self-affirming and self-punishing. What ever happens is philosophical. And totally embodied. That is to say, what ever becomes of the thinking, it is done with an ice pick.

> *Leave hard feelings back*
> *down there.*
> *Hammer your pitons in*
> *high on the rock face.*

In case you think I am exaggerating, here is a passage from *After Romulus*, in which Gaita reveals himself to be hanging by a rope in shifting weathers. I am not going to analyse it: the poem will simply put it out as a kind of natural object, with all the allusion to physical stress it employs.

> *My mother's failure to understand this aspect of my father's moral identity was not, therefore, reason to think that she was morally slack, 'a characterless woman.' But even someone who takes the Socratic perspective has only occasionally a full understanding of what is revealed to him from it. His sense of the reality of good and evil waxes and wanes. That is partly why remorse feels like a bewildered remembrance as much as a shocked realisation that anything in the world could have the kind of importance that wrongdoing can when its nature is fully exposed. Plato tells us that philosophers, by which he means lovers of wisdom, are clinging in recollection to what they have seen.*[7]

The poem became inevitable the day I fell in upon Gaita in London, about six years ago. I had been living in Rome and had spent time in the Alps. He was alone in the Bloomsbury flat, missing his wife, as I have never known a man so lovingly to miss a wife from whom he was not estranged. The upshot was that I ended up cooking for him! Meanwhile, he had something special to show me, which few others had seen. On his tiny TV we sat down and watched the final cut of *Romulus*. He was restless all the way through. The intensity of the film, seen small, is immense. The forces in it want to

---

[7] Gaita 2011, 186–87.

break out. My first thought, afterwards, was that I had seen a Russian film. I mentioned Chekhov – thinking of characters that wait in slow time in vast bare places for their fates to unfold. The film also reminded me of the furious Shakespearean stories of Stanislaw Lvov, especially his version of *Macbeth*.

After a while we settled down to look at the book I had with me. He lit up. It was a big illustrated book of that superlative place, that quintessentially sublime site, which he knew like the back of his hand. Mont Blanc, the highest peak in Europe, towers above Chamonix, a village first settled in the fifteenth century by wintry monks. Mont Blanc has a tilting, round summit, like the heave of a shoulder into the sky rather than what you would call a peak. Several glaciers descend from it, grinding down between forest and escarpment, trees that have crashed and rocks that have become rubble. Out from the hulk of Mont Blanc, among a world of snowfields, ice walls, ridges and precipices, are the Aiguilles, the sheer, red granite needles that shoot up from valley and glacier. Taken together, the white mammoth and the ecstatic spires, you are face to face with the absolute.

Such is the presence of the absolute it's impossible not to find yourself contending with several questions.

> *Is there a God?*
> *What is my value?*
> *How am I here?*
> *What is the mountain?*
> (This last question I phrase as a koan, a Zen riddle designed to help get beyond the suffering that is endemic to dualistic thinking).

A few weeks previously, no climber myself, I'd gone up one of those needles by cable car. It was the Aiguille du Midi, which has a viewing platform that feels level with the lazy white hump of Mont Blanc, innocently lit on that mid-winter afternoon.

I stepped to the edge of the platform and looked down.

Later, that night, as the sun left the mountain and its terrible weight seemed to slip into the unconscious, I tried to tell my diary what had happened.

Down I had wished to go. All the way down, and with a snow-dive out over the valley, before falling like a stone to my death.

Such was my swoon, the bliss of the fall.

I described that long instant in full, and sent it to Gaita.

That's how I felt! he exclaimed, as soon as we met.

CHAPTER 2

He'd been thrilled to hear I was going to Chamonix, where he'd spent so many years climbing up and scrambling around, making a life on those needles and out on the steep slopes you can see along the valley. Not climbing mountain peaks, I should add. He has always eschewed the competitive collection of peaks in favour of the pleasure of reaching the zones that had long ravished him from a distance. Climbing to inhabit Beauty, you might say, while keeping a foothold amid Terror. Physically philosophizing the Sublime.

From up there you can see how the world was made! he said.

And you will be able to walk on La Mer de Glace! (the glacier that comes down into the village one peak away from Mont Blanc).

Start climbing
with its terrible white
shoulder over your shoulder.

The Sea of Ice below you
the ice-pick in
your frozen hand

and with each step
a secular hymn:
Father, Mother, Fall.

Climb until
you are frost.
Gain in crystal weight ...

II

La Mer de Glace is receding these days, but when Shelley arrived in the summer of 1816, in tow with his beloved Mary, who was carrying an early draft of her novel, *Frankenstein* – it's on the glacier that her creature pleads for the help and understanding that is not given to him – the glacier came right up to the road. Shelley felt the sea of ice was all the time expanding – 'inexplicably dreadful' – and that one day the whole world might become a mass of frost.

He was in a frenetic state, overloaded with much that had not found its way into his writing. Back in London he had abandoned his first wife Harriet, along with his two daughters. In due course Harriet would drown herself. He and Mary had eloped with their child, little William, along with

Claire, Mary's eighteen-year-old stepsister, who was pregnant to Byron while being loved by Shelley. Shelley, forever idealistic about what was possible in relationships, tended to look skyward. On the way to Chamonix he wrote *The Hymn to Intellectual Beauty*.

As they came across France the villages seemed to be still smouldering from the Napoleonic wars. The world had been turned upside down and it only remained for the courageous in love to strike out for their own lives. Closer to the Alps, they glimpsed the peaks, and shuddered. To Mary the mountains seemed to increase in height and beauty – 'higher one would think than the safety of God would permit.'

At the Hotel de Ville de Londres, right at the edge of the glacier, the three of them plus the one on the way, slept. As if this was not scandal enough Shelley added to it when he signed the hotel register. Under the 'occupation' column he wrote, in Greek, *Democrat, Philanthropist and Atheist*.

Shelley, once face to face with the mountain – its sheer mass and cruel simplicity – could think of nothing else: 'I never knew I never imagined what mountains were before. The immensity of these ariel summits excited, when they suddenly burst upon the sight, a sentiment of exstatic wonder, not unallied to madness.' He was filled with awe; at the limits of his own intelligence; at the massive, impersonal forces. His great poem, *Mont Blanc*, which recounts the layers of geological chaos, is a kind of warding off of madness as it enacts a heroic confrontation between sensitive mind and brutal matter:

> *For the very spirit fails,*
> *Driven like a homeless cloud from steep to steep*
> *That vanishes among the viewless gales!*
> *Far, far above, piercing the infinite sky,*
> *Mont Blanc appears, – still, snowy, and serene –*[8]

Shelley asserted what no other English traveller dared to put into print: the mountain confirmed the *non-existence* of God. All it could affirm was 'The secret strength of things / Which governs thought.'[9]

And that is the thing, I feel, the secret strength of the things that takes someone onto the actual mountain – upon which, by the way, Shelley seems not to have actually stepped, although in a cultural sense he never really left. By the time Gaita arrived a century and a half after Shelley's revolutionary

---

[8]   Shelley 1847, III, ll. 9–13, 232.
[9]   Shelley 1847, V, ll. 13–14, 234.

CHAPTER 2

times, the poet was all the vogue again. *The Pursuit*, Richard Holmes' passionate biography of Shelley (from which I have been plundering) was published in 1974.[10] I bet some of Gaita's young contemporaries had it tucked away in their tents: Shelley's radical idealism suited their era, as did the poet's everlasting faith in love. South of the Alps, Shelley settled a while in Rome, where he delivered his generation's greatest translation of Plato's *Symposium*, that timeless discourse on love, on the notion of our yearning to meet our other halves, a dreaming of love that entails the One. Need I go on? Not here, but the poem *will* go on, as it must. Reading Gaita, you can't miss his tender references to Plato; even when he is arguing against him he seems to be extending a hand, a muscular arm, like Michelangelo's Adam, towards a transcendental love which he continues to insist is not religious. The poem might give some body to this riddle in Gaita.

The Hotel de Ville de Londres has gone now. The philosopher's generation of climbers, those around Shelley's age I mean, camped in a field down along the way. They were there all summer, without facilities. A whole field of youngsters hell-bent on putting themselves to the test, and living communally while loving the mountain to bits. By the end of their stay the place was a quagmire, if not a cesspit. And overhead – the sound of choppers, as it was in Vietnam. At the end of each day they swung on down to collect the wounded and sometimes even the dead the mountain had claimed. Come the next morning, and everyone was collecting their gear to partner up and go out again. It was incredible, Gaita told me, it was like a war-zone.

Soldiers of the mountain, the daredevil fit young men. The poem, as it climbs, will have to pause on obdurate, reckless pride as well as courage. One day, on the high slopes, having worked his way around an avalanche, the weather started to close in. We will have to turn back, his partner said, looking at the storm clouds racing towards them. They were on a traverse to the Aiguille du Midi.

The other climber was relatively new to the game: fear was building like the storm. They could signal for help, a helicopter could pick them up from where they were. Oh, no, Gaita insisted, that would be too *embarrassing*!

Shelley, just a few days before arriving in Chamonix, was boating with Byron on a lake in Switzerland. He was usually fine in a boat talking his head off until 'the ladies' brains whizzed with giddiness about idealism.' But on this day Shelley's talk became unsettled, as the boat they were on began to sink.

---

[10] Holmes 1974. The main citations are at 342, 339, 327, 334–35.

A SENSE FOR HUMANITY

'My companion, an excellent swimmer, took off his coat, I did the same,' Shelley recalled, 'and we sat with our arms crossed, every instant expecting to be swamped.' Shelley knew that Byron knew he could not swim. But the last thing he was going to do was signal any need for help: 'I felt in this near prospect of death a mixture of sensations, among which terror entered though but subordinately ... I knew that my companion would have attempted to save me, but I was overcome with humiliation ...'

I told this story to Gaita and he laughed. He said that, once, he *had* almost agreed to a helicopter rescue from a hut near the peak of Mount Cook. He had two cracked ribs, which was going to make it difficult to leap crevasses on the way down. As it happened, a small plane was scheduled to deliver supplies when the blizzard passed: he and his partner hitched a ride back. 'That,' he told me, 'didn't count as a rescue.' And it was also because no one easily called it a rescue as the chopper came to deliver supplies: they were just using it to get a lift back.

This is the thing: mountains exist to test one's capacity for humiliation. They bear witness to the secret strength of things that govern not just thought but feelings – especially feelings that are too painful to express, and the full expression of which might trigger an avalanche in the self. The mountain is there to pit oneself against, the better to secure oneself, after a fashion. If you survive the mountain you can survive anything, even if you have done so by lying against the ropes. Not for nothing have great mountains in ancient cultures been named Mother. The Mountain calls and wholeheartedly you go; you give yourself to it on pain of death. Death in the arms of the mountain may be what you desire. Death-in-life, and life-in-death is what great White Mountains are.

But I am going too quickly, I know, and too romantically for my own good. The poem must not be allowed to go overboard here. The whole experience of taking one's sorrow to the mountain also entails leaving many things behind: the hearth, the sapping human-creature comforts, the succour of mothers and wives. The slow walk up towards the mountain solicits the classic mode. Each step *outwards* is a new step, a kind of glad start, to use Wittgenstein's lovely phrase. You are walking into fresh-ness; the physicality of the world is sharp, sharpened, as each step is individually valued, as you move in the direction of self-sufficiency and contact with something much bigger than the self.

Gary Snyder, the Zen poet-ecologist who trained his mind and body in mountains, has a fine word for the physical reality of the path underfoot. *Riprap*. It's a Rocky Mountain term for a cobble of stone laid on steep,

CHAPTER 2

slick rock to make a trail for horses in the mountains. It is the full physical reality of the path as you go into the mountain wanting to leave your ego behind. And as you do you start to discard some of your own self-talk; its all too familiar grammar shifts as you go. Being up there, out there, with Nature lying all around, solicits the new grammar. Snyder goes on, citing Thoreau: 'The Spaniards have a good term to express this wild and dusky knowledge, *Gramatica parda*, tawny grammar, a kind of mother-wit derived from that ... leopard ... ' The leopard was 'this vast, savage, howling mother of ours, Nature, lying all around, with such beauty, and such affection for her children, as the leopard; and yet we are so early weaned from her breast to society.'[11]

The point is that you are, in a Zen sense, not homeless, not abandoned, precisely because what you have is the whole universe. A man might become something else on a mountain. One with no argument with Nature, even his own nature, riddled as it is with madness, loss, fear or both. Of the wind, you might say. Breathing and all seeing of the world as it is – all around.

Zen Master Dogen asks: 'Are you going to try to improve yourself or are you going to let the universe improve you?'

Come back to Chamonix, and the inevitability, or not, of the mountain tending one in the classic mode, whatever the knot of self-anguish. John Ruskin, the great critic who was often mad, found solace at Chamonix. The place made him feel sane when it allowed him, an *ethical* being through and through, to escape from his parents who persecuted him with their *moralising*. Ruskin needed to live near a mountain that healed. As a young man, while lying on a mossy rock in the valley of Chamonix, when he had born witness to the storm clouds breaking over the mountain, giving birth to that famous passage about the thunder, the cloud cloven by the avalanche, the white stream emerging like slow lightning, the Aiguilles breaking through, the spire of ice, the dome of snow and so on – a celebrated passage in which 'a celestial city' is revealed to him, 'clothed with the peace of God.' But it was much more than that. It could 'turn the human soul from gazing upon itself.'[12] And it did so, he came to realise, because 'the stones of Chamonix,' the geology of it all, the mountains themselves, their 'violent muscular action' on the body of the earth – *their* spirit was a constant saying of 'I live forever.'[13]

---

[11] Snyder 1990, 83.
[12] Rosenberg 1961, 19.
[13] Ruskin 1988, 104–05.

And so with Ruskin's reverence for the truths of all things there: moss, lichen, birds, trees – 'the pine is trained to need nothing, and to endure everything.'[14] He loved clouds second only to rocks: 'Our whole happiness and power of energetic action depend upon our being able to breathe and live in the cloud.' Even when he himself felt 'as unstable as water,'[15] Ruskin knew that realism was the basic intention of Romantic art – a project that dissolved the dichotomy between the romantic and classic.

Ruskin wanted truth and accuracy in drawing, respect for the detailed facts in nature, including their animate inter-relationships: see the 'socialised' nature of the tree, its powers of accommodation to other trees; and plants, how plants 'helped' the other, thus 'intensity of life is also intensity of helpfulness.'[16] The Alps were not-self yet alive, a truth that artists could render by acts of the imagination, the spiritual encounter of the human spirit with matter, as witnessed in the greatest painters, most notably Ruskin's hero, Turner, whose active engagement with the Alpine topography was unsurpassed. This because *power* in art depends on a basic principle: 'to describe rightly what we call an ideal thing, depends on its being thus, to [the artist], not an ideal but a *real* thing.'[17]

What does this sound like? I think it sounds very like a philosopher we know placing the notion of goodness in the embodied world. Ruskin's power as a critic drew from a great painter's imaginative engagement with the mountain. As does Gaita's power as an ethicist: its natural terms of appraisal are strikingly symmetrical with those summonsed by the mountain. They are the terms he adopted in his first remarks about the ravishing mountains to be climbed, when he was shaping his romanticism about nature into the classic mode, hailing the mountain as worthy of reverence in its own right, deserving of our gratitude, soliciting our best selves and so on.[18] Furthermore, the poem will feel entitled to place these terms of appraisal beside Gaita's most elevated and abstract philosophical arguments for absolute good. In this light, the poem will relish the preface to the second edition of *Good and Evil: An Absolute Conception*, written long after the doctorate done in the physical company of the Alps, but where

---

[14] Ruskin 1988, 92 and 97.
[15] Rosenberg 1961, 147.
[16] Ruskin 1988, 109.
[17] Quoted in Rosenberg 1961, 17.
[18] See Gaita 2002, 149–53.

the morality itself strikes the keynotes which have already been brought to the mountain. Thus, it too is worthy of *reverence* because it is a *gift*, like life itself, and so inspiring of *awe, mystery, beauty* that it makes sense to speak of the *sacred*, whether one is *religious* or not. It is *revelatory*. One might *wonder at its goodness*, so to speak; one is drawn to it *beyond reason*, you might almost think of it as something that can be *loved*. There it is. In all its uniqueness – out there as a *guide, yet a strange guide it is that puts obstacles in our way and then suggests ways around them*. But this is its way. To live a fully examined life in its presence requires *an ethic of renunciation*. At the same time – and as it can be on the mountain – one calls into play *an ethic of assertion*, which upholds the virtues of *autonomy, integrity, courage, nobility, honour* and *flourishing* or *self-realisation*.

And so on. Everything is complex, interwoven, all mind-heart. And this form, I am thinking of it as a kind of double living thing – call it morality/mountain, mountain/morality – which can be as *intractable* as the remorse that is proper when one violates a person/creature/thing's pristine nature. And this double thing is as *sublime*, say, as justice. 'I try to reclaim the wondrousness of it for philosophical reflection,' Gaita writes, referring to the notion of justice applied to Eichmann, and as he does you can feel him positioning himself, as so often, in the pure air of the Alps.[19]

Conceptually, maybe what I have just proposed will be enough to drive some philosophers mad. Well and good. They might set off with the poem.

III

On one climb, back then, Rai had to stay the night on a ledge high up on an aiguille. An eagle might have been comfortable on it – a rock face that looked out on the approaching storm, and which then received, in the course of the night, the bolts of lightning.

Kahkkkkk, Rai goes, hitting the air with his knife hand. The lightning struck the rock in line with their heads.

Eventually the storm passed, and they hung there, until the sun came up.
But what did you do all night? How did you pass the time?
We talked.
What about?
He laughed.
Life and death, of course.

---

[19] Gaita, 2004, xv–xvii.

A SENSE FOR HUMANITY

'Mountaineering is degraded,' we read in *The Philosopher's Dog*, 'unless the prospect of death is lucidly accepted.' The chapter is called 'Sacred Places.'[20]

I am calling him Rai again now, because his writing in *After Romulus* is a summons to intimacy. The poem must embrace him accordingly. The need for, in the end, a plain healing poem, became freshly apparent to me when I came to the several passages in what I would call Rai's *Mother Book*. There are several painfully revealing statements, *cris de coeur*, I can't get out of my head. My friend has, with the hardiness of a rock climber, not foolhardiness, I hope, prodded me to worry for him.

The first comes after a passage that paints a startlingly primitive image – a passage that seems to invite us to feel that Rai had a kind of primal relationship with the mountain. He gives us an image of himself as a desolate creature of the wild, as much abandoned to the icy wastes as Frankenstein's creature. It is a passage which, consciously or unconsciously I do not know, can only be fully imagined to a background howl of grief. Only then, are we expected to experience relief.

'In 1974, filthy, having lived for two months in a tent in Chamonix where I was mountaineering, I turned up unannounced at her front door in Homburg. I fell in love within seconds of our meeting. Though I had not seen her since I left Germany in 1950 and my skin had been so darkened by the sun reflecting off the snow and ice that I was often mistaken as an Indian, she recognised me straight away. "Raimond!" she exclaimed, "What a surprise!"'[21]

This woman is his mother's sister, Maria. They have kept in touch ever since. Then the statement that jolts: 'I fear her death because I know that I will again experience the death of my mother, and the numbness will not protect me from the pain as it did, to some degree, when my mother died.'

('Fog always, and the snow faded from the Alps,' Ruskin cripplingly lamented, at 'his loss of faith in nature.')

The second statement from Rai comes a few pages later; it is, in part: 'My longing becomes, painfully, more intense as memory fades ...'

The chapter 'An Unassuageable Longing' offers no solace, psychologically speaking. No resolution of whatever is there by way of guilt, remorse, anger, grief: the alpine wastelands stretch ahead. The poem would treat this chapter as a *passage* of writing – a traverse, a climb, a fall, a riprap progression, an application of tawny grammar that has no progression

---

[20] Gaita 2002, 144.
[21] Gaita 2011, 204.

CHAPTER 2

as the philosopher *who is a poet unacknowledged to himself* lets time pass, makes nothing happen. We can only stand on the edge with Rai, not quite knowing how to broach his predicament, except perhaps to press on with the poem that encompasses as much as it can.

In the poem you will come to a koan carved into a rock. 'Before your mother and father met, show me your original face. What is your original face?'

Snyder's teacher would say: 'Don't explain it to me. Don't give me a philosophical interpretation of it. Don't talk about it that way at all. Show it to me.'

Here the poem might have to start again, or at least move into a new section I would want to call *Native Sutra*, the creation of which I would see as a gift-offering to a friend who so needs us to attend to his never-ending anguish over the events and losses of his childhood, and to the struggle it has been to find the right categories to do justice to each of his parents, as well as the ambivalences and ambiguities of his own sufferings. In *After Romulus* he is so naked about this need that it is natural to think, I think, of him as perhaps a suitable case for treatment. In *After Romulus* he tells us that his dear friend, Anne Manne, draws his attention to the 'distancing nature' of his philosophical mode, especially with regard to his ability to tap into a fully open, and possibly remedial contemplation of his mother as a source of his suffering. Many readers and viewers of the Romulus memoir, Rai reports, have looked for his wounds. Rai's response to Manne is to recount how he never doubted his mother's love, any more than he was unaware of the solace provided by her sensual presence. He says that he has had no 'anger or resentment to vent,' his 'chronic melancholia and yearning' notwithstanding. He goes further: even if such feelings existed in his 'unconscious,' he insists, they would have showed up in his writing.[22] But this is a classic form of denial. At the risk of impertinence, I feel that the first session of any consultation where even the smartest of philosophers undertook to do some emotional work as distinct from more thinking would expose it as such. Rai's construction also stands as a reminder of the tenacity with which he eschews the figure of Freud or anybody in the healing wake of Freud. Yet who am I to say? No more than a caring friend. And when the potential therapeutic subject is possessed of uncommon clarity, honesty and courage, by what criteria should another order of consciousness be asserted, or insisted upon, even in the name of someone's best interests?

---

[22] Gaita 2011, 221–23.

Still, it seems to me that what also comes through these passages – and which might be helpfully elucidated with the right pitch in the right poem, crampons and all – is a heightened awareness of someone not being able to *endure his suffering reduced*, in the manner Roland Bathes described in his posthumously published book about the loss of his mother.[23] Barthes defends his own totalisations, even to the point of clinging to his suffering. Anything but have it *stolen* from him.

Well and good then, the poem has to work with the climber's absolute sense of totality, of possession and self-possession, and his reluctance to cancel one thing into another, his insistence on all that the mountain is and must remain even as everything, with the living and dying all around, keeps on changing. To my mind, an exemplary method for sustaining this sense of reality is offered by Zen Buddhism, especially the formulations of Zen Master Dogen, an alpine thinker if ever there was one. Zen is also marvellously compatible with what I would call Rai's naturalism, his low-key appreciation of nature, its creatures and landscapes in various forms. Herein lies a realm of solace, he has often told us: in an outward direction from the self, rather than from within. The poem, with Dogen, can have its Platonic/Socratic dimensions – throwing its lines out to such a figure as Rai, one who believes as much in loving kindness as the Buddha, even if he seems lacking in kindness towards his own self. But the poem is also compelled, as naturalistically as Ruskin, we might say, to be responsible to its own traverses. It has to be let do its rope tricks in the ice and snow, the better that they be experienced for the tricks that they are, acts of rarified mind, and mind only, worthy of silence. The world in its beauty and strength, and with the secret strength of its things that governs thought, is as it is. Rai often writes in this spirit of hard acceptance. His mode is an aspect of his wondrous gratitude for the preciousness of life.

Then, sooner or later, the poem will come back to the hut, where we – myself as a poet and friend, the reader and maybe the poem's subject – will make the tea, then taste the tea.[24]

---

[23] See epigraph from Roland Barthes's *Mourning Diary* (2010, 71).

[24] For those interested in this apparent aphorism, in the *Lankavatara Sutra*, sometimes considered the holy grail of Zen, there are two key teachings. One is that 'that everything we perceive as being real is nothing but the perceptions of our own minds.' The other is that 'the knowledge of this is something that must be realised and experienced for oneself and cannot be expressed in words.' In the words of Chinese Zen masters these two teachings became known as 'have a cup of tea' and 'taste the tea.' *The Lankavatara Sutra* (2011, 3–17).

CHAPTER 2

The poem
can't keep saying.

You and the mountain
can't keep climbing.

Having refined distinctions
treat them like snow plumes.

You just need to
go out each day

face the weather
for a good time

be strong in the rain
come back into the kitchen

taste the tea
taste the rain.

Meanwhile, the poem would have had to make its own riprap, its ground for a creation dance on the mountain. 'The green mountains are always walking; a stone woman gives birth to a child at night,' as Dogen says in the *Mountains and Water Sūtra*, a supreme teaching text for being *at home* in the *whole* universe. There is no time to go on about this here, and if I did it would sound as if the poem was out to push Rai Gaita so far East many would not recognise him, and he might not even recognise himself. Just let me say, though, that Dogen's Sūtra, a discourse on process, has it that 'the idea of the sacred is a delusion and an obstruction: it diverts us from seeing what is before our eyes;'[25] and that 'if you doubt mountains walking, you do not know your own walking.'[26]

---

[25] Snyder 1990, 103.
[26] *Moon in a Dewdrop: Writings of Zen Master Dogen* (1985, 97–9).

Chapter 3

SOPHIE'S CHOICE

Alex Miller

I've been greatly affected by *Romulus, My Father*, and by my friendship with Rai in ways I will probably never adequately express. Both have been late gifts in my life. The impression of the book, which has persisted with me most strongly, is of Rai's mother's unhappy life and her tragic death, when her beginnings had seemed to me to have been so promising. Indeed the influence of *Romulus* and of my deepening friendship with Rai continues to play an evolving and increasingly important part in my life.

After revisiting Frogmore with Rai and Col McLennan, a Murri friend from Queensland, to whom Rai was showing his country, I recently wrote the following to Rai in an email: It was very moving walking behind you across the wheat field coming down from the abandoned house yesterday evening. I had a deeper sense of the tragic beauty of that landscape and your childhood as a part of it than I've ever had before. And I thought to myself how wonderful it is that you've made sense of that past of your parents and your father's friends and given it a real presence. I think it is a truly heroic thing you have done, and I mean this in the old sense of the way in which shiftless peoples and tribes founded their stories of their own pasts in order to cherish their forebears and celebrate their lives and deeds, and by doing so gave a deeper meaning to their own existence in the present. The creation of story. It is magical and beautiful. And to think of you as a young boy writing that story of the struggle between good and evil in the guise of your hero Elvis. It is as if you were announcing your own future – the old people, and I mean our own old people of the North, would have said the gods gave you the gift of the story. And none of this would have been so if you had flinched from the whole truth of your family's history at Frogmore, terrible and frightening though so much of that history was. I have never before understood quite so clearly as I did yesterday evening why you had to reveal all the deeply private pain of that time. But that is what all the great

CHAPTER 3

foundation stories do. They tell of the irredeemable tragedy as well as the triumph of life. And that is what makes them great, and gives to them the lasting significance they have for all of us.

When Rai told me he had titled his essay on his mother, 'An Unassuageable Longing' – Helen Garner's expression for her sense of Rai's emotional state as a result of the loss of the nourishment of his mother's love at an early age – I thought of Emily Dickinson's image, 'The craving is upon the child like a claw it cannot remove.'

This essay is a personal reflection on Rai and our friendship, and it also looks at the effect on me of *Romulus* and of Rai's essay on his mother. I've titled it 'Sophie's Choice' because it is in the circumstances of their beginnings that friendships, and indeed all our relationships, establish the enduring qualities of their character. It is in the inception of relationships that we most often experience the earliest nurturing of something enduring within ourselves, something which forms a deep connection that remains with us – the deepest of all these emotional beginnings for us is, of course, in our mothering. To find a friend is often to find something in oneself that one was not fully conscious of before, something which the friendship brings more fully into the light – something that is the result of the nurturing acknowledgement of the other.

If it had not been for Sophie Halakas I might never have met Rai and my life would have been the poorer for that. Rai's influence on me has been immense. Some time – I'm not good with dates – after my wife Stephanie and I moved to Castlemaine ten years ago, Sophie Halakas, the owner of our local fruit shop and the matriarch of her large Greek Australian family, asked me if I had met Raimond Gaita. I told her I had read his books and that I greatly admired his work, but that I hadn't met him. In admitting this to Sophie I felt as if I were admitting a fault. 'You should give him a call,' she said with a quiet insistence that confirmed my sense of being in the wrong for not having met Rai already. 'You are both writers,' she said, 'and you would like each other.' Sophie spoke to me, a stranger, with more than a hint of reprimand that day, in a tone that implied, *This situation is not as it should be and we had better see to it that we set it to rights as soon as possible.* Charles Dickens would have put her in a novel. You can't know Sophie for long – a day or two at most – before also knowing she is actively concerned about the moral quality of the community she lives in, and has every intention of seeing to it, if she can possibly manage it, that her community reflects her own sense of what is right. In this, as in a number of other ways – though with a very different delivery and style – Sophie holds a number of values in common with Rai. As I left her shop that day, with my bag of beans and potatoes, I said to myself, Well, I'd better get in touch with Rai Gaita before I go in there again.

When it came to making the call, however, I was shy about picking up the phone and out of the blue ringing the author of such imposing masterpieces as *Romulus, My Father*, *The Philosopher's Dog*, *A Common Humanity*, and the intimidatingly dense and scholarly work, *Good and Evil*. Why would this writer and thinker, who I also knew to be the Professor of Moral Philosophy at London University, and whose essays and public statements had given him a commanding presence in the intellectual life of Australia, why would he want to hear from me? Surely he would already be far too busy with the pressing demands of a richly elaborate international private and public life? How should I seem to casually break in on this? Would I say, 'Hi Rai, Sophie from the fruit shop told me to call you.'

I am a coward about these things so I avoided the fruit shop for as long as I could. But we needed fruit and vegetables and eventually I could avoid it no longer and I went in. Sophie, who was not always there, was at the counter that day. She greeted me as I came through the door. 'Hello Alex,' she said. 'We haven't seen you for a while.' Her gaze followed me around the shop and when I arrived at the counter with my basket of vegetables, she weighed and packed my things in silence. Only when I'd paid and she was handing me my change did she at last look directly into my eyes. 'So,' she said. 'Did you get in touch with Rai Gaita?'

'No,' I said. 'I'm sorry. I'll call him today. I promise.'

'Good,' she said. 'I think you should.'

After this encounter I was more intimidated by the thought of fronting Sophie again than I was by the thought of calling Rai, so I phoned him. He said that for some time Sophie had been urging him to call me. We arranged to meet for a coffee. I can't remember what we talked about at our first meeting but on my way home I wondered why I'd thought Rai Gaita would not be as his books are. What had made me think that the man who had written about Jack the cockatoo and Gypsy the dog, would be a haughty and difficult highbrow and not the warm, humane, caring person he is in his books? A man, that is, motivated by a modest, but passionate, determination, not so very different from Sophie Halakas' own determination, to see to it that, in so far as he is able to influence these things, the community he lives in is a decent one, is a community, in other words, in which people and animals, and indeed all things, are respected simply for what they are and *because* they are, because they share with us our being-in-this-world.

CHAPTER 3

Rai Gaita, I realised after our first meeting in the cafe, was a practical philosopher for whom the congested moral qualities of the life we live from day to day provide the principal focus and ground not only of his thinking but also of his actions. As I walked home from the cafe I knew that I had met a man who was not only a very great writer (something I had already discovered for myself) but who was also a great human being.

I'm not a Christian, and dislike all varieties of proselytising religion, but I'd be a fool to imagine that my thought has not been influenced by the imprint left on me and on the culture I inhabit by two thousand years of Christianity; by the shaping conviction, that is, that the struggle between good and evil is the principle moral focus of human society and the rule of the good the measure of its moral health. Though Rai would almost certainly not express it as I do here, from my reading of his books and essays I knew him to have spent his most serious intellectual energies in dealing head-on, as it were, with this subject, and I knew that his judgements on questions of good and evil would always be nuanced and complex. I did not expect my own judgements to be as keen as his. Even though as a novelist I'd been concerned for my entire writing life with the intricate dilemmas of private and social morality. Would our views on these things be at odds, I wondered? I had liked Rai at once and was anxious to discover that we shared some deep common ground, so that our friendship might flourish. I was, of course, looking in the wrong place.

After my meeting with Rai I couldn't wait to go into the fruit shop again. But Sophie was too quick for me. Before I could deliver my punch line, she said, 'Rai was in just now, Alex. He said how much he enjoyed meeting you.' – I realised it wasn't Dickens, after all, but was Trollope who would have put her straight into a novel. Her manner assured me that arrangements in Castlemaine had been adjusted a significant step closer to her ideal. It wasn't long after this that Rai and I were shovelling gravel together at Shalvah and walking in the rain over his old Baringhup home country and he was telling me of his childhood and taking me to his sacred sites, showing me the implements his father had used, the beautiful wrought iron gates he had made and the old shed on the farm where his father had worked and where as a boy Rai himself had turned the handle of the home-made tool for twisting the hot straps of iron. These were scenes that reminded me of my own early years as a farm labourer in England when I had become joyfully intimate with the skills and the hand tools of those days. I was very aware while shovelling gravel with him and visiting his father's old work sites with Rai (these events occurred on different days but were of the same feeling) that he and I both loved physical work and the peculiar quality of mental contentment and wellbeing that comes with it. There was a connection between us in this that was deeply important to me and which I knew also to be deeply important to Rai. We might not be going to agree on every social and moral question, but we would both delight in shovelling gravel and loading his ute with firewood for my Rayburn. I knew I could rely on that. I knew I could rely on him.

Our friendship has flourished since then in action and in talk, and we have done a great deal of both. Rai and Yael have travelled with me to the Stone Country, in the Central Highlands of Queensland, where they met the dear friends on whom the characters in two of my novels were based. Rai was overcome with emotion and wept when he stood among the stone arrangements of the sacred playgrounds of the Old People, in that strange and mysterious opening in the bendee scrub at the heart of Jangga country, to which Col McLelland, elder of the Jangga, had invited him. And I was reminded that day of the depth of Rai's love of country around Shalvah, a place as sacred to him as the stone arrangements in the wild bendee scrub are to Col and his people. Rai and Yael and I lived together, cooked and ate and travelled together in that sublime country for a week during which we came to know each other at an open level of trust and intimacy I have rarely experienced. Although ours is a young friendship in years, it is one of the most important and influential of my life. I quite often feel ambivalent and uncertain about my decision to live away from the city in the quiet country town of Castlemaine (Sophie's town) but whenever Rai and Yael are at Shalvah I feel reassured and less ambivalent and more aware of having been admitted generously into a special love of country – just as I did when I was first invited by Col McLelland to journey with him through his country in the hinterland of the North. When Stephanie and I moved back to Melbourne for our daughter's last two years of schooling a few years ago, Rai wrote to me from London, 'Don't get too fond of Carlton, mate. I want to grow old with you in the bush.' It is a thought I too cherish. Not growing old (I think I've already done that) but continuing to enjoy our friendship.

Rai's complex and deeply passionate attachment to the country of his childhood has its roots not only in his love and admiration for his father but also, and no less deeply, in his longing to reconnect the broken threads of his love for his mother. It is a longing that has been a powerful source of inspiration for him. Without that longing we would not have *Romulus, My Father* or his courageous and deeply moving essay about his mother, 'An Unassuageable Longing.'

CHAPTER 3

During our journey around Rai's home country he took me to the cottage he rented in Maldon where he wrote *Romulus*. 'I wrote it in five weeks,' he said – he may even have said three. 'It was already written in my heart,' he explained. As we sat in the car looking at the cottage I was thinking of Rai's mother and remembering Colm Toibin's heartbreaking story 'A Long Winter,' in which the father and the boy search for the mother who has run away from them, a story pervaded by that sense of guilty responsibility that all children endure for the failure of love in the family, and by a longing to recover the lost love of the mother. The mother is never found, of course, in such stories and we are left with her poignant absence as a powerful presence. Writers are often inspired to write by an irresistible urge to recover what has been lost. This urge may not be fully conscious at the time of writing; it is the process of writing itself that uncovers the poignant, the impossible, and the heartfelt necessity of responding to the longing and makes the longing more immediate, bringing the absence into the presence of the writer. It is Henry James at that pivotal moment in his life, returning to America after thirty years a migrant in England and anxious to know if he is going to be able to recover the America of his early years that is to be so important for him.

The separation of writers from their homelands (their mother country) and their mothers, has often been the source of the inspiration for masterpieces of literature – and by literature I mean all forms of writing. *Romulus* is one of the finest examples of this intense lucid masterpiece of family emotion, of love and the failure of love to be enough, in which the author writes above him or herself under the influence of what we once happily called inspiration, and what Rai called writing from the heart.

Romulus was surely an important part of the beginning of a new chapter, or perhaps more accurately a new stage, in Rai's return to his home country, in which the move to Shalvah was also an important act of recovery for him. The landscape around Shalvah is not only rich in sites of deeply cherished incident with Rai's father, but is also rich in sites of sacred significance for Rai's mother and her tragic history, places intimately associated with her suffering and her final despair. Reading Rai's essay on his mother it is impossible to believe that his unassuageable longing will not continue to be a powerful prompt of memory and imagination for him, a precious source of energy and inspiration for his writing. The story, I believe, is not over yet. When he began writing *Romulus*, Rai said to me he did so wanting to write about his mother, but he was not able to do it at that time. His mother, of course, was to become the great absence of the story, the poignant presence of her despair and loss. Some of the greatest works of literature are about those very things the writer cannot say but which haunt the work with the poignancy of their absence. It was his mother's tragedy that had most deeply affected me in the book, and had left me with a longing for the resolution of her absence in her son's life. We are only a few pages into *Romulus* when we encounter the young girl of sixteen, sensitive to the cultural values and educated in the ways of the German middle class. She enjoys Shakespeare and opera and is prone to melancholy and asthma. That she falls in love with the intensely romantic blacksmith six years her senior, his unsettling gaze and his hard muscles, the challenge to her values of his contempt for what he considers to be her snobbishness in loving such things as Shakespeare and opera, terrify her parents – they think of *Romulus* as a gipsy. From their cultural perspective this is just about the most damning thing they could say about him. In the recounting of their meeting the young girl's doom is foretold, almost in the tones of a classical tragedy. The portent of those few opening pages is as powerful as anything I know in literature. It is what first grips the reader, and it is what holds the reader until the end – or I should say, which held this reader to the end. Christine dies in chapter 8, two thirds of the way through the book, but the unresolved conflicts her life and death have left behind remain for me the source of the book's energy to the very end – the last two words of the book are 'my mother.' A foreshadowing of the long essay that Rai has at last found himself able to write and an acknowledgement of the presence of the mother's absence as the guiding spirit of the book that was written in the author's heart before a word was set to paper.

What parent could remain unmoved by the scene in *Romulus* when the boy Rai tells the headmaster of St Patrick's that he does not wish to see his mother if she should ever again visit him at the school? The tragedy is that of an educated and refined European woman who loses everything in the move to the Australian bush, an environment for which she was totally unfitted and which left her no room or opportunity in which to even begin to change or to nurture her natural gifts. Unlike Hora and Romulus, there is nothing Christine can do. There is no place for her to turn to. There are many father son books but there is none I know of that carries a greater tragic force than *Romulus*. It was the move to the Australian bush in the early fifties that drove Christine into the arms of madness and other men. The irony is that it was she herself who chose to come to Australia. It was for her as Virgil said, *We make our destinies by our choice of gods.* For the migrant, surely destiny is determined by the choice of destination. We, people, all of us, are capable of breaking. Breaking emotionally and spiritually I mean. The break, when

CHAPTER 3

it comes, will take a different form in each of us and will reveal where our weakness has lain all along. Given a nurturing environment in which there was room and opportunity for Christine to gather her strength I cannot believe she would have been pushed to the point where she displayed the symptoms of the defeat of her reason.

Trustingly, with an extraordinary generosity that I've learnt to treasure in our friendship, Rai sent me an unedited draft of his essay on his mother in early April. The chapter is written with great courage and honesty. It is written with a confessional honesty far beyond anything I would be capable of if I were ever to write about the private emotional wounds of my own family's history. When I'd read the chapter I was greatly moved by it and wrote to Rai at once:

> I have just finished reading your chapter. It is very beautiful and deeply moving. I was gripped by it and wanted it to go deeper and deeper into the elusive life of your mother – I wanted it to find her. And it was terrible in that she remains unsighted in the tragedy. It is a grand and wonderful piece of writing. I could never write of such intimate moments in the life of my parents and myself, but I am glad you have found the courage – or sufficient cause – to do it. It took me through the emotional and historical landscape of your life in Central Victoria once again – the landscape of *Romulus* – like a tour you needed to make, going back and revisiting *Romulus*, still haunted by what had remained implicit in that book – for all this, the tragedy of your mother that you render explicitly here, was already in the book and was, more than anything, what moved me when I first read it. The presence of her absence was at the core of that book. I am very grateful to you for writing this, Rai, and I can understand your need to do it. To look again and know, once and for all, that you can never know her.

People who write – or for that matter who attend sessions of psychoanalysis – are almost always surprised by how much of the seemingly irrecoverable we are able to recover once we begin to write. Memory opens up under the stimulus of our close attention. It takes courage to write memoir, more courage I believe than it does to write fiction, where one hides one's intimate sins behind the mask of make-believe. All art, I believe, is engaged in a search for truth. But for Rai truth is a sacred good and he is incapable of consciously falsifying for effect – as, say, a fiction writer or a painter will often do. It is, I believe, that for Rai truth itself is the work of art. While truth may be sacred to him, it is not a given but must be striven for. And for this courage is required. Also the courage to fail. The courage to find that the truth may not be available to us. Rai's search for truth in his books – in all his books and in his daily life – is a conscious striving that is beautiful and good and which is often nearly impossible, is elusive and is sometimes difficult beyond words. The richness of his mind is exemplified for me in that we can never know in advance what he thinks but must hear from him. It is a great privilege for me to know myself his friend, and to know the friendship and love I feel for him is cherished by him in turn. I hope you'll forgive me, Rai, for this inconclusive personal meander. You can tackle me on some of my obscurities next time we're shoveling gravel from the back of your ute at Shalvah or collecting firewood for my Rayburn.

Chapter 4

ROMULUS, MY FATHER AND THE AUSTRALIAN LITERARY IMAGINARY

Brigitta Olubas

In this chapter I want to consider *Romulus, My Father* as a work of literature, to think, as literary critics do, about what kind of book it is and what its significance might be for Australian readers today and in the future. An approach focusing on the 'literary' qualities of a work of memoir might perhaps be seen to effect an evacuation of truth from the work, to rely on a sense of it as mere 'text,' or empty narrative form, as lacking, or not requiring, a tenacious hold on the world. This is not the approach I want to take. Rather, in response to the ways Gaita's book sets its readers to consider the question of the truth of a particular life, I want to consider what kind of truth literature provides, to set the literary and the aesthetic weight of the memoir, of this memoir, alongside its commitment to truth, to veracity. Nor do I want to reduce the issue to a question of genre. Rather, I want to take seriously the question of the place and the work of the genre of memoir in the literary imaginary of a nation, to devote attention to the way it presents to us our world and the places where we live.

In his commentary on this memoir, Raimond Gaita insists on its commitment to truth in terms that differentiate it from literature:

> There is no single reason why I wrote *Romulus*, but I wrote it partly because I wanted to bear witness to, rather than merely record, or even celebrate, the values that defined my father's moral identity. Considered purely as literature, separable from the strict truthfulness of its narrative voice, my book does not have much to recommend it, I think.
>
> I am certain that the way people have been moved by it is inseparable from the fact that they believe it to be entirely without fabrication.

They recognize, I believe, if only instinctively, that it bears witness to the values it celebrates. The integrity of witness seldom, if ever, survives invention, however honourable the motive for it might be. Were *Romulus* exposed as fraudulent, or seriously mistaken, no publisher would recommend that it be reissued as fiction (Gaita 2007, viii).

The concern here is, I think, more with the signal force of truth than with the nature of literature. However Gaita reiterates the distinction a little later, writing about the decision not to use voiceover in the film, when he writes that 'witness is essentially in the first person and by real rather than fictional persons' (Gaita 2007, ix).

The distinction between the real and the fictional is an important one; however I want to propose here that in a different sense, and with particular reference to *Romulus, My Father*, truth and literature are not at odds with one another, and that it is the work of memoir to bring them compellingly together. I want to look at how this happens with *Romulus* in the first part of this chapter where I consider more broadly Gaita's investigation of questions of truth in a national context and suggest some of the implications of this for our understanding of what I'm calling the Australian literary imaginary – the domain within which we read and apprehend the literary. I then want to take up another aspect of memoir: its significance as a form of writing in response to death. Gaita of course reminds us of the genesis of this book in the eulogy he wrote for his father's funeral; but in his further writing about the memoir his attention has turned, or returned, not so much away from the figure of Romulus, but rather towards the more hidden or less accessible figure of his mother, Christine. The long essay, 'An Unassuageable Longing' which concludes his 2011 collection *After Romulus* is the fullest account of this return, but it is everywhere evident in Gaita's commentary on his memoir in the years since its first publication. The figure of Christine has also preoccupied many of the readers of *Romulus*, as Gaita makes clear in a story recounted in that essay and elsewhere, of a reading he gave at the Sacred Heart Mission in Melbourne:

> [There], five or six girls, prostitutes in the area, not one of them yet twenty, asked me again and again to read about my mother. I read to them passages that I had not read before or since in public because they are painful for me. In my mother's troubled life they saw something of their own (Gaita 2011a, 203).

CHAPTER 4

Thinking about the relation of memoir to death provides a way for me now more directly to address Christine, whose death and life have haunted the narrative for me as they have for many other readers. It suggests moreover a way to read her story into the ethical structure of the memoir, into the sense of truth it works to present to its readers, and to try to understand why her story is so important for me as an Australian reader. Before moving on to these considerations, I want to note two distinctive features of this book from the perspective of a literary critic: firstly its moral weight and secondly its foreignness.

As a philosopher, Raimond Gaita brings to his writing an admirable, enviable clarity of thought and expression, but more than this he brings to its subject matter and its cadences a sense of substance and of moment that is unusual in Australian writing. In my several decades as a literary scholar in the field of Australian literary studies, I have rarely come across anything like its unapologetic sense of its own weight of purpose, its *gravitas*, its sense that what it is presenting to us really matters. And what matters is the imaginative and ethical, but also the narrative and poetic, dimensions of human experience, the sense that this book gives of the crafting of a self in the course of a life's story. Here, that creating of a self is not an abstract or imponderable process; it is utterly tangible, full of the weight and consequence of words, as well as of the substance of everyday living. This sense of *gravitas* derives in part, from the ponderousness and – for readers of Australian fiction at least – the unfamiliarity of the terms being put into play: concepts of truth, honour, integrity. It also derives, I would suggest, from the solemnity with which the protagonists are invested: their sense of their own significance and destiny, not simply the tragedy of their stories, though this is part of it, but also the force and dignity of their everyday actions, that impels us to a sense of 'character,' as Harold Bloom has articulated it:

> [O]ur word 'character' still possesses, as a primary meaning, a graphic sign such as a letter of the alphabet, reflecting the word's likely origin in the ancient Greek character, a sharp stylus or mark of the stylus's incisions. Our modern word 'character' also means ethos, a habitual stance towards life (Bloom 2002, 4).

Gaita's focus on recreating the daily lives and ethics of the characters in his memoir has at its heart a compulsion not simply to speak to the facts of these lives, but to address directly the truth they embody, a truth he has described as poetic or tragic as distinct from novelistic or fictional:

> When I reflected on what I had written I realized it had little in common with the kind of biography that naturally takes a novelistic form. Because of its emphasis on character, fate and affliction, I thought of it as a kind of tragic poem, in that extended sense in which the ancient Greeks spoke of poetry. In *Romulus* I say that tragedy as a literary genre shows calm pity for the affliction it depicts. I hoped that my book could show that same calm pity for the people whose story it told. I hoped that it could show that though all of them were to some degree broken by their suffering, in none of them was their humanity diminished by it (Gaita 2007, xvii).

Poetry and tragedy here draw weight from the work they do in the world, which Gaita explains in another essay 'The Pedagogical Power of Love' as the task of 'the understanding of the human condition,' the pondering of 'what life means to us,' a process he argues which must be tied to specific locations: to homes, communities, landscapes. And he draws fervently on the expressive capacities of the poetic imagination in his account of his own luminous grounding in the landscape of his childhood, experienced as a form of 'epiphany,' and fundamental to the writing of the memoir. As he explains:

> If I had not found myself whole again in my love of the landscape of my childhood, I could not have written *Romulus* in the way that I did. It's not just that I could not have written the passages describing the landscape with the same feeling. The entire tone and mood of the book would have been different (Gaita 2008).

The process draws, moreover, on the force of tragedy:

> I hoped that the story I told would be one whose events and characters would be bathed in the light and colours of that landscape. I hoped that in the telling of it I could achieve the same calm pity that I attributed to tragedy as a literary genre (Gaita 2008).

In these claims, we find literature partaking of the weight of truth, becoming indeed a locution of, in Gaita's own terms, *witness*, a place where we can '[see] something of [our] own' (Gaita 2011a, 203).

A second distinctive feature of the work as I see it for an Australian literary critic is the way it peoples the familiar, desolate landscape of national memory with the voices, the bodies and the stories of non-Anglo Europeans. Raimond Gaita has said that he has been surprised by readers who have responded strongly to the 'immigrant story,' as he hadn't set out

CHAPTER 4

to write a work of social commentary. I would suggest rather that *Romulus, My Father* shows us something of the ways that an 'immigrant story' is a matter of imagination, of ethics, and of literature, rather than social commentary in any narrow sense. The foreignness of this family, visible from the start in the cover photograph of the original Text edition, and audible throughout in the reported speech of its protagonists: the at times unfamiliar lexicon as well as the non-Anglo voicings of familiar words. Again, for me this was utterly new, a point brought home graphically when I watched the film: sitting in the cinema I was struck with the realization that I was looking at, indeed I was witnessing, a landscape I recognised and with which I had identified since my earliest childhood as 'home,' but now for the first time – here is the moment of witness – this landscape was occupied by people who looked and sounded like my own family: smoking, drinking coffee, washing eggs, talking or laughing intemperately. *Romulus*'s commemoration of this European migrant family was for me an act of generosity, providing new ways for me as an Australian reader to imagine my place and the place of my own family in the story of the nation.

Gao Xingjian, in his speech delivered at the Nobel Jubilee symposium on 'Witness Literature' in 2001 presents an account of literature as profoundly connected to truth, arguing that 'literature testifies to human existence, and ... truth is the minimum requirement for such literature. Literature is subservient to nothing but truth' (Xingjian 2006, 49). In other words, for Gao Xingjian, the truthful relation of literature to the particular lives it records is amplified and animated by its capacity to testify and bear witness. In some important ways, this sense of witness is akin to the question of political truth, a point debated at length by Gaita in his *Quarterly Essay*, 'Breach of Trust: Truth, Morality and Politics,' which explores the question of political mendacity in relation to national belonging. Gaita is concerned in this essay to establish a sense of civic responsibility as a mode of thoughtfulness and openness, a way of being in the nation that is grounded in family, culture and community, through the medium and practice of conversation. The essay argues that our connections to and relations with those around us, together with our modes of speech and expression both public and private, determine and underpin our relation to truth. Gaita is not of course arguing that truth is in any way contingent or dependent on specific circumstances, any more than Gao Xingjian is, but is reminding us rather that truth must be grounded in human contact and understanding, in attending to others, in self-expression, and in our response to the places we inhabit.

Gaita is careful to distinguish the sense of connection to the nation he is expounding, which he describes as 'love of country,' from an assertive and divisive nationalism. This distinction is grounded in his sense of individual conscience, which is 'a fundamental constraint on national identity' (Gaita 2004a, 36), a political insight with the gravest ramifications: 'That states must recognize the individual voice of conscience, and that this is one of the things that distinguishes patriotism from jingoism is one of the lessons to be learnt when we reflect on the Holocaust' (Gaita 2004a, 37). This sense of national belonging is also characterised by its forms of expression: it is 'a lucid and truthful love of country,' to be distinguished from 'its false semblance, jingoism – corrupt ways of dividing the world between them and us' (Gaita 2004a, 39). So truth cannot be separated from its expression, nor from political acts, and the clarity generated by truth produces insight and 'lucidity' as well as veracity.

Gaita's 'love of country' sits moreover at the heart of an ethical response to pressing political matters and recalls his twenty-first-century readers to the grave and defining national moments of the Mabo judgment of the mid-1990s:

> To reveal the depth of the wrong done to the Aborigines when they were dispossessed of their lands ... one needs to appeal, not to the values of citizenship, but to love of country. By rejecting the claim that the notion of *terra nullius* applied when Australia was settled, the High Court's Mabo judgment in effect acknowledged that Aborigines could love the land so deeply that their forcible displacement from it would lacerate their souls (Gaita 2004a, 38).

He is, moreover, quite explicit about love of country as a mode of being that laces together the different kinds of connection people experience across their lives:

> It is just a fact of human life that many – perhaps most – people develop deep attachments to places and to institutions. This is one of the fundamental ways in which identity is formed – through putting down roots. ... The human soul needs warmth, and for most people that comes from belonging. For most people their deepest attachments are local, to a particular part of a country, perhaps a farm or a town, sometimes a city. They may realize that their sense of belonging is wider than this only when they are abroad and discover just how pleased they are, if they are Australian, to hear an Australian accent. This is

CHAPTER 4

not a superficial thing: poets sometimes dry up in exile. For many people, less fortunate than Australians, the realization might come when they have lost their country and live under foreign occupation, denied the right to speak their language, to honour their national institutions, fully to remember their past and to pass on its treasure to the future generations. In such terrible circumstances, people realize that responsible love of country will seek protection by force of arms for what is loved and is owed to future generations (Gaita 2004a, 40).

Community is thus more than just the setting for the action of the memoir; it grounds the nature and consequences of truth as a form or mode of testament. This approach gives force to the painstaking account of the moral qualities and the work ethic of 'the men and women I had known as a boy growing up in Central Victoria in the 1950s,' in that community – a set of shared practices and experiences, an ethos – provides an imperative to truth; in compelling us to speak straight, it presses us into the national and the human frames where truth is tested.

The memoir also takes up the idea of *character* as a means to articulate an understanding of the self as constituted in relation to the other, and this is seen most intensely in the friendship Gaita describes between his father and Hora, a friendship understood primarily in terms of conversation. Gaita makes two significant points in his account of that friendship: firstly that the self is formed in relation to others, and is thus porous and incomplete, part of a more expansive relation to the world around it. The self is forged through the diverse acts and modes of belonging. It is formed in friendship and work, and is thus social, material and quotidian, and it belongs to others – to the community – in fundamental ways as a consequence of these practices. It is most distinctively through the operations of conversation that these relations come about. Conversation draws us into the orbit of otherness, where the self is opened up to different perspectives and points of view. The second point is that this provides for truth, and connects truth to the details of particular lives as they are lived, based in practices of honesty and a certain directness: 'To be straight was not merely to tell it straight, but to tell it from a self made straight by its obedience to ethical imperatives.' And: 'For my father, truthfulness was [not an abstract principle, but] a condition of human interchange, a condition of conversation' (Gaita, 2007, xvii). Friendship and community are thus defining modes in terms of the self that is formed, and also in terms of the possibilities for truthfulness and authenticity being sustained at a national level. Both *Romulus* and 'Breach of Trust,' then, focus on the idea of conversation as a practice that attends, indeed testifies to our specificity and location in the world; to the detail and matter of our daily existence, across the reach of our lives, and also to our modes of locution, to the words we speak, hear and read. For me, the experience of watching actors in the film of *Romulus* playing characters speaking to each other in ways that were both deeply familiar in terms of my own life and family, and also utterly unexpected in terms of established conventions of representing national experience, worked to transmit this specificity of locution. And it is on this basis that I am proposing that we view this experience of veracity or witness as a property of memoir as a literary form in relation to *Romulus, My Father*.

I now want to consider the place of Christine in this story. As a genre centrally concerned with the story of a life, memoir privileges the family home as a primary site at which the self is formed, in terms of the coherence and development of the child, and of course as the locus of memory and inheritance. In this memoir, it is precisely this locus that is bereft of Christine. This point is also eloquently made by novelist Alex Miller, in a letter from which Gaita quotes in a revised version of the 'From Book to Film' essay included in *After Romulus*: [Your mother] … seemed, of all of them, to be the one truly displaced person … She was an exile in a way that none of the others were' (Gaita 2011a, 162-63). Miller makes his point in relation to the film: 'I had not seen this before and I believe it is part of the greatness of the film to have given it to us' (Gaita 2011a, 163), but I want to propose that this exiled, unhoused dimension of Christine is central to the memoir's account of her story as well. With the literal and symbolic absence of Christine, the domestic space of the home is occupied instead by Romulus and his friend Hora, who take responsibility for the care of the young Raimond. This care is by no means confined to the domestic realm; it opens up within the family unit the imaginative and affective capacity for grace and forgiveness, as can be seen in the compelling account of father and son working together to build the headstone for Christine's grave:

> In the summer sun we did our remorseful work. We dug the foundations, carried sand from the creek at Carisbrook, mixed the cement and built the monument. My four-year-old daughter Katie played among the graves, guaranteeing that we would not yield to morbidity. At one point my father rested on his shovel and cried. 'Memories,' he said.

CHAPTER 4

> With shaking hands he rolled a cigarette which he smoked to help control his tears, and he spoke compassionately of my mother's troubled life. Working together, our sorrow lightened by the presence of a young girl representing new life and hope, we came together as son and husband with the woman whose remains lay beneath us (Gaita 1998, 113–14).

I looked at this scene in an earlier discussion of this work (Olubas 2007), and argued there that:

> We are faced here with a complex and yet utterly prosaic temporality, where family relations are determined by labour on behalf of another. The persistence of loss, the impossibility of closure over the death of a mother, frames an understanding of family relations in terms of generation as a mode of interrelation. The interment of Christine draws her story and her loss into the present of the telling, and sets it alongside Gaita's memories of the parental care exercised by Romulus and Hora – the sewing, the cooking, the buying and growing food – that work to fill the maternal spaces rendered bereft by Christine's emotional distress and incapacity.

There is a solemnity and solidity, indeed a gravity, in this scene that is absent from the accounts given in the memoir of Christine inside houses or dwellings. Threaded through the memoir is a sense of her persistently uneasy habitation, compounded by a sense of confinement that she displays when she is inside a house; a profound disquiet in the face of the domestic spaces that are at the same time configured with ease and a sense of rightness around Romulus, Hora and the boy Raimond. Indeed Christine is seen in constant flight from each of the family homes. In none of these dwellings is there the sense of solidity for her that we find in the grave scene. It seems to me that as literary readers we need to make sense of Christine's death and burial but also and at the same time to make sense of her absence from the family home. With this in mind, I want to think further about the grave scene, and to examine some of the ways it brings her into the heart of the memoir, and its literary ambit; I want, more precisely, to propose that Christine's grave and the family home are tightly bound together and that this binding is in itself important. The connection is also apparent in Gaita's continued meditation on the story. His essay 'An Unassuageable Longing' opens with a graphic and affecting scene in which he recounts his own act of retracing Christine's steps away from the house towards a site that is akin to a grave, on a night of heightened emotion, his motivations mysterious even to himself:

> [W]ith no conscious thought I drove to Frogmore. I climbed through the wire fence surrounding the remains of the house. From there, with no sense of what I was doing or why, I walked half a kilometre across a paddock, my feet crunching on the wheat stubble, almost white by the light of the moon, and lay down next to a log in a swamp area. As is often the case, there was no water in it.
>
> More than fifty years earlier, a few days after she returned to Frogmore from the hospital in Maldon following a failed suicide attempt, my mother left the house without telling my father or me and spent the night in that same swamp, lying beside a log. …
>
> She came back to the house (I cannot say she came 'home') the next morning. My father and I were hysterical with grief because we thought she lay dead somewhere in the paddocks, but she refused to tell us what she did that night or why. She told us only that she had stumbled over a log and cut one of her shins. She said that she had been demoralized and had slept the night beside the log. I doubt that she slept (Gaita 2011a, 168–69).

Gaita's stricken and unthinking act is to return to the literal site of Christine's unhousing, a site that itself suggests both bed and grave. With this act he brings together past and present grief, commemorating the utter isolation of this figure lying on the ground beside a log, by taking its place a half century later and thus re-enacting the burial anticipated that night by her son and husband. The layering of loss and grief across generations, returning us over and over to the same place, which is the place of burial, suggests something of the force of the grave, as Derrida has reminded us in his meditation on the ghostly appearance of Hamlet's father on the ramparts of Elsinore, asking: 'What goes on between these generations?' (Derrida 1994, 5). In order to examine this question more closely, I turn to an observation by the Australian literary scholar and novelist Gail Jones from her 2006 essay 'A Dreaming, A Sauntering: Re-imagining Critical Paradigms' about the nature of literary writing and the relations of veracity it engenders. Jones writes:

> Maurice Blanchot, commenting on Kafka, suggests that the belief that writing is an observation which is also an act is a form of *confidence*,

CHAPTER 4

> almost metaphysical confidence, in the face of bureaucratic phantasms and desolating injustice. It is, in Blanchot's words, 'fidelity to the work's demands, the demands of grief.' There is a solemnity to this statement that is very compelling: it suggests that all writing, in a sense, is an assertion against loss, a wish to commit to the figure, or figuration, what seems otherwise assigned to wordless compliance or surrender. Yet the work's demand here implicates or assumes a kind of redemptive drive, a promise of reparation within words themselves (Jones 2006, 15–16).

The sense of literature, of 'words themselves' as a mode of confidence in the face of phantasm or injustice, and of literary attention as a 'fidelity to … the demands of grief' expresses something very close to the way I want to think about the question of Christine. For me, the memoir refuses – or fails – to account for her as a separate character, but it nonetheless insists with profound empathy, with sorrow, on the very full significance of her place in the story, her unspeakably difficult life and death, and their role in ordering the lives and deaths of those around her. In the face of this desolation – the cigarette smoke, the 'memories,' the child playing around the grave – the memoir takes on the confiding force of writing, and of literary attention.

Gail Jones appends to this rich moment from Blanchot an argument about the force of what she calls 'signifying absence and the trope of disintegration' (Jones 2006, 16) not, I think, in order to fetishise the dead or ghostly figure but rather to attend to the roundness of its loss. She continues, moreover, to embrace the figure of the ghost as a point of uneasy presence that requires us 'to assess the claims the dead have on us to be heard and acknowledged' (Jones 2006, 17). Raimond Gaita uses similar words to Jones when he describes the part played by his grief over Christine in writing the book:

> Only recently … have I come to realise fully how much I wanted to write about my mother, Christine. I should have realised earlier. For some weeks after I had decided to write the book, I wrote only a few pages of notes. Then for my fiftieth birthday one of my daughters, Katie, gave me a tape of songs she liked and hoped that I would like. It included songs by Emmy Lou Harris. For reasons I still do not fully understand, the song 'Goodbye' (with its refrain 'I can't remember if we said goodbye') summoned the ghost of my mother. For at least a week I brooded on her and played the song repeatedly. I then rented a cottage

at Maldon, fifteen minute's drive from the farm on which I grew up, and began to write (Gaita 2007, xii).

Writing the book becomes possible only when Gaita acknowledges, insistently, his forgetting of Christine, his mistaking of her loss, voiced in the repetition of forgetting and of loss: 'I can't remember if we said goodbye.' This voicing brings the *in*consequence of Christine's loss back into the orbit of memory, and back into a gripping proximity to the home. It recalls at the same time, the story Gaita tells only later, in 'An Unassuageable Longing', of his re-enactment as an adult of Christine's act of self-burial from his childhood, drawing us yet again to reflect on 'what goes on between these generations.' Now consequent, Christine's ghost takes on material form through the labour of writing, and as such, this moment constitutes a reiteration of that scene of father and son making her headstone beside her grave, with daughter Katie again providing the note of grace.

Without making too much of Christine as a haunting and haunted figure in the narrative, I want to propose, in the terms that Gail Jones provides, that there is another dimension of veracity in the unutterable force of her story, drawing the desolation of her melancholy into some 'kind of redemptive drive, [or] promise of reparation within words themselves.' This is something like Flannery O'Connor's 'The Story of Mary-Anne,' an essay I turned to when I first wrote about this book, in the way it insists on grace and ghostliness, on persistence, loss and locution in its attempt to think through the question of how to write about goodness and a life of goodness. What Gail Jones's insights have given me now is a way of thinking as well about loss and about a life of difficulty, and the significance and force of the grave at the heart of *Romulus*, a way of understanding why as a reader I return so often to the scene I've just considered.

In order to think further about the proximity Raimond Gaita establishes between memoir and grave, I want to turn to another literary scholar, Robert Harrison, in particular to his reading of burial as the site of the literary in western culture. Harrison proposes that: 'As the primordial sign of human mortality, the grave domesticates the inhuman transcendence of space … [marking] human time off from the timelessness of the gods and the eternal returns of nature' (Harrison 1994, 23). 'The surest way' he tells us, 'to take possession of a place and secure it as one's own is to bury one's dead in it' (Harrison 1994, 24). In its function as the site of burial, the house grounds the larger structures of city and state: 'the ancient city was built on the foundations of the ancient house and … the ancient house was

CHAPTER 4

built in turn upon the ancestor's grave' (Harrison 1994, 25). Thus nations and empires 'repose on ... [these] human – call them humic – foundations' (Harrison 1994, 27).

The work of Gaita's memoir – to bear witness to the truth of his father's life – also insists on the centrality of his mother's grave. And her loss sits inside, beneath and around the home that is maintained with such care by Romulus and Hora. As Robert Harrison argues:

> If a house, a building, or a city is not palpably haunted in its architectural features – if the earth's historicity and containment of the dead do not pervade its articulated forms and constitutive matter – then that house, building, or city is dead to the world. Dead to the world means cut off from the earth and closed off from its underworlds. For that is one of the ironies of our life worlds: they receive their animation from the ones that underlie them (Harrison 1994, 36).

In other words, Christine's grave in this memoir teaches us something hugely important about 'love of country,' and about how we occupy our homes and live in our communities; it teaches us, that is to say, about what the Australian literary imaginary might be. The searing specificity of attachment to place that Gaita articulates both in regard to the devastations of *terra nullius* and to the humbler story of his own family speaks to the obligations attendant not only upon the lives of individuals, communities and cultures, but also upon their deaths. This is why Christine's story is so much at the heart of this memoir: it is because the grave itself in its doggedly material dimensions, is absolutely central to the literary capacity of memoir. For the final word on this, I turn once more to Robert Harrison:

> In giving voice to the wound of mortality itself, literature houses or gives a home to even the most desolate kinds of grief. It gives us back that which we keep on losing, namely a cognizance or recognizance of our passionate and mortal natures. Hence the intrinsically posthumous character of the literary voice. ... Works of literature, then, are more than enduring tablets where an author's words survive his or her demise. They are the gifts of human worlds, cosmic in nature, that hold their place in time so that the living and the unborn may inhabit them at will, make themselves at home in their articulate humanity – all thanks to the ultimate gift of the earth, which renders their testaments possible (Harrison 1994, 14–15).

Chapter 5

THE TIME OF FRIENDSHIP

Helen Pringle

I'll begin with time. Joseph Ratzinger tells a story of his friend Romano Guardini out walking one day in Munich's English Garden. Guardini was approached by a boy who asked him the time. In German, the usual expression is 'Wie spät ist es?' that is: how late is it? The elderly Guardini was seized by a melancholic reverie, wondering, 'Indeed, what time is it? How late has it gotten at this hour of my life?' (Ratzinger 2004, 4). Ratzinger's retelling of the story of Guardini leads in to an extraordinary reflection on the nature of time and eternity, prompted by the question, 'What in general is this thing, time?' (Ratzinger 2004, 5). Or, as Nina Simone asks, 'What is this thing called time? Where does it go, what does it do? Most of all, is it alive?' And who knows where the time goes.

The question at issue for Ratzinger with this thing called time concerns its relation to eternity, and hence our understanding of God and of our relation to Him. Eternity is probably most commonly understood as being outside time, like something one would plop into after the very last day. For Ratzinger however, this cannot be right. Eternity understood in that common view as a kind of non-time would not be eternity. So Ratzinger explains that eternity is better understood as a power over time. He means power – at least as I understand the point – not as domination, but power as a holding, an encircling tenderness towards the world and to the time of the world.

This relationship of a tender care seems to be the kind of power involved in Romulus Gaita's workmanship as characterised in his son's book. Raimond Gaita writes of his father: 'He was so at ease with his materials and always so respectful of their nature that they seemed in friendship with him, as though consenting to his touch rather than subjugated by him' (Gaita 1999, 97). Or again, it seems to be the mode of life of Vacek, who lived near the Gaita family, living 'in that landscape as though in friendship with it' (Gaita 2002, 16). It seems a rather odd way of speaking to characterise a relationship with craft materials or with a landscape as one of 'friendship,' but I think it is comprehensible if we think of friendship as a particular form of relation to time, rather than confine it more narrowly to a relation between persons, in which however it finds its finest shape.

The true friend

As I understand Joseph Ratzinger's perspective, the relation that is characteristic of eternity is that of friendship, whose archetype is the love of friends for each other. In his homily immediately preceding his election, Ratzinger marked out this relation:

> a mature adult faith is deeply rooted in friendship with Christ. It is this friendship that opens us up to all that is good and gives us a criterion by which to distinguish the true from the false, and deceipt [sic] from truth ...
>
> The Lord addresses these wonderful words to us: 'I no longer speak of you as slaves ... Instead, I call you friends' (John 15:15). We so often feel, and it is true, that we are only useless servants (cf. Luke 17:10). Yet, in spite of this, the Lord calls us friends, he makes us his friends, he gives us his friendship. The Lord gives friendship a dual definition. There are no secrets between friends: Christ tells us all that he hears from the Father; he gives us his full trust and with trust, also knowledge. He reveals his face and his heart to us. He shows us the tenderness he feels for us, his passionate love that goes even as far as the folly of the Cross. He entrusts himself to us, he gives us the power to speak in his name: 'this is my body ...' 'I forgive you ...' He entrusts his Body, the Church, to us ... The second element Jesus uses to define friendship is the communion of wills. For the Romans *'Idem velle – idem nolle'* (same desires, same dislikes) was also the definition of friendship (Ratzinger, 2005).

This last phrase from the Romans is a reference to Sallust's histories, and reads more fully: *'Nam idem velle atque idem nolle, ea demum firma amicitia est,'* 'For to like the same things and to dislike the same things, only this is a strong friendship' (Sallust 1921, 34: xx.4). Sallust writes this in the course of telling the story of Catiline addressing his army and fellow conspirators. Cataline rallies his men by saying that friendship is about liking and disliking the same things, from which it follows that whatever misfortunes befall one also affect, and afflict, the other.

This saying from Sallust's histories is quoted again in Benedict XVI's encyclical *Deus caritas est*. Indeed, the saying is a staple of classical Catholic discussions of friendship more broadly, with the source usually given as Cicero. Aquinas had misattributed the saying to Cicero, writing, 'it is reckoned a sign of friendship if people "make choice of the same things" (*Ethic.* Ix, 4) and Tullius [Cicero] says (*de Amicitia*) that friends "like and dislike the same things"' (Aquinas, *Summa*, II–II q.29a 3c, quoted in Schwartz [2007, 44] and in Orsuto [2006, 278]). I think it is important to note that the saying, and its acceptance and approval by various writers, does not seem to mean that we should feel towards our friends as we feel towards ourselves. The Catholic discussions of friendship did accurately attribute to Cicero the view that we should stand ready to do *more* for our friends than for ourselves – even unto death: *dulce et decorum est, pro amico mori*, say.

This conclusion is movingly set out in some medieval Islamic texts, such as the parable of the friends in al-Ghazali's *On the Duties of Brotherhood*. Al-Ghazali claims that the covenant of friendship (or of brotherhood) confers on your brother-friend a right to 'your property, your person, your tongue and your heart – by way of forgiveness, prayer, sincerity, loyalty, relief and considerateness' (al-Ghazali 1976, 21). Even to oblige your friend to ask for any of these things is, al-Ghazali says, 'the ultimate shortcoming in brotherly duty' (al-Ghazali 1976, 22). The duty of a friend is to bear the burden of the other, even to put oneself before the other, in the sense of going first when facing danger or harm. The Levinasian ethical gesture of 'after you' is here superseded by the gesture of 'I will go,' that is, go without stint. Al-Ghazali writes that self-sacrifice is one of the fruits of the highest stage of brotherhood, the rank of *siddiq*. He gives the example of a Sufi fraternity condemned to death, one of whom, Husayn al-Nuri, ran forward to the executioner, putting himself before the others, and saying, 'I wished that my brothers rather than I should have that moment to live' (al-Ghazali 1976, 27).

This story and the rigour of its demands seem to present a rather bleak picture of friendship, hardly likely on first glance to be much of an inducement to form such a relation with another person. Al-Ghazali however does not think of friendship as a joyless dirge. In some ways it is for him a relationship that one actually can taste, and can be savoured as a delicacy: 'I feed a morsel to a brother of mine and find the taste of it in my own throat' (al-Ghazali 1976, 27). Over a series of essays on medieval accounts of friendship, Mother Adele Fiske charted the image of the friend as *paradisus homo* and of friendship as a garden, in which 'death is already conquered and paradise, the presence of God, regained' (Fiske 1965, 436).

CHAPTER 5

One of the things that is most emphasised in these accounts of friendships is the mutual delight that friends take in each other's company. In this context, the criticisms that have been made of the classical understanding of friendship by Jacques Derrida and others like Maurice Blanchot seem misplaced. These critiques see the classical portrait of friendship as a relationship of the Same, rather than with an other. For example, Blanchot argues, 'Greek *philia* is reciprocity, the exchange of the Same with the Same, but never an opening to the *Other*, discovery of the Other [*Autrui*] insofar as one is responsible for them, a recognition of their pre-eminence, an awakening and disillusionment by this Other [*Autrui*], who never leaves me in peace, enjoyment (without concupiscence, as Pascal would say) of their Height, of that which always makes the other closer to the Good than "me"' (Critchley 2006, 16).

However, I take it that the phrase, 'to like and dislike the same things,' does not mean that we choose our friends as Narcissus might, but rather that the relation of friendship generates or gives rise to mutuality. Or, that friendship over time gives rise to a sharing in the secrets of our self that is made possible in becoming friends *in time*. As Kant writes in *The Metaphysics of Morals*, 'Moral friendship (as distinguished from friendship based on feeling [*ästhetischen*]) is the complete confidence of two persons in revealing their secret judgments and feelings to each other' (Kant [1797] 1991, 261; see Critchley 2006, 12). This secret sharing of a deep friendship (so well captured in John le Carré's *Perfect Spy*) carries with it the danger of 'indifference or deafness' to the outer world, as C.S. Lewis noted in characterizing real friendship as 'a sort of secession, even a rebellion' (Lewis 1960, 80).

These considerations help to illuminate the way in which we can be said to have and not to have friendship, or to be friends, with animals. I am resistant to the idea that our relationship with animals can be best or appropriately thought of as friendship. Part of my uncertainty comes from my father, who is a heretic in this matter, as in much else. Although he is a religious man, he says that he does not want to be 'saved' if animals are not also, saying this not out of any great love for animals in general, but out of a sense that a God or an order created by God that does not include dogs, say, cannot be that of a just, wise and loving God, or constitute a just order of love.

While we often talk about 'man's best friend,' it is not always clear who is the friend in such a phrase. In the dialogue *Lysis; or Friendship*, Socrates broaches this problem in exploring unrequited love. The argument in *Lysis* is that we cannot be properly said to be lovers of those who do not return our love:

We were saying that both were friends, if one only loved; but now, unless they both love, neither is a friend.

That appears to be true.

Then nothing which does not love in return is beloved by a lover?

I think not.

Then they are not lovers of horses, whom the horses do not love in return; nor lovers of quails, nor of dogs, nor of wine, nor of gymnastic exercises, who have no return of love; no, nor of wisdom, unless wisdom loves them in return. Or shall we say that they do love them, although they are not beloved by them; and that the poet was wrong who sings –

'Happy the man to whom his children are dear, and steeds having single hoofs, and dogs of chase, and the stranger of another land'? (Plato 212c–e).

And yet Raimond Gaita's *The Philosopher's Dog* speaks powerfully of the tender presence in the life of the child of animals like Jack the cockatoo or Orloff the dog (Gaita 2002, 5-15). But the book does not set out any extended exploration of the relation between animals and humans as a relation of friendship, even if there are elements of reciprocal care in the relation. In this context, some of the finest literary pictures of friendship are presented in children's books of relationships *between* animals, as metaphors of human connection, as in an exquisite episode from Kenneth Grahame's *The Wind in the Willows*, in which the Rat and the Mole are hurrying homeward along their path (Grahame 1908, 101-02). The passage is remarkable for the tender but wrenching longing for home and the past, as well as the gentle understanding of friendship as a sharing of quiet joys between friends or companions on the road.

Friendship, time and loss

Friendship in the world might provide an intimation of paradise regained, but in the world it is a relation that takes place in and over time. We *can* and do speak about falling in love, and mark the point or points where it happened. But it does not really make sense to speak of falling into friendship, or of its suddenly appearing. Friendship between persons seems to be necessarily a bond that has a relation to duration. People may turn to, or 'make,' friends for advantage or pleasure, but they continue to cultivate a friendship because of the virtue of the other, and the classical discussions

CHAPTER 5

suggest that only a friendship based on mutual recognition of virtue over time is real or true friendship.

This can be clarified a little more by reference to Cicero's great work on friendship, *Laelius, de Amicitia*. The work was written by Cicero around 44 BCE, *after* his work on old age, *de Senuctute*, and it is set around 129 BCE. The context is a discussion of Laelius with his sons-in-law. Laelius had 'lost' his friend Scipio Africanus – lost to death that is – and he is concerned with how he can bear this terrible loss. The oldest friendships ought to be the most delightful, and indeed some durability or endurance of the tie must be present for the relation to be considered a friendship: 'many pecks of salt must be eaten together to bring friendship to perfection' (Cicero 1887, 50). True friends are 'old friends' who have become open to each other. In this way of thinking, it seems that the friendships of children cannot count as friendships in the deepest sense, and that friendship between persons is an important aspect an adult relationship. Anna Akhmatova famously wrote of her 'friends of the final levy' (Dyurmen, August 1942, in Akhmatova 1992, 431).[1]

Most classical accounts of friendship insist on the slowness of friendship. Cicero's *Laelius* for example claims that even becoming friends is something to be approached with considerable slowness and caution. Medieval Catholic authors took this to an extreme, with Aelred of Rievaulx's *Spiritual Friendship* making an argument for the need of a kind of warden of the heart to ensure that 'They are worthy of friendship in whose very selves there is reason why they should be loved.' And this gatekeeping certainly seems prudent given the danger of ex-friends divulging our secrets to the world (Aelred of Rievaulx 2010, 1.20, 59), whether carelessly or maliciously.

And friendships do break down, often spectacularly, as attested in colourful fashion by the title of Norman Podhoretz's memoirs, *Ex-Friends: Falling out with Allen Ginsberg, Lionel and Diana Trilling, Lillian Hellman, Hannah Arendt, and Norman Mailer* (1999). William Blake's poem, 'To H[ayley],' poignantly portrays the breaking of the relation between friends:

> Thy friendship oft has made my heart to ache:
> Do be my enemy – for friendship's sake.

Many classical discussions of friendship include sections on how to handle the breakdown of a friendship, as in Cicero's advice:

---

[1] The translation of the phrase is by Stephen Fortescue.

> Such friendships are to be effaced by the suspension of intercourse, and, as I have heard Cato say, to be unstitched rather than cut asunder, unless some quite intolerable offence flames out to full view, so that it can be neither right nor honourable not to effect an immediate separation and dissevering (Cicero 1887, 55).

In this context, there seem to have been formal procedures for the renunciation of friendship and its duties in the Roman republic and empire (see Rogers 1959).

Going far beyond the breaking down of friendship or friendships, however, is the loss of a friend to death. For Cicero, 'real friendships are eternal,' with the paradox that these real friendships are only made through time. Derrida seems to point to a resolution of this paradox by understanding first that the discourse of friendship is very often a mourning or lamentation for a lost friend (*Work of Mourning* 2001, 115), where friendship in the world is conducted under the ordinance of time, in which friends are 'lost,' whether it is Scipio Africanus or Hobbes' sweet friend Sidney Godolphin (Hobbes [1651] 1996, 3–4, 484).

In a very cynical sense, a friendship could then be said to be complete: dead men tell no secrets. But of course, few people breathe a sigh of relief when their friends die because of knowing that their secrets are now safe (they are probably on the hard drive anyway). The discourse of friendship seems to reach its greatest flowering in the loss of the friend. Cicero writes, in the person of Laelius:

> For he, indeed, who looks into the face of a friend beholds, as it were, a copy of himself. Thus the absent are present, and the poor are rich, and the weak are strong, and – what seems stranger still – the dead are alive, such is the honor, the enduring remembrance, the longing love, with which the dying are followed by the living; so that the death of the dying seems happy, the life of the living full of praise (Cicero 1887, 19).

Laelius concludes that memories of his friendships are his consolation, with friends and friendship becoming eternal in memory.

This understanding of friendship constituted in memory is suggested in Ratzinger's meditation on time, whereby eternity is not a form of timelessness or non-time but a relation to time, a relation that reconciles it – and its wounds – in an encircling love. Ratzinger asks,

> can we come up with some idea of time gathered up into a final definitive state, a state in which it is not revoked but finds the valid way for it to

CHAPTER 5

continue to exist? I think that our reason can derive some help from the concept of *memory*. Men and women can interiorize the time that is passing by, give to it a continuing existence on a new level in which, on the one hand, it ceases as a time that passes, but yet, on the other hand, is given a continuing existence, a kind of eternity (Ratzinger 2004, 24).

In this kind of eternity, the suffering that has borne the wounds of temporality is reconciled as a form of wisdom rather than as inexplicable affliction. The wounds of time can then be taken to express the pain involved in the movement to perfection and wholeness – or in the loss of a friend.

Friendship and virtue

The starting point of this essay was a passage from *Romulus, My Father*, in which Raimond Gaita paints a portrait of Romulus' friend Hora, and talks of coming to know what friendship is:

> The philosopher Plato said that those who love and seek wisdom are clinging in recollection to things they once saw. On many occasions in my life I have had the need to say, and thankfully have been able to say: I know what a good workman is; I know what an honest man is; I know what friendship is; I know because I remember these things in the person of my father, in the person of his friend Hora, and in the example of their friendship (Gaita 1999, 74).

This passage raised a question for me, as a mother as well as an academic, of how a child learns to be a good and a true friend, especially perplexing in the age of Facebook, when amassing 'friends' seems to have taken the place of stamp collecting as a child's hobby. At any rate, it is not immediately clear from this passage or from the book how children can *know* friendship from examples of it.

This is the problem about which Alexander Nehamas has written a charming essay, an essay the more troubling for its charm. Nehamas conjectures that contrary to classical accounts, virtue has very little to do with friendship, and that one might be taken up in a deep relationship of friendship with a reprobate. He is arguing against the classical view that friends seek the good of friendship for its own sake, not for the sake of something external to it, such as pleasure – and that hence, only good people can have true friendships. The view that goodness is linked to the trueness of friendship is also implied in this passage from *Romulus, My Father* concerning the relation of Hora and Romulus at Frogmore:

When Hora was at Frogmore he and my father often talked into the early hours of the morning, the kitchen filled with cigarette smoke and the smell of *slivovitz*. They talked to each other in Romanian, which I understood reasonably but could not speak. To me they spoke in German until my teenage years when, to accommodate my foolish embarrassment, they spoke to me in English. Their individuality was inseparable from their talk – it was revealed in it and made by it, by its honesty. I learnt from them the connection between individuality and character and the connection between these and the possibility of 'having something to say,' of seeing another person as being fully and distinctively another perspective on the world. Which is to say I learnt from them the connection between conversation and Otherness (Gaita 1998, 72–73).

Gaita writes elsewhere, in the context of exploring trust, of the importance of the 'answerability,' where 'the constantly modulated answerability of flesh-and-blood individuals to one another, individuals who must answer the challenge "Why are you doing this?"' (Gaita 2004a, 12) gives weight to morality. The answerability of friends to each other is a moral relation on this view, inseparable from the pleasure of friendship. In *After Romulus*, Gaita writes of the risk of conversation as suddenly finding ourselves answerable to a 'call to seriousness': 'That is a burden inseparable from the joy of having found someone with whom we can really talk' (Gaita 2011a, 27).

Alexander Nehamas argues in contrast that friendship is not a moral good, and that 'friends' activities are often trivial, commonplace and boring, sometimes even criminal' (Nehamas 2010, 267). This conclusion is made in the context of a discussion about how hard it is to *see* friendship, even in paintings, say, of which friendship is the ostensible subject. Novels are even less promising in this respect. Nehamas gives the example of the friends Bouvard and Pécuchet in Flaubert's novel, a pair of blockheads who bore and even disgust their own creator. Mark Polizzotti's introduction to the novel, notes Nehamas, makes a comparison to the friendship of the Three Stooges, that is, a comparison to lives and activities of 'unredeemed [and seemingly unredeemable] insignificance' (Nehamas 2010, 273), such lives as are mirrored in a song of banality like 'Life Gits Tee-Jus Don't it?'[2] The activities of friendship in this view might be tedious, or even criminal and cruel. Nehamas notes that the friendship of Thelma and Louise becomes stronger and appears 'more admirable *because* of the bad things they do [together]' (Nehamas 2010, 276). In a similar vein, Dean Cocking and

---

[2]   I owe this reference to James Smythe.

CHAPTER 5

Jeanette Kennett cite the actions of the friend Dave in helping his friend to dispose of a body in the Australian film *Death in Brunswick* (Cocking and Kennett 2000, 279–281ff).

Classical expositions of friendship would see such stories not as exemplars or even as examples of friendship but as perversions of the relation. In Cicero's *de Amicitia*, Laelius warns that 'Wrongdoing is not excused if it is committed for the sake of a friend.' For instance, the friends of Tiberius Gracchus did not support him – and rightly did not support him – in his fomenting of civil unrest. Cicero holds it as a 'law of friendship' that friends do not ask their friends to do a wrongful deed – and it follows for him that 'the friendships of evil men must be suppressed' (although it is not clear how that suppression was to be accomplished). 'For to like the same things and to dislike the same things, only this is a strong friendship' – but if both of them like pillage and thieving, this is not a strong friendship, nor one that deserves to last over time. It is not enough to refer to the joys of company as lying at the basis of friendship, for criminal friends may enjoy great larks together. Cicero cannot even bring himself to call such comradeship by the name of friendship: 'were one to feel bound to do all that friends might desire, such connections ought to be considered as not friendships, but conspiracies' (1913, 7). Cicero's discussion in *de Officiis* makes clear that friendship is a relationship of men of like character, the unifying in plurality of those who have 'the same virtuous desires and purposes.' So in terms of same likes and dislikes, Cicero does not have in mind that both of them like their eggs scrambled rather than boiled, say.

The fact that Cicero's conception of friendship differs from a modern conception does not of course amount to an argument against the modern perspective, and it is a difficult question to grasp what renders the modern conception as an inappropriate example from which we might gain knowledge of friendship. The example might teach stupidity in the case of Bouvard and Pécuchet, or criminality in the case of Thelma and Louise, but does it teach a mistaken idea *of friendship*? I think the answer has something to do with the way friendship stands in regard to time. A friend of my son referred to him in charming if somewhat faltering grammar as *'un amico de cuore,'* a heart's friend, meaning to convey something of the sense of the established lasting-ness of the relation, both in its longevity and in an expectation of its permanence over time to come.

Perhaps the very duration of friendship over time grants a glimpse of the power of eternity, such that a true friendship is a kind of philosophy, philosophy as the practice of consolation. At least this might be the case where the friendship is one of equals and one conducted with thoughtfulness and seriousness. That is, where what Plato calls 'the bonds of friendliness and fellowship' are the very stuff of conversation, as appears in Gaita's account of Hora and Romulus. Where this is the case, friendship is not just one relation among others, but reveals something fundamental about who we are. Although friendship makes us vulnerable to time, and the losses it exacts on the levy of friends, its thoughtful practice simultaneously enables us to withstand that vulnerability. It becomes a practice of the good life, in time, and saves us from despair.

Politics, Law and Society

Chapter 6

A POLITICAL FRIENDSHIP

Robert Manne

A few years ago, Rai and I participated at a panel at the Melbourne Writers Festival on the subject of friendship. In the course of the discussion, the Chair of the session asked whether the friendship between us ever involved discussion of non-intellectual matters. We were both very amused by the question, at the idea that a friendship as long and as deep as the one between Rai and me could possibly have been conducted entirely on the intellectual plane. It goes without saying that friendships are not like that. On the other hand, it is true that throughout our wonderful friendship one persistent dimension has been the political vision that we shared at the beginning and the ways that original shared political vision has influenced a part of what we have thought and written about over the years. In the brief space available to me in this chapter, what I will speak about, inadequately, is the nature of what I will call our political friendship. Yet here one caveat is important. As a philosopher, one of the questions Rai has wrestled with throughout his life is the problem of the relationship between an absolute morality of good and evil in the life of individuals, and the realm of politics, where both a concern for consequences and the willingness of political actors to dirty their hands seem inescapable and intrinsic to the practice. In what I say here Rai's attempts to resolve this tension – that is to say his formal contribution to political philosophy – is not at all my subject. The story I will tell is about the origin and evolution of a political friendship. In essence it is the story of the friendship of two moralists born shortly after the end of the most barbaric period in the history of humankind – one a philosopher, the other an historian – whose parents' lives had been shaped in different ways by the great European catastrophe. My hope is that it might shed some unexpected light on Rai's thought for those who know him only or mainly through his writings.

I have said before and will most likely say again that I first encountered Rai at the University of Melbourne in (I think) 1967. The occasion was a lunchtime discussion on the topic of existentialism. There were three speakers. One was a lecturer in philosophy, Max Charlesworth. The second was a flamboyant postgraduate in the field of fine arts, Patrick McCaughey. The third was Rai. In his comments, he revealed a theoretical depth and complexity and, even more strikingly, a level of seriousness and a purity of spirit, which I had never before encountered in someone of my own age. I felt about him then a kind of awe that almost half a century later I still feel.

In circumstances I cannot recall, it was not long before we became friends. From the first, the friendship had what I will call a political dimension. The simplest way of describing that dimension is to say that by the time we had graduated from the university we had discovered that both of us instinctively associated ourselves with the tradition of thought that we have since come to call left-wing anti-communism. It is the tradition of thought associated at that time with Hannah Arendt, especially with her great seminal work, *The Origins of Totalitarianism*, with George Orwell and particularly with his essays rather than either *Animal Farm* or *Nineteen Eighty-four* and with Albert Camus, in particular, as he was defined by his break with the more theoretically accomplished Parisian thinkers – Jean-Paul Sartre, Simone de Beauvoir and Maurice Merleau-Ponty.

This tradition to which Rai and I were drawn can be best defined in the following way. At its centre there existed the traditional left-wing concern for social justice and equality and a belief that the most just form of society was a democratic but genuinely egalitarian socialism. The belief in socialism as the political form for the realisation of social justice had however become complicated because of the understanding that in our era the most radical attack in history had been mounted on the autonomy and the dignity of the individual human being and that this attack had been mounted from both the Right, by the German Nazi state, and from the Left, by the Soviet Union under the dictatorship of Stalin. What drew Nazism and Stalinism together was what Hannah Arendt had rather dramatically defined as a genuinely novel form of government, totalitarianism. The desire for social justice, the belief in socialism, situated us firmly on the Left. The belief that since the defeat of Nazism in 1945 the totalitarian threat came from the descendants of Stalinism, in the Soviet bloc or China, situated us (but especially me) among the anti-communists at the University and beyond, most of whom were neither socialists, except in the most tepid sense, nor on the Left.

CHAPTER 6

To put things like this suggests both far greater clarity than existed at the time – the thought of most people when young is rather protean and chaotic – and also probably exaggerates how far our political visions overlapped. And yet it was that eventual overlap that did form the basis of our political friendship at the time and which has indeed endured. Let me try to recall as faithfully as my memory allows its most important elements.

The first element was the centrality of the Holocaust. As undergraduates, we had both already judged that the Holocaust represented the most radical attack on the autonomy and the dignity of the human person in the history of humankind and also the most extreme expression in history of a special kind of exterminatory racism. In my case that understanding was grounded in the fact that my parents had fled from Europe to Australia; that, in one way or another, the lives of all my grandparents had been lost; and that, as I grew to learn, the Nazi state had attempted to remove my people from the face of the Earth. Although I do not recall ever discussing the issue, I am almost certain that the centrality of the Holocaust to Rai's moral and political thought was connected, in addition to intellectual grasp and sensitivity to the nature of the event, to the fact that his mother was German and that the Holocaust was a German deed. When in his philosophic work Rai has subsequently written about the paradoxical relationship between community, patriotism and treason, the example of the anti-Hitler plotters who expressed their patriotism through their 'treacherous' activities is the case that invariably comes to his mind. Later, the centrality of the Holocaust in Rai's thought and life gained another dimension, through the great love of his life, his Jewish wife, Yael.

Historians now argue that it was in the 1960s that the Nazi campaign to exterminate the Jews was transformed in common understanding – from one of the most terrible of wartime atrocities to the seminal myth of evil for our era. They also argue that in this transformation of general understanding, the publication of Hannah Arendt's *Eichmann in Jerusalem* played a significant part. Whatever the truth of both these claims, it is certainly true that this book, and in particular one extended passage, has since the late 1960s played a part in shaping our general worldview, our political friendship and, on one occasion, our informal intellectual collaboration. The passage occurs towards the end of the book. In it, Arendt is trying to explain first the meaning of genocide and, shortly after, why she believed it proper that Eichmann should be hanged. The most important sentences are these:

> It was when the Nazi regime declared that the German people not only were unwilling to have any Jews in Germany but wished to make the entire Jewish people disappear from the face of the earth that the new crime, the crime against humanity – in the sense of a crime 'against the human status' – appeared ... And just as you supported and carried out a policy of not wanting to share the earth with the Jewish people and the people of a number of other nations – as though you and your superiors had any right to determine who should and should not inhabit the world – we find that no one, that is, no member of the human race, can be expected to want to share the earth with you.

The significance of this passage to both of us was, much later, at least in part responsible for our intervention in the question of genocide and the stolen generations. In 1937, one of the Aboriginal protectors, who proposed a policy of separating 'half-caste' children from their mothers, had enquired of his colleagues: 'Are we going to have a population of 1,000,000 blacks in the Commonwealth or are we going to merge them into our white community and eventually forget that there were any aborigines in Australia?' Both Rai and I heard in this question an echo of Arendt's words about genocide being the decision taken by one human group not to share the earth with another. Because of the influence of Arendt, both of us saw in these words and the associated interwar Western Australian and Northern Territory policy of 'breeding out the colour' of the 'half-castes,' either a genocidal plan or what I came to call the structure of genocidal thought. What shocked us about the policy was of course not physical cruelty but the conceptual arrogance of racists who sincerely believed that they were driven by concern for the wellbeing of a lower race, whose disappearance from the face of the earth would represent no great loss. For this reason, both of us were also greatly affected by the comment of one of the protectors, James Isdell – that it was of little importance if 'half-caste' babies were taken from their mothers. Like animals, Isdell observed, 'they soon forget their offspring.' For Rai, Isdell's comment took us to the very heart of racism – the sense that other lesser races do not feel as we. I suspect that Rai's concern for the question of Aboriginal child removal had another purely personal element. As readers of the wonderful essay on his mother in *After Romulus* will understand, he knew that the child's pain at the loss of a mother was lifelong and 'unassuageable.'

One other enduring influence of Arendt's *Eichmann in Jerusalem* on Rai was the comment she reported Justice Landau making at the opening of

CHAPTER 6

the trial's proceedings. Despite the facts of his case already being known, and the incommensurable evil of the crimes he had committed being altogether indisputable, nevertheless, as Landau demanded, as a human being Eichmann was owed justice and therefore a solemn trial. It is near the heart of Rai's moral philosophy about the preciousness of human beings that even the most evil criminal must not be shot down as if a rabid dog.

Another author we came to share was George Orwell. For some time this was not so. Orwell was the most important influence on my politics. What I learnt from him was how socialism, patriotism and anti-communism could be combined in what seemed to me at the time a compelling and coherent political worldview. Rai was initially sceptical. He was more drawn to Sartre or Camus than to Orwell. His resistance requires a little explanation.

George Orwell was one of the authors of choice of the anti-communist circle at Melbourne University, known oddly enough as the Australian Labor Party (ALP) Club, who had been educated by two of the most politically influential academics of that era, the Czech Jewish anti-communist, Frank Knopfelmacher, and the Irish Australian poet, Vincent Buckley. Both Knopfelmacher and Buckley had a marked impact on Rai, Knopfelmacher in particular. He regarded Rai as impossibly naïve from the political point of view but also as perhaps the most brilliant student of his generation. He was also largely responsible for Rai's movement from psychology to philosophy. Although I more or less joined the Knopfelmacher-Buckley ALP Club circle, Rai never did. For Rai, the influence of Knopfelmacher was balanced by that of another fine university teacher, Geoff Sharp, the founder of *Arena* and a man of the left. It was indeed because of his suspicions of the ALP Club circle that Rai was for some time altogether uninterested in Orwell. I still remember, or at least I think I remember, the day that he announced the discovery that he had been wrong.

The passage that converted him then, and which has stayed with him throughout his life, occurs in the essay called 'Looking Back on the Spanish War.' Orwell reports that he was getting ready to snipe at fascists across the trenches. He spotted a soldier from the other side in full view who, as he ran, held up his trousers with both hands. 'I refrained from shooting at him ... I did not shoot partly because of that detail about the trousers. I had come here to shoot at "Fascists;" but a man who is holding up his trousers isn't a "Fascist;" he is visibly a fellow creature, similar to yourself ...' Rather typically, Orwell asks 'what does this incident demonstrate?' and answers 'nothing very much,' although he also urges us to accept that for him it was unusually affecting. For Rai, in fact, it has come to mean a very great deal.

I suspect that it was a single phrase – 'fellow creature' – that was responsible for Rai's Orwellian conversion.

Throughout Rai's work attentiveness to passages like this one that others, even their own authors', have allowed to pass almost unexamined become seminal, providing means of opening the eyes of his readers to worlds of meaning. The woman, M, who thought Vietnamese did not have a feeling for children like Westerners, provides his window onto the meaning of racism. The Dutch woman who, having learned that three Jews who she had been protecting but no longer could, had been murdered, and who argued on a television documentary that the Nazis had turned her into a murderess, provides the window through which we can understand the character of remorse. The nun in the mental hospital who he observed as a young man provides a window onto the meaning of uncondescending care for the afflicted. And the passage on the fascist holding onto his trousers reveals the fellow creatureliness of all other human beings, in other words, of our common humanity.

Orwell was for Rai as he was for me an important influence in showing, at a time when Sartre had declared all anti-communists bourgeois swine, the inescapability of anti-communism to any vision of a humane politics of the left. At the time we were undergraduates, while much of the illusion about communism had already worn off – it was after all a decade since Khrushchev's anti-Stalin speech – an uncompromising anti-communism for those whose politics were situated on the left was still a reasonably unusual position. Although we shared this position as undergraduates, we arrived at it in somewhat different ways. In my case, as a young man whose political identity was shaped by the Holocaust, what I needed was to be convinced, as I was, by Orwell and Arendt and by Knopfelmacher and Buckley, about the essential similarity of the regimes of the extreme right and extreme left whose central purpose was the destruction of human dignity and autonomy and whose central institution had been the concentration camp. In Rai's case, if I understand him now as I did not at the time, there was not only the influence of books and teachers but also the profoundly important influence of his father Romulus and even more of his father's great friend. Hora was a refugee from the new communist state of Romania and had therefore experienced the meaning of communism, as Eastern Europeans were wont to say, 'on his own skin.' In Rai's fine essay on Hora in *After Romulus*, he tells of how he sang to Hora a song about working class scabs. Hora, probably correctly, thought it to come from a communist songbook. For a month or so Hora refused to speak to Rai. In *After Romulus* Rai argues that Hora's silence

CHAPTER 6

is best explained in the following way. 'Hora was, I came to understand, simply unable to speak, and ... that the impossibility in question was ethical. Hora thought that if I had become so superficial, so morally unserious, as not to care that I had become a fellow traveller with mass-murderers, then there was nothing to talk about.' Rai, who at that time was more naturally left-wing than I was, in addition, was called to moral and political seriousness because of the behaviour of a fine man.

What it is fair to say is that when we arrived at the university both Rai and I were unclear where we stood on the communist question. By the end of our undergraduate days in the late 1960s we knew. The position that we had arrived at separated us intellectually from most of our generation on the left where the prevailing moods were either pro-communism or anti-anticommunism. Hostility to all communist regimes remained a dimension of our political friendship throughout the years of the Cold War and beyond. I was not alone in being unwavering on this question. More quietly, so was Rai. Let one example suffice. The Chinese authorities offered to publish *Romulus, My Father* in translation on the condition that certain passages with an anti-communist flavour were excised. Rai refused. I would have been astonished had he agreed.

As students, the most important political event for both Rai and me was undoubtedly the Vietnam War, concerning which there was a polarisation of attitudes not seen in Australia since the Spanish Civil War and not even remotely replicated during the invasion of Iraq. There were many questions raised by the war that were debated with passion and frequently intelligence. Was the war in Vietnam in reality a civil war into which the US and their allies had intervened to advance their imperialist interests? Were the communist forces in the south puppets of Hanoi or truly independent as they claimed? Were the Vietnamese Communists agents of the Soviet Union and/or China, whose victory would represent a potent defeat for the Western cause in the Cold War? Or were they the true representatives of anti-colonial Vietnamese nationalism, as their Western supporters claimed? And more generally: Under what conditions could one think of wars as just? What was the relevance to the justice of the war of the vast technological disparity between the warring parties? How far had the technocratic mindset and scientific jargon of the mandarins in Washington disguised the nature of what was being done? Was it treasonable, as the pro-communist Labour Club at one moment agreed to do, to send funds in support of the National Liberation Front, that is to say the enemy at time of war? And was it right for the university to use its supposed traditional immunity from the police activities of the state to provide national service draft dodgers with sanctuary?

Both Rai and I discussed all these questions often deeply into the night. The questions raised by the war have never left us. According to my memory, the one question that dominated our discussions was whether a war could ever be regarded as just if its prosecution could be known in advance to involve the taking of innocent life. Rai was already grappling with problems that would remain at the centre of his thought – the impermissibility of evil acts no matter what the circumstances; the intentional killing of an innocent human as the most obvious instance of an evil act; and most radically of all – even though at that time Socrates had not yet become for him the central teacher – that it was better to suffer evil than to do it. Rather feebly but nevertheless stubbornly, I resisted Rai on the question of war on the practical ground that under contemporary conditions no war, no matter how just, could ever be fought without the knowledge that its prosecution would inevitably involve the taking of innocent life. It was fundamental to these discussions that neither Rai nor I was ever tempted by pacifism. For both of us the recent war against the Nazi state was almost self-evidently just.

This argument between us was never resolved. What is perhaps interesting is that it shows something about the very early origins of Rai's anti-consequentialist philosophic life mission, his exploration of the irreducible conflicts between politics and morality, and his rejection of the most familiar attempted resolutions: classically Macchiavelli, who thought of politics and morality as existing in entirely separate realms; in our own age Isaiah Berlin, who tried, rather superficially in Rai's view, to reconcile the apparently irreconcilable realms of politics and morality through nothing more than his core idea about the existence of incommensurable systems of value. More recently, if I am not mistaken, for Rai the question of the clash between politics and morality has been complicated by the introduction of a third element, namely law.

In general, at the University of Melbourne two camps formed over the Vietnam War. The majority of politically engaged students and staff opposed the war on the ground that the communists were nationalists and that the United States and its allies imperialists. A minority of anti-communist students and staff supported it on the ground that the Vietnamese communists were the pawns of the Soviet and Chinese totalitarian enemy and that the United States was the leader of the Free World. Rather awkwardly, neither Rai nor I was able to associate ourselves wholeheartedly with either camp. Both of us regarded the war as unjust. Both of us regarded

CHAPTER 6

the North Vietnamese communist regime as abhorrent. At the time Rai wrote with his friend Arnold Zable an article fiercely attacking Ho Chi Minh's behaviour during the time he worked against the French as an agent of the Comintern. For my part, even though I was always opposed to the war, I spoke at public meetings against the supposed independence of the National Liberation Front from Hanoi. Both Rai and I marched in the early 1970 moratorium against the Vietnam War. As Rai was able to remind me some time ago, we gravitated towards a banner – probably of a Trotskyist group – which proclaimed: 'Neither Washington Nor Hanoi.' The political intention of the banner was utterly unrealistic. But it accurately reflected the ambivalence of two young left-wing anti-communists. In later times, as I moved into the anti-communist camp more deeply than Rai ever did, I found myself on one occasion tempted by a case that had been made by the serious scholar, Guenther Lewy, in defence of the American side during the Vietnam War. I am profoundly grateful that after a short conversation with Rai, I was no longer tempted.

For those who were educated under the shadow of the Second World War, an utterly improbable expectation had inserted itself into the Western political imagination – namely that wars would be fought between powers representing the forces of good and evil. What I think both Rai and I realised at the time of the Vietnam War was that this was rarely if ever true. It was not even true of the Second World War where in order to defeat Nazi Germany, Britain and the United States were, rightly, allied to the monstrous Soviet Union under the dictatorship of Stalin. In Vietnam we opposed a war waged against a regime we despised. The same would be true in 2003 when we both contributed to a book Rai edited on the invasion of Iraq, which Michael Heyward at Text suggested we call: *Why the War Was Wrong*. In neither the case of Vietnam nor Iraq case was this opposition comfortable.

The political friendship between Rai and me has extended to the present, where both of us are involved in the struggle against global warming. For reasons that this essay might help explain, Rai was invariably an ally, sometimes very actively, sometimes through his friendship, in many of the controversies in which I became involved – the mid-1980s debate about the communist journalist, Wilfred Burchett; the 'Demidenko' affair; the stolen generations; the question of asylum seekers and many others. Discussion of all this must wait for another time. Yet one more thing needs to be said. During the time I was editor of *Quadrant* Rai wrote a monthly column which he called 'Turnings of Attention.' Eventually the columns formed an important element of Rai's book, *A Common Humanity*. In my opinion the 'Turnings of Attention' columns – truly profound and original reflections on contemporary questions produced month after month – represent one of the more astonishing achievements of recent Australian intellectual life. The column was nonetheless deeply resented by the *Quadrant* old guard, who, we learned, organised a secret campaign called G.R.O.G. – get rid of Gaita.

Happily, as this collection proves, in this ambition the *Quadrant* old guard singularly failed. All those who have contributed are, in one way or another, in Rai's debt. I know I speak for us all when I say to Rai – thank you.

Chapter 7

INTERNATIONAL LAW'S COMMON HUMANITY, OR ARE PIRATES NECESSARY?

Gerry Simpson

> ... you alone of Italy's sons has dared
> To epitomise mankind in three instalments
> What style! What wit! What a performance!
>
> Catullus

The idea of a humanity, against which crimes can be committed and in the name of whom these crimes can be punished, occupies an equivocal place in the history of international law. Provoked in part by Rai Gaita's reflections on Nuremberg and Eichmann in his essay 'Genocide and the Holocaust,' this chapter offers a brief anatomy of humanity in its various (juridical) guises. In particular I want to say something preliminary about a relatively novel legal category called 'crimes against humanity,' and how this relates to a more established category known as 'war crimes' and an even older category (perhaps the oldest in international law) inhabited by people we have wanted to call 'enemies of mankind.'

Humanity

In an article entitled, 'Why there is no International Theory,' Martin Wight, the neglected international relations scholar, argued that philosophers (and he meant here political philosophers, in particular) had taken very little direct interest in the organization of human relations in the international sphere (Wight 1960, 35-48). International relations, or the realm of the international, either had generated a set of concerns to which second-rate philosophers had dedicated themselves or was one in which first-rate philosophers had produced second-rate work. He was thinking, perhaps, of Kant's disappointing sketch of *Perpetual Peace* or Hume's merely descriptive asides on the balance of power. He might have added, had he lived longer, John Rawls anti-climactic *Law of Peoples*, a late work featuring little of the persuasive originality of his earlier work, and a book in which political liberalism, in its encounter with the brute realities of international political life, seems over-compromised (Rawls 2001).

From an international lawyer's perspective, this absence, or Wight's reflections on it, might seem counter-intuitive because international law, among all legal practices, perhaps is most susceptible to philosophical self-reflection. It is *possible*, after all, to practise company law or the law of secured transactions without engaging in discussions about the possibilities and limits of the field or about its 'lawness.'

I don't mean to suggest that such lawyers don't experience forms of dissonance about their legal and ethical practice (indeed, it almost goes with the territory) but this – most often – takes the form of angst (should I be making so much money working for this corporation?) rather than analysis (is this field of law internally coherent? Or externally enforceable?).

If Wight is right (and he was writing half a century ago) this malaise is odd for another reason because, of course, we live in at least two places simultaneously: a national political and ethical space defined by territory, sovereign exclusivity and nationality, and an international sphere distinguished by either a fragile cooperation between these various sovereigns or, in a deeper version, a vision of a world society or common humanity.

I want to think about this *common humanity* here through the twin lens of a chapter from Raimond Gaita's book of the same name (Gaita 2000) and through the doctrines or invocations of 'humanity' found in international law – particularly in a largely novel sub-species we now call, hubristically, international criminal justice (I mean by this, war crimes trials and so on).

Before I say more about this, perhaps I should describe (with a view to offering some sort of rejoinder to) one typical explanation for this apparent weakness in international political theory, which may also be a deficiency in international law itself. The international legal system as it has existed since, say, Westphalia in 1648, is marked by a form of anarchy (hence Hedley Bull's defining study: *The Anarchical Society* [2002]). There is not one sovereign but many (the idea of multiple *de jure* sovereignties was identified in relation to the Italian city-states as early as the 1300s by the

CHAPTER 7

Italian law professor, Bartolus (1313–1357) and his student, Baldus (1327–1400) (Koskenniemi 2012b, 3, 22; Koskenniemi 2012a, 47–63).

This affirmation of sovereignty at Westphalia, can be thought of as a defeat for a grander conception of (international) law as the basis for a world society. The autonomy of political units within Europe became the foundation for a narrower idea of international community and a guarantee *against* projects that saw international law's destiny in federation, perpetual peace, an updated *res publica Christiana*, a future world government (tyrannical or benign) (Abbé de St Pierre, 1713; Kant, 1795) or a return to the spiritual and temporal dominance of the Holy Roman Empire (Saint-Pierre [1713] 2009; Immanuel Kant [1795] 2007). Westphalia instated, then, a form of pluralism – a living side-by-side – that was the antithesis of the clash of absolutisms that was said to have led to the Thirty Year War. Sovereigns could do what they liked internally but they were forbidden from imposing values on other states (whatever the merit of these values).

Holy war, we might say, is international law's original wound. And that is why contemporary projects to eradicate evil or terror often think of international law not as a way of doing the right thing but as an obstacle to it. Think of Tony Blair's speech at Sedgefield in 2004 where he says, sounding like a history professor, that the 9/11 attacks had crystallised his doubts about the Peace of Westphalia (Blair, March 5, 2004).

So, in the absence of a single locus of constitutional authority (the Westphalian ideal) – the argument goes – no political and legal order can flourish. Political life, and an ethics of that political life, can exist, in a strong and meaningful form, only in a society underpinned by law and government (think of the way in which Machiavelli approached the question of law: necessary in city-states, sentimental distractions in international relations or, in a more optimistic vein, Kant's view in *Perpetual Peace* that republican constitutionalism would have to migrate outwards from internal state practices before taking shape as a sort of transnational civility buttressed by commerce and diplomacy: the EU, in its pre-bailout days, was once the model for this sort of thinking).

This argument against international law, often, is supplemented by the belief that international society is too ideologically plural or culturally fragmented to support a set of ethical precepts or, even, a legal order. All this, in turn, gives rise to a debate with which international lawyers are resentfully over-familiar. It begins with a question: is international law really 'law?' John Austin (1790-1859), of course, responded in the negative. A typical conversation around this theme will sound a bit like an exchange from a scene in Thomas Mann's *Magic Mountain*, in which Settembrini, Naphta and Hans Castrop, the novel's central figure, are discussing the future European order (Mann 1980).

Settembrini, the Italian liberal, argues for a truly international law:

> The important thing is that above the explicit jurisprudence of nation states there rises a higher jurisdiction empowered to decide between conflicting interests by means of a court of arbitration.

Naphta responds:

> Courts of arbitration! The very name is idiotic! In a civil court, to pronounce upon matters of life and death, communicate the will of God and man, and decide the course of history! – Well, so much for the 'wings of doves.' Now for the Eagle's pinions.

Or, to put this in starker terms, when the Austro-Hungarians, in 1914, presented Serbia with a set of demands it couldn't meet, the Serbs responded by suggesting that any differences arising out of the assassination of Archduke Ferdinand might be settled by the Permanent Court of Arbitration in The Hague. This quixotic gesture reads like a scene from Karl Kraus.

But at least some of this response to the problem of international law – the bathos implicit in going to court instead of going to war – revolves around Settembrini's idea of a higher jurisdiction representing 'humanity.' The question is can we return to Humanity without at the same time returning to Empire?

I want to come at the problem of 'humanity' a little indirectly by describing what the Finnish international lawyer, Martti Koskenniemi, has called 'the structure of international legal argument' (Koskenniemi, 2006).

International law has long been split between its apologetic and utopian limbs; or, to put it in the terms legal theorists might employ, its positivist or voluntarist face and its naturalist inclinations. As Koskenniemi has argued, this split is not incidental but constitutive. It is not a choice international lawyers make but a life they lead or a professional practice in which they engage.

International legal argument is always a dual appeal to the sovereign (representing concrete politics and consent or embedded practices) and to justice (representing transcendental values or ethical absolutes).

So, the tradition in the history of international law has been to juxtapose a textual, consensual tradition represented by Vattel, and emphasising state

CHAPTER 7

consent in the formation of norms, with a more cosmopolitan orientation grounded in the common humanity of people and going back to Vitoria (1485–1546) and Suarez (1548–1617), each arguing for a natural law encompassing Europeans and infidels or, even, in Vitoria's case, Indians.

This, in turn, may have reflected an earlier division in Roman conceptions of international law between a technical *ius gentium* (facilitating relations between Rome and the foreigner) and a more Stoic sensibility in which universal reason would form the basis for a world community of 'mankind.' These debates are repeatedly enlivened by contemporary UN interventions.

Cicero is thought to be the originator of the idea that pirates are *hosti humanis generis* or 'enemies of mankind.' This may well represent the first appearance of 'mankind' or humanity as a category capable of acting in some way as opposed to a political ideal to be strived for or an immanent state or prospect to be identified in the entrails of the current imperfect order.[1]

Note here two vitally important features of humanity as in 'enemies of mankind.' First that it is capable of taking unified political action, second that there are figures outside this apparently comprehensive category. This, then, can be understood as inaugurating a struggle over humanity between a wholly inclusive cosmopolitan ideal of human fellowship on one hand and a humanity that E.H. Carr thought of as a mere provisional 'harmony of interests' or an effect of empire. This struggle continued to play out over the recent war in Libya between those who believe that what we witnessed was a humanitarian war and those who viewed it as the latest in a line of imperial interventions.[2]

So far, I have described a highly stylised opposition between the international law of barely civil sovereigns opportunistically pooling their self-interest and an international law of a global humanity armed with norms of human decency sitting above state desire or national vanity.

And within this latter category a further split emerges between humanity as an inclusive world community; and humanity as a particular configuration of political forces acting in its name against 'outlaws.' Anyone who is attracted to, and yet repelled by, the phrase 'international community' will understand this division.

---

[1] Is there a sense in which Cicero's stoicism works against his attitude to piracy? Or is humanity somehow established, as a category, in its engagements with its enemies?

[2] Cosmopolitan projects have a habit, after all, of being wedded to highly specific politics. Suarez's natural law may have been prompted by his loyalty to the Catholic Church and its need for a theory of 'intervention' in English religious politics on behalf of (a papal) humanity: Koskenniemi 2012a, 51.

Crimes against humanity

The development of crimes against humanity in the twentieth century offers a microcosm of some of the themes sketched so far. Remember the whole idea of law as a form of judgement standing over sovereigns had been sidelined up to this point. Westphalia expressly rejected a structuring principle that was to become central from Versailles onwards: namely the idea that inter-state relations, and in particular war, can be organised on the basis of some sort of centrally enforced accountability for illegal acts. Justice was thoroughly relativised. If international law began in 1648, it did so in a forgiving, agnostic mood, introducing us to sovereignty as a form of forgetfulness:

> ... That there shall be on the one side and the other a perpetual ... Amnesty, or Pardon of all that has been committed since the beginning of these Troubles, ... but that all that has pass'd on the one side, and the other ... during the War, shall be bury'd in eternal Oblivion. (Treaty of Münster Art. II).

By the twentieth century, this Westphalian fusion of sovereignty and amnesia had become deeply unfashionable. Oblivion has given way to war crimes trials – all this in the midst of a fetishistic culture of compulsory commemoration.

There is barely time for even a synoptic account of how all this happened. The story of humanity begins at Versailles with the decision to indict the Kaiser for offences against international morality (a phrase reminiscent of Bentham's dismissal of international law itself) and the sanctity of treaties. The Kaiser who thought he had merely started a war found that he had committed a crime. Meanwhile, the war's winners were no longer simply the temporary beneficiaries of fate but the guardians and creators of a new legal order. Hitherto ad hoc, provisional coalitions of particular interests were transformed into the 'international community.' War had been displaced by 'pest control.' Enemies had become criminals.[3]

This is, if you like, the politico-juridical background to the momentous decision on the part of the Allies in Moscow, and then implemented later at Nuremberg, to charge the Nazi leadership with the crime of aggression and war crimes. But the mass killings (not yet properly understood (or at least fully absorbed) as a policy of eradication) prompted the articulation of a new

---

[3] The phrase is Carl Schmitt's (2003, 123).

CHAPTER 7

category: crimes against humanity. What did it mean, though, to commit a crime against humanity?

I think two separate trajectories meet here. One involves the consolidation of 'humanity' as a juridical category or the revival of the ideal of a global community of human beings (going back to Suarez and Vitoria) and, of course, the identification of enemies of that community (15 years later Eichmann was to be characterised as a latter-day pirate, after all). These are, to put it crudely, the political antecedents of crimes against humanity.

The second trajectory tracked a concern (perhaps, an obligation) to offer a juridical response to the moral problem of The Holocaust. I now want to turn to this second trajectory while keeping an eye on the first. With crimes against humanity we need to ask: What work is this new category trying to do? What special offence or injury is being captured here?

Frances de Menthon, one of the French Prosecutors at the Nuremberg war crimes trial in 1945, was assigned, in his opening statement, the task of defining humanity. The context was a trial in which a more or less new legal category – crimes against humanity – had to be created to encompass a horrifying system of abuse and murder created by the Nazis in the mid-thirties. The existing category of 'war crimes' was inadequate and under-inclusive. There was a spatial imperative (those Nazi crimes committed against Germans fell outside the category of war crimes, a category applying only to crimes committed against foreign soldiers or civilians), a temporal imperative (war crimes were committed only during war) and a moral imperative (a special level of baseness had been reached and it required a new language and new law) (See Simpson, 2012).

De Menthon believed that 'crimes against humanity' might refer to three qualities. The first was the idea that certain acts were crimes against human beings regardless of their race, religion, national affiliation or ethnicity. This was international criminal law in its human rights mode, and it was an inspiration for two 1948 landmarks: *The Genocide Convention* and *The Universal Declaration of Human Rights*. The Frenchman's second version revolved around the idea of crimes against humanity as crimes materially affecting one particular group but somehow committed against all human beings; to use the language of the International Military Tribunal (IMT) these were crimes that 'shocked the conscience of mankind' and such crimes ultimately incited the agents of mankind into adopting a variety of now – familiar responses: universal jurisdiction over war criminals ('Eichmann in Jerusalem'), international tribunals (Milosevic in The Hague) and the concept of 'prosecute or extradite' found in treaties like *The Torture*

Convention and *The Apartheid Convention* ('Pinochet in Piccadilly') The third, and most radical, concept of humanity imagined it as a unified, indivisible, and inalienable category that resisted attempts to divide human beings into 'more, or less, human,' and deplored political programmes that demanded that a person's humanity be forfeited or alienated. The Nazis' greatest crime, then, as Hannah Arendt remarked, had its origins in an effort to abolish this category of humanity through a programme of mass murder, slavery and deportation whose governing principle was the imperative that the Jewish people was to be destroyed and whose governing methods were marked by a combination of industrial murder, savagery, extreme cruelty and relentless humiliation. It was a crime, as she put it, against the order of mankind.

But this special 'crime against humanity' has been variously diluted, misapplied and mischaracterised almost from its inception. The relationship between it, The Holocaust and another crime, genocide, is especially cloudy.

Gaita in his essay, *Genocide and the Holocaust*, seems concerned to make two distinctions. One is the distinction between war crimes and crimes against humanity, the other is a more controversial distinction between genocide and the Holocaust.

First to war crimes and crimes against humanity: as Gaita puts it, the destruction of the Jews was not the latest in a line of political crimes in history. The Jews were not 'enemies,' they did not occupy land sought by the Nazis, they were not scapegoats. So what happened to them were not war crimes or breaches of minority treaties. As he puts it, and anticipating the second distinction:

> They were killed because they were judged unfit to inhabit the earth with the master race. The ruthless determination to hunt and to kill them in all the corners of the earth, if possible, distinguishes the Holocaust from other forms of genocide, as they are alleged to have occurred in colonial times (Gaita 1999, n. 3, 131).

Yet, the assimilation of the Holocaust and crimes against humanity to the category 'very bad war crimes' is found everywhere in political culture (*Schindler's List*, which I haven't seen, is a prime exhibit here for Gaita). Interestingly, the opposite problem occurs, too. Whenever a British or Australian soldier is indicted for war crimes offences, the cry goes up that our soldiers are not Nazis, that this or that act might have been a dereliction of duty or a reckless murder but it hardly bears comparison with the paradigm case: The Holocaust.

CHAPTER 7

Before we consider the special case of The Holocaust, it is important to offer an initial distinction between war crimes and crimes against humanity. But if crimes against humanity are not simply aggravated war crimes to what might they refer? Here I want to offer some possibilities largely drawn from legal doctrine.

The term 'crimes against humanity' might encompass, in 1945, the killing of Germans *by Germans in Germany*. This killing was, after all, not legally cognizable in some sense. It was neither a war crime (then at least) nor a crime against peace, but rather a deformity of sovereignty, or perhaps not a deformity but the realisation of sovereignty as the right to massacre one's own citizens without interference from other sovereigns. On this view, crimes against humanity are about space. But this might seem too local and jurisdictional, perhaps arbitrary.

An alternative view might think of the category, 'crimes against humanity,' as a way of capturing the particularly grave atrociousness of certain acts committed against civilian populations *during war*: Poles, Belarusans, Hungarians and so on. This is what the International Military Tribunal judges were getting at in 1946 and this is what Gaita worried about when he said that the term crimes against humanity 'invites the misconception that the Holocaust was marked by extreme inhumaneness' (Gaita 1999, 132) or a particular scale of atrocity rather than being different in essence. For Gaita, The Holocaust was not simply a by-product of war or an incident of generalised atrocity or an especially bad mass killing: a grave breach of the Geneva Conventions to put this in legal dialect.

Sometimes, crimes against humanity have been thought of as a way of applying an international penal code to the problem of atrocity outside the context of war. It is striking in this regard that there is no mention of war in the International Criminal Court (ICC) Pre-Trial Chamber's Arrest Warrant decision in *Gaddafi*. This is crimes against humanity in their temporal mode. Crimes committed in times other than war-time.

Finally, there is a tendency to distinguish 'their' crimes against humanity (organised, deliberate, intentional, representative) from our 'war crimes' (accidental, incidental and aberrant). During the Trial of Klaus Barbie in Lyon in 1986, the French defined crimes against humanity as heinous acts committed 'in furtherance of a national socialist ideology.' And there has always been the temptation to use 'humanity' in this way. So according to the Lyon court, crimes against humanity could be committed only by Nazis (this excluded, from this category, French torture in Algeria or Vichy collaboration). Thus the purpose of a war crimes trial is to declare of the prosecuting party: 'we, at least, are not Nazis.'

At Nuremberg, the Allies were careful to link jurisdiction over crimes against humanity with waging of aggressive war. Only the Axis powers could commit crimes against humanity.

As Robert Jackson, the American Prosecutor said at the time:

> We have some regrettable circumstances at times in our own country in which minorities are unfairly treated. We think it is justifiable that we interfere or attempt to bring retribution to individuals or states only because the concentration camps and the deportations were in pursuance of a common plan or enterprise of making an unjust or illegal war in which we became involved (Marrus 1997, 45).

So at Nuremberg, there is an effort to make jurisdiction over genocide dependent on some link to aggression. Only states that are aggressive *and* genocidal are subject to international legal scrutiny. In the case of Libya there was a reversal of sorts: crimes against humanity were uncoupled from the existing civil war (presumably in order to avoid any complication associated with defining this war). When it comes to crimes against humanity, in 2011, the ICC spoke as if there was no war in Libya. In 1946 the IMT spoke as if there was *only* war. In both cases crimes against humanity are decontextualised. This picture was further complicated by the introduction of the crime of genocide into public international law in 1948.

Recent international legal definitions have tended to focus on the widespreadness or systematic nature of an attack on a civilian population during which a particular act (say, murder or deportation) occurs. Thus crimes against humanity are distinguished from war crimes by their scale and intensity and by the absence of war as a necessary pre-requisite for conviction. And they are distinguished from genocide by genocide's requirement that the killers or torturers possess a special intent to destroy in whole or in part a particular national, ethnic or religious group.[4]

I think what has happened is that international legal definitions, which have steadily become more expansive, have moved away from Arendt's crime against the order of mankind or genocide's associations with the annihilation of whole groups.

The finding of genocide in, say, the *Krstic* case at the ICTY is not the sort of crime against humanity of which either Gaita or Arendt speak.

---

[4] See e.g. Articles 6 and 7 of *Rome Statute of the International Criminal Court.*

CHAPTER 7

The Srebrenica massacre, officially designated a genocide by the ICTY (International Criminal Tribunal for the former Yugoslavia) and the ICJ (International Court of Justice) (a rare combination), would not, I think, qualify as *this sort of* crime against humanity (the Gaitan version). General Krstic was guilty of complicity in the killing of the boys and men of Srebrenica (in other words a part of the Bosnian Muslim population of Eastern Bosnia who in turn were part of the Bosnian Muslim ethnic group: in other words, two parts of a whole). This is an awful killing and, arguably, a genocide under the terms of the convention, but it falls some way short of seeking to remove a people from the face of the earth.

So, The Holocaust seems incapable of capture by the legal definitions. Maybe this is not so surprising given the ambiguous origins of 'crimes against humanity' and 'genocide' in uncertain moments of legal innovation. And maybe law's universalising impulses and technocratic demeanour make it unsuitable to this task in any case. In law everything must have a precedent and be a precedent for something else. And yet, at the same time, atrocity is often described as unprecedented or unique.

The definition of 'crimes against humanity' in the International Criminal Court statute, for example, falls hopelessly short of saying anything about The Holocaust's essence. Gaddafi's acts look to me like the sorts of crimes referred to by Arendt when she talks about 'excesses of war' and this precisely was what the Holocaust was not. Its mysterious combination of banality and evil is best represented, according to Rai Gaita, through scrupulous remembrance and acts of moral and, often, literary imagination.

There is a passage in 'Genocide and The Holocaust' where Gaita discusses whether law can speak *at all* to these moral catastrophes, whether it might be the case that law makes an assumption about common humanity that these crimes deny or – and this is of course a related point – that somehow there is an incommensurability between the distinctive evil of the camps and the routines of legalism. He describes, too, the way in which chroniclers of the Warsaw Ghetto kept journals believing that their descriptions of the privations of ghetto life would appeal to a 'common humanity' later to underpin applications of legalism at Nuremberg and in Jerusalem. The camp survivors, he goes on to say, suspected either that this common humanity had been destroyed by the Nazis or that a totalitarian conception of common humanity might have led to the Holocaust itself.[5]

---

[5] Gaita quotes Sara Horowitz who writes: 'The Ghetto writers anticipate the outrage of the future reader – outrage based upon the shared values and common idea of

This arresting comparison takes us full circle to my discussions about *humanity* in the first part of the chapter. In international law it continues to play this dual role. On one hand provoking and justifying humanitarian interventions – military, monetary, judicial – against groups and individuals beyond or excluded from humanity (the recent indictment of Muammar Gaddafi may be an example of humanity in its most instrumental guise and adopting its more imperial cast). On the other hand, there is the humanity that seeks to recognise and come to (legal) terms with special harms done to the idea of collective human flourishing. This latter project has been the subject of the second half of the chapter: an insubstantial but, I hope, useful gloss on the work of Raimond Gaita's 'A Common Humanity.'

What we have in the end then is a legal problem about categorizations, a political problem related to the uses of humanity as an ideological project and a moral problem implicating language, history and punishment. When it comes to assaults on the dignity of human beings, as in law so it is in life, we seem always to be making a distinction that doesn't quite capture our best intuitions, always grasping for languages just out of reach.

Acknowledgements
Thanks to Catherine Gascoigne for her help in preparing this chapter.

---

civilisation. Generally they remain untroubled by the suspicions which plague survivor reflections that these values were killed by the Holocaust, or indeed brought on by it' (Gaita 1999, n. 3, 145–6).

Chapter 8

'EVEN THE MOST FOUL CRIMINALS ARE OWED UNCONDITIONAL RESPECT'

The Ethical Lawyer and the Ideal of Respect

Steven Tudor

Introduction

Readers of Raimond Gaita's *Good and Evil: An Absolute Conception* are likely to be struck by a sense that it was written out of a deep, serious and personal engagement with its subject. That individual voice helps to set *Good and Evil* apart from – and sometimes put it in creative tension with – much of modern academic moral philosophy. Perhaps part of the reason for the book's distinctive tone and perspective is revealed by Gaita in his Preface to the second edition, when he says that *Good and Evil* '"registers" three "experiences," "marks" three "encounters."' This marking, he says, 'is, in all three cases, a kind of testimony' (Gaita 2004b, xii).

The first of Gaita's encounters was with a nun who tended patients at the psychiatric hospital where Gaita worked as a young man. The nun, attests Gaita, manifested a compassion – indeed, a saintly goodness and love – toward the patients that was 'without a trace of condescension.' This showed Gaita, he says, that the incurably mentally ill 'are fully our equals' (Gaita 2004b, xiii). The inclination – for me, at least – to say '*nonetheless* fully our equals' is very strong, but, as I read Gaita's testimony about the nun, to be able not even to think 'nonetheless' is part of what it would mean to see human beings as the nun showed him they could be seen.

Another of Gaita's marked encounters was with remorse. Gaita does not refer to his own experience here, but cites several examples from fiction (such as Raskolnikov in Dostoevsky's *Crime and Punishment*) and non-fiction.

Perhaps the most arresting example of remorse that he presents is that of the person he identifies as a Dutchwoman, who was interviewed in *The World at War*, the 1970s television documentary series about the Second World War. This woman had harboured some Jews in her home, but, because of her connection with the anti-Hitler underground, she could not let them stay for more than two days. She found out later that they were caught and transported to Auschwitz. Because of what she saw as her complicity in their deaths, she saw herself as a murderer, and blamed Hitler for turning her into one.[1]

Gaita presents this as an example of remorse, not because of the forensic accuracy of the woman's self-description as a murderer (no court of law would convict her of murder and surely no fair-minded person would judge her to be guilty of a moral equivalent of murder), but because of the depth and seriousness of her recognition of the reality of the people who had died, partly due to her actions, however excusable and non-murderous those actions in fact were. Remorse, says Gaita, is 'a pained, bewildered realisation of what it means (in a sense interdependent with *what it is*) to wrong someone' (Gaita 2004b, xiv). Thus, to argue that this woman ought not to feel remorseful because she is not to be morally blamed for the deaths of the Jews she had sheltered is to assume that, prior to encountering her remorse, one can have a sure grasp of the general concept of what it is to wrong another person and so can then bring that understanding to bear in judging the reasonableness of her particular remorse as a case of self-assessment. Instead, as I read Gaita, it may sometimes be the case that our understanding of what it can be to wrong another is conditional upon our recognition of authoritative examples of remorse (though such recognition need not entail uncritically endorsing the terms of the remorseful person's self-assessment). Gaita's reading of remorse thus challenges us to be open to a richer, subtler and more troubling conception of the ways in which we can understand what it is to wrong another.

---

[1] It would appear that the woman was Christabel Bielenberg, who was in fact an Englishwoman of Anglo-Irish descent, married to a German lawyer, Peter Bielenberg, and living in Germany as a German citizen during the war. Her husband was associated with the anti-Hitler underground within Germany. He was arrested and imprisoned after the failed attempt on Hitler's life on 20 July 1944, though he was released before the end of the war. The relevant part of the interview with Christabel Bielenberg appears in *The World at War*, Episode 16, 'Inside the Third Reich: Germany 1940–1944' (Thames Television, 1973). Christabel Bielenberg also wrote a memoir, *The Past is Myself* (2011). In a chapter entitled 'A Jew Story,' she relates the story of her temporary harbouring of a Jewish couple in early 1943. 'I loathed myself utterly,' she writes, for allowing the couple only 'two miserable days of grace,' though she does not there speak of being a murderer nor, indeed, mention the couple's subsequent capture and transportation to Auschwitz (2011, 122). *The Past is Myself* was adapted for BBC Television by Dennis Potter. See Potter, *Christabel* (1988).

CHAPTER 8

The other encounter Gaita notes in the Preface was with the way in which the judge presiding at the trial of Adolf Eichmann strove to ensure that the trial's sole purpose was to do justice, and that this meant, among other things, that justice was owed to Adolf Eichmann, the individual human being. It is my encounter with this encounter of Gaita's that is the prompt for my contribution to this volume.

Gaita's encounter with the judge's sense of justice was, he tells us, through his reading of Hannah Arendt's *Eichmann in Jerusalem* (Gaita 2004b, xiii; see also Arendt 1965). At Adolf Eichmann's trial in Jerusalem in 1961, the prosecutor sought to turn the event into a show trial, in which all the crimes perpetrated by the Nazis and suffered by the Jews would be paraded before the world for the political benefit of the Israeli government. The presiding judge, Justice Landau, resisted this effort and kept the trial of Adolf Eichmann focused on the individual accused and the specific allegations against him.

Gaita notes, in *A Common Humanity*, that it is 'a commonplace of legal practice ... that no criminals are so foul that they may be denied justice' (Gaita 1999, 54). And yet, as Gaita also notes, that even the 'chief architect of the Final Solution' was owed justice for his sake, as a human being, represents 'one of the sublime features of our system of criminal justice' (Gaita 2004b, xiv). Gaita sees this commonplace yet sublime aspect of the criminal law as an expression of a broader moral principle, 'the affirmation that all human beings are owed unconditional respect' (Gaita 1999, 54). And that means insisting that 'even the most foul criminals are owed unconditional respect' (Gaita 1999, 10). (Again, one has the sense, reading Gaita, that those who truly understand such unconditional respect have no need for the qualifying word 'even').

My particular interest here is with what this sublime aspect of the law might mean for individual lawyers and judges. What sort of moral encounter might it involve for them, and how may lawyers respond to the challenge to engage in an infinite and not-quite-graspable moral task as part of their everyday work? How is this aspect of the animating ethics of the institution of law related to the ethics, both professional and personal, of the individuals who maintain that institution?

As far as I know, Gaita has not addressed these particular issues in any of his writings, but my aim in this chapter is not to predict – or critique – what I think Gaita might say about them. Rather, I want to try to understand better what it might mean for lawyers and judges to encounter, through reading Gaita, a personal and even disturbing moral challenge in the idea of unconditional respect for all criminal defendants – 'even' the worst among them.

One quick preliminary word about terminology. Only a person convicted of a criminal offence can, strictly speaking, be called a criminal. However, I take it that Gaita is referring to both accused persons and convicted offenders when he speaks of 'criminals' being owed unconditional respect. I further take it that the unconditional respect owed to a convicted person is essentially the same as the unconditional respect which is owed to an accused person – or, indeed, to the unconditional respect which is owed to the most upright and innocent among us. Some lawyers might readily concede that we should respect accused persons, because, after all, in our system they are presumed innocent and may yet be found not guilty. Such 'benefit of the doubt' respect is, by definition, not available to convicted persons, even though some other basis for respect may be thought to come into the picture once an accused is found guilty. However, the unconditional respect that I understand Gaita to be talking about is lost if we start pointing to an accused person's presumed innocence as its basis. For brevity's sake, in what follows I will simply use the word 'defendant' to cover both accused persons and convicted offenders.

The sublime

When Gaita describes Justice Landau as giving 'voice to one of the sublime features of our system of criminal justice' (Gaita 1999, 54), he intends high praise for the law. Many lawyers would no doubt be quite pleased to hear such praise. Some might even feel a touch of pride in the thought that their daily work helps to maintain one of the most important aspects of our legal tradition.

However, Gaita's praise should give us pause for thought. He did not say that the law's unconditional respect for each defendant was part of the law's 'noble calling,' or reflected a 'foundational principle of procedural fairness,' or was 'essential to the protection of fundamental human rights' – though I do not think he would simply deny these propositions as such either. Instead, Gaita chose to describe the law's expression of unconditional respect as something *sublime*.

It is, of course, by no means easy to get the measure of the sublime. One way to elicit something of a sense of the sublime is through Kant's evocative descriptions of the sublime in nature in *The Critique of Judgement*. There he says that the sublime is 'what is beyond all comparison great' (1952, 94/248) and speaks of '[t]he astonishment amounting almost to terror, the awe and thrill of devout feeling, that takes hold of one when gazing upon the prospect of mountains ascending to heaven, deep ravines and torrents raging there, deep-shadowed solitudes that invite to brooding melancholy' (120–121/269)

CHAPTER 8

and oceans disturbed and 'threatening to overwhelm and engulf everything' (122/270).

These are certainly arresting images, but perhaps we also need here to consider Iris Murdoch's moral revisioning of the Kantian sublime in nature. In her 1959 article, 'The Sublime and the Beautiful Revisited,' Murdoch suggests that 'we think of the spectator as gazing not at the Alps, but at the spectacle of human life' (Murdoch 1997, 282). This spectator, she says,

> faced by the manifold of humanity, may feel, as well as terror, delight, but not, if he really sees what is before him, superiority. He will suffer that undramatic, because un-self-centred, agnosticism which goes with tolerance. To understand other people is a task which does not come to an end (Murdoch 1997, 283).

With Murdoch's moral sublime, one's attention turns from the enormity and power of nature to an infinite openness to the manifold, never-finally-graspable reality of other people. The vast scale shifts from physical heights and depths to the 'infinity' of an incompletable task, and, rather than being overpowered by nature, we become 'un-selfed' by the openness that the task of loving attention to other people requires. That unending process of un-selfing and attending is, of course, for most of us by no means easy, and the prospect of it should induce in most of us an unsettling awe.

It is not, then, pleasure and pride that lawyers and judges should feel on hearing that their daily work partakes of the sublime. Rather, perhaps they should feel astonishment, awe, and even a kind of fear – for, on this view, they seem to have a direct and daily responsibility to engage in an infinite task, beyond full comprehension, and one which requires an 'un-selfing' of the kind that many would not see as coming naturally to lawyers.

Perhaps we should not expect too much from ordinary lawyers and judges in this respect. Kierkegaard once said that 'to express the sublime in the pedestrian absolutely' was 'something only the knight of faith can do' and thought it was so rare that 'it is the one and only marvel' (Kierkegaard [1843] 1985, 70). How, then, are ordinary lawyers and judges to express this rare and marvellous sublimity of the criminal justice system in their daily work?

In order to begin answering this question, I want first to unpack a little further what respect and unconditional respect are understood to be.

The varieties of respect

To respect someone is to *behave* toward them in a certain way or to have a certain kind of *attitude* or *feeling* toward them. One can use the word 'respect' as a verb (as in 'I respect my teacher') for both act and attitude. But the noun (as in 'I have or feel respect for my teacher') is usually used only for the attitude. Of course, act and attitude often go together. One can (and often should) perform the act with the attitude. But one can sometimes respect someone in the act sense without feeling or having respect for them. Often enough, *showing* one's felt respect is a key part of the act of respecting someone, such that to let one's lack of feeling of respect show undercuts the act. But that need not always be so. Further, there may be situations where there is no occasion to respect someone in the act sense, though one can very well have an attitude of respect or feel respect towards them.

As *action*, to respect someone can involve either positive or 'negative' acts (or both), though this distinction is not rigid, and a 'negative' act may well involve just as much deliberation, effort and care as a 'positive' act (hence 'omission' is not an optimal concept in this respect). In both cases, we restrain or withdraw the self as we take the other person into account, and thereby recognise or acknowledge them. In positive acts of respect, one makes the other person's interests and desires count in one's deliberations, sometimes equally with one's own interests and desires, but sometimes less and sometimes more. Positive acts of respect can sometimes involve satisfying the other person's preferences or complying with their commands, depending on the nature of the relationship. As a negative action, to respect someone is to defer to them, to let them be, to tolerate them, or, as Kant famously but obscurely put it, not to treat them merely as a means (Kant [1785] 1997, 38/429).

The *attitude* of respect for someone involves a kind of 'affective understanding' of them. It is a felt way of seeing or construing them. We can distinguish two quite different modes of attitudinal respect: what we can call social respect and moral respect. *Social* respect for a person involves seeing or appraising them as having some sort of impressive, admirable, dignified, or prestigious quality or qualities (whether by virtue of their given status or their own achievements) – and one consequently has feelings of esteem or admiration toward them.

Moral respect, on the other hand, is different and a lot harder to pin down, but as we are now heading into sublime territory, this sort of difficulty is to be expected. Starting negatively, we might say that the understanding that partly constitutes moral respect is not an appraisal or assessment of the person's dignity, prestige or impressive qualities. Instead, I understand that the other person is a fellow human being, is one with whom I share a common humanity, as Gaita might put it. I sense that here is a human life, with all its thoughts and feelings, quirks and commonalities, virtues and vices, experiences and dreams, fears and hopes, doings and sufferings, and so on. I don't pretend to 'know all the details' about the other person; I simply understand or appreciate that here is a human being and their life.

Similarly, the *feeling* that helps make up moral respect is not admiration or esteem. It is perhaps a 'cooler' feeling, and yet it is not some sort of thin, attenuated derivative of rich, substantive esteem. More positively, we might say that when we feel moral respect toward a person, that feeling is more like a sort of awe or wonder at the simple fact of that person. 'Here in front of me is a life – a human being and their universe: is that not astonishing?' – or so we might try to express it.

Moral respect as unconditional

Another way to mark the difference between social and moral respect is to see social respect as something that can be lost if the person respected no longer presents as dignified, prestigious, estimable or having some admirable quality. Respect has to be earned, some people are fond of saying (as if they themselves were all the more admirable for not selling their respect cheaply), and where that is so it can just as easily be lost.

Moral respect, in contrast, cannot be earned or lost by those to whom it is owed. When we see the other person as owed moral respect, we recognise that they cannot ever lose that. That recognition is indeed part of the sense we have of the respect we feel. It is this incapacity to be lost that I understand Gaita as referring to (at least in part) when he speaks of 'unconditional' respect. To say that respect is owed to everyone unconditionally is to say that we are not released from the duty of respect by virtue of anything a person does or suffers. No matter what foolish, arrogant or evil deeds they do, everyone is owed this respect. And no matter what misfortune, suffering or affliction befalls a person, they are still owed this respect.

In relation to wrongdoers, that unconditional nature of moral respect means, among other things, that they are, as Gaita puts it, always owed justice or may never be denied justice. Another way to put it is to say that even the worst criminal wrongdoers can themselves be wronged, or be the victims of injustice, in how they are treated. Some may be tempted to deny this and say that, for at least some extreme offenders, no wrong can in fact be done to them because any suffering that could be imposed on them would be morally permitted as part of their just deserts. However, the attitude of unconditional respect maintains that, no matter how severe a person's just deserts may rightly be (and even if it amounts to the death penalty), it is not without limit and so does not encompass all and any possible sufferings. This means that the imposition of some sufferings would be unjust and a wrong done to the wrongdoer. Thus, even if death were a person's just deserts, he or she could be wronged in how that punishment was carried out (for example, if it were accompanied by humiliating degradations or torture). Moreover, inflicting that undeserved and wrongful harm on the criminal wrongdoer is not wrong simply because unbridled vengeance tends to demean or corrupt those who impose it. It is wrong because it wrongs the person upon whom it is imposed. Further, such unconditional respect for criminal offenders need not be based on a supposition that even the worst criminals must have at least some good in them and that it is that goodness which we respect. Unconditional respect is not a limit on the concept of how bad or evil a person can be; it is a limit on what the proper recognition of vice, wrongdoing or evil permits in response. Unconditional respect thus need not stop one loathing the evil that a person has done, or that person's character as the root of that deed, or, indeed, the person him or herself if enough of his or her character merits being loathed. But, at the same time, unconditional respect does constitute a limit on such righteous or justifiable loathing, a limit which not only prevents such loathing from getting out of control, but also conditions the quality of that loathing itself, so that there is a kind of respect even as one loathes another. In addition to the sense that even the gravest wrongdoer can him or herself be wronged, that respect can include a sense, or acknowledgement, that committing a seriously wrongful act is itself a calamity for the wrongdoer him or herself (and not simply because of the unhappy consequences the deed may bring in its wake for the wrongdoer, such as social rejection or punishment).

Gaita speaks of all human beings being *owed* unconditional respect. This way of putting it brings into relief those who owe the respect as well as those to whom it is owed. The duty is unconditional in the sense that the one who is duty-bound to give respect cannot be released from this duty because of anything done or suffered by the one to whom respect is owed. (I will leave aside here the question whether anyone may ever be released from this duty because of what they themselves suffer. Perhaps among the greatest moral saints are those who, despite their own afflictions, continue to accord respect to even the worst of wrongdoers.)

Gaita, as I understand him, does not ground unconditional respect in the idea that it is a fundamental human right to receive respect. Though it is a duty grounded in the humanity of those to whom it is owed, it is not simply a matter of recognising a prior right to receive respect. Indeed, the duty may be part of what helps to ground talk of fundamental human rights, such that a person's right to receive respect is in part a consequence of others' duty to give respect.

CHAPTER 8

The preceding several paragraphs have sought to articulate at least part of what it is for moral respect to be unconditional. What the respect itself amounts to, substantively, is a distinct, though related, question. It is related, of course, because the unconditional aspect of such respect must inevitably shape and animate its substantive content. As to that substance, a key question is whether the duty of unconditional respect is a duty to respect others in the action sense or a duty to have respect for others in the attitudinal sense, or both. It is, perhaps, easier to fulfil a duty to act in a certain way than a duty to feel a certain way, in that one can perform one's duties of conduct grudgingly and still do one's duty, but one cannot grudgingly feel moral respect and still say that one's duty has been duly acquitted in the same way. Indeed, some might argue against the idea of duties of feeling, on the basis that feelings and attitudes are not something that we 'do,' but are rather something that we experience or undergo, and so are not amenable to being commanded. This seems to rely on too rigid a distinction between will and emotion, and to overlook the idea that there can at least be duties to *cultivate* certain feelings and attitudes. Nonetheless, it seems fair to say that what it means to fulfil – and hence to *attempt* to fulfil – duties of conduct and duties of feeling will be importantly different.

Perhaps we see here something of what is sublime in the ideal of unconditional moral respect. Perhaps we should concede that it is virtually impossible for ordinary people truly to feel moral respect for all human beings, no matter what they have done. At best, most of us might manage to respect most others in action (i.e. do the acts that respect them) because we think it morally right to do so (however such rightness is understood). But truly to *feel* moral respect universally and unconditionally seems beyond ordinary human capabilities. Or, at least, it is so extremely rare that it is something for moral saints rather than ordinary folk, who cannot help but fall back into assessing the qualities of others and measuring out due respect accordingly. Of course, many moral ideals are practical impossibilities. That, however, is not something we can take comfort in, with the thought that, as ideals, they are something 'other-worldly' and not meant to be realised in the everyday here and now. On the contrary, depending on the attitude of those living in the here and now, such ideals can exert a strong moral pull on the realm of the ordinary and can radically transform it. That we might only ever strive toward but never attain such ideals is indeed part of their sublime nature.

Be that as it may, I want now to return to our lawyers and judges and how they are to carry the burden of law's sublime respect for all defendants.

Is lawyers' conscientious professionalism enough?

Let us accept that it is indeed one of the most sublime aspects of our legal system that all criminal defendants – 'even' the most foul among them – are owed unconditional respect. When a legal system fulfils its duty of according unconditional respect to defendants, what does this mean, in practice? At a minimum, it means that each defendant entering the criminal justice system is given a fair trial (with all the particular rights that this entails, such as proper notice of the charges, the opportunity to cross-examine prosecution witnesses, the opportunity to call his or her own witnesses, and so on) and, if duly found guilty, is given a fair sentencing hearing, and, finally, does not receive unjust punishment. Underpinning and partly animating this procedural dimension to unconditional respect for defendants, there is, or should be, a communicative respect as well. This communicative respect involves the legal system seeking to engage with and address the defendant as a rational and responsible person, capable of understanding and answering the charge (see Duff 2009). (Where a defendant is not in fact sufficiently rational or responsible, for example due to mental illness or immaturity, then this does not license withdrawing respect. Rather it means that a different order of respectful discourse is called for.)

A legal system which respects all defendants in these ways is indeed something to be earnestly desired. But what is required of the individual lawyers and judges (and others) who put such a system into practice? Are they required simply to ensure that the various procedural rules are scrupulously followed in every case? Or are they also required personally to have an *attitude* of moral respect, to *feel* moral respect, for all defendants?

Those who would answer 'no' to this last question might argue that if the lawyers and judges are indeed running that system effectively, then that is enough to ensure that all defendants are getting the respect they are owed. So long as the lawyers and judges do in fact conscientiously and successfully maintain that system, then what does it matter what the individual judges and lawyers themselves feel? To the individual defendants processed by the system, it should not matter at all (so the thought may go) what the lawyers and judges themselves think. So long as the rules are the right ones and are scrupulously followed, the individual defendant will be treated with due respect.

Now, one line of response here is to say that in fact it *does* matter, that more is needed than simply that the rules and practices are working. This is because (on this view) we are dealing not with a machine but with a human process in which human beings are engaging and communicating with each other. 'The system' only really treats defendants with respect if the people who run that

CHAPTER 8

system – who *are* that system – *show* them respect. The rules themselves don't do it, and if the human operators of the system don't themselves show respect for the defendants, then, even if the rules are scrupulously put into practice, the system itself will fail to accord the right kind of respect owed to all.

On this view, it is not merely that the individual defendants will, often enough to matter, tell that the people processing them don't actually have respect for them. That is probably true, but the deeper point that this approach presses is that because the law is itself a human practice and not a machine, it requires the judges and lawyers who both represent and embody that system to enact the values the system is meant to realise. Thus, on this view, the system needs judges and lawyers to show respect to all defendants, in order for the system itself to work. The relationship between the system and its human operatives is too intimate for 'the system itself' to do the work alone.

Note that this approach is consistent with a certain degree of 'faking it.' Legal professionalism, that is, requires of the lawyer only that they act 'as if' they have respect for each of the defendants they deal with. That is to say, on this view, it is part of one's professional role to play the part of one who has respect for all. Just as doctors and nurses need to have a caring bedside manner regardless of their true feelings, lawyers need to have a respectful 'desk-side' manner – it is what the role demands, and the true professional plays that role well. Sincerity is not the issue, on this view. What matters is a commitment to conscientiously presenting the kind of face that the role requires. Professionalism means that we need to provide what our role within the system requires and not let our personal attitudes and emotions distract us from that task. It may be tolerable enough for sensationalist tabloid writers to whip up horror, rage and vengefulness in their readers. But those who have to run the system cannot afford to let such emotions distract them from presenting a respectful face to all defendants, even when meting out condign punishments.

For the individual lawyer, then, it might seem that, while privately they may loathe the defendant, to fulfil their important role they must stick to the rules which say that the defendant has a right to a fair hearing and must not let their true feelings of revulsion, contempt or pity show through. 'Even if I don't personally have much respect for him,' the lawyer may think, 'I respect the legal system that respects him, and so I will do everything I can to ensure that the system works.'

We can call this the 'quarantine' approach. The idea is that the lawyer should keep their private feelings and attitudes towards defendants separate from their professional dealings. In their professional conduct they should uphold the legal rules that require that all defendants be treated justly, and, in their outward demeanour, they should show appropriate respect. One can be a good, conscientious, even exemplary lawyer by doing this, while keeping hidden one's private disgust, anger and disrespect.

But perhaps this way of putting it is too stark. We often enough engage socially with others in more or less formal or predictable ways which purport to express respect and politeness, but which we all know do not necessarily express our inner feelings – but which we also all know do show that we are genuinely trying to maintain a polite and civil relationship, whatever our inner feelings may be.

Kant observed in this respect that we often practise certain social graces which are

> only externals ... which give a beautiful illusion resembling virtue that is not also deceptive since everyone knows how it must be taken. Affability, sociability, courtesy, hospitality, and gentleness (in disagreeing without quarrelling) are, indeed, only tokens, yet they promote the feeling for virtue itself by a striving to bring this illusion as near as possible to the truth. By all of these, which are merely the manners one is obliged to show in social intercourse, one binds others too; and so they still promote a virtuous disposition by at least making virtue fashionable (Kant [1797] 1991, 265/473–474).

On this approach, in observing the manners expected in certain situations, we do not so much 'fake it' or deceive anyone, since we all know that our mannered behaviour is intended as such and, very importantly, reflects a deeper moral commitment to social harmony and respect, even if that sits alongside private disapproval and even disgust. This sort of self-aware observance of good manners need not undermine our integrity; indeed, it most likely promotes it.

Thus the defendant in the dock may well know that the judge personally thinks he is an awful person, and yet may appreciate that the judge makes it a point to address him as *Mr* Smith (and not simply as 'the prisoner') and observe all the strictness of legal procedure to ensure he is treated with respect by the process in which they all play a part.

Must the ethical lawyer personally feel unconditional respect?

A different approach is to say that it is even better, morally, for the individual lawyer or judge actually to *change* their attitude so that they are not keeping it hidden or quarantined or are not simply being professionally well-mannered.

CHAPTER 8

It is better, on this approach, that one should not merely treat defendants *as if* they were worthy of unconditional respect but also come to *have* this attitude oneself. That is, one should not merely uphold the rules that respect all defendants; one should actually *have* respect for all defendants oneself. On this view, you will be a morally better person if you have such respect, and you will be an ethically better lawyer as well.

Let us accept that such a lawyer is a morally better person than the merely conscientious and well-mannered lawyer. Is there, however, also a *professional* duty to have such feelings? Many would say that this is something beyond the call of duty, in the sense that a lawyer who did not have such feelings of respect would not be guilty of any professional or generally moral misconduct. Instead, such felt respect for all defendants is something supererogatory – morally admirable but not morally required.

However, a very common feature of those who perform acts of supererogation – or, at least, who strive in their direction – is that they do not see their efforts as an optional extra, but rather as something they *must* do. From this perspective, such felt respect is not a matter of generosity, mercy or grace, but is something necessary or owed. Moreover, such people will also often say – and, indeed, be expected to say – 'It's what anyone in that situation would do.'

And yet, because it is virtually the province of moral saints truly to have equal moral respect for all persons they encounter, we know that most lawyers, like most people, will very often fail to live up to this ideal. Though many will be able to act conscientiously and with professional good manners, and so support a legal system that respects all defendants, they themselves will often enough have to quarantine their deeper feelings in order to act professionally and keep that system going.

To admit to the inevitability of most lawyers' failing to reach the ideal of truly feeling unconditional moral respect toward all criminal defendants is not, I hope, to indulge in cynicism or a wet-blanket 'realism' about human frailty. Rather, it is intended simply to be a recognition of the nature of moral ideals: we ordinary folk who are less than saints see the world in the light of such ideals, and we strive toward them, but we do not expect to realise them.

Where, then, does this leave the rules of the legal system that require unconditional respect for all defendants? Perhaps one way to be reconciled to the virtual inevitability of failure is to view the legal procedural rules as a concrete distillation of the attitudinal ideal that I cannot realise. As rules of conduct, the rules form a minimum threshold which can guide my actions should I fail – as indeed I will at some point – truly to view all defendants with unconditional moral respect. The rules also serve as a reminder and a prompt – even a goad – to continued striving to realise unconditional respect for all defendants.

This may sound like an odd way to treat legal rules – almost like a religious sublimation of them into some sort of moral call from on high. Rules and their conscientious following are thought by some philosophers to constitute a low-grade kind of morality. The truly wise and virtuous are not, on this view, fixated on rules, which are for moral novices to start with and for the morally wise to master and then transcend. Only the morally dull-witted will stick to the rules as if they were the very stuff of morality. The exemplars of virtue will trust their practical wisdom and their attuned affective understanding of particular situations, rather than fall back on general rules to provide the answer to the question of what they are to do in any given case.

But in the case of the legal rule that all defendants are owed a fair trial, perhaps we have a sublime rule that may in fact outstrip the moral virtue and wisdom of any single individual or, at least, the moral virtue and wisdom that comes with a Bachelor of Laws degree. Because the legal rule is itself sublime, perhaps it is more than what any individual might 'master and then transcend.' If this is so, perhaps there is less shame for a lawyer in admitting that they cannot always *feel* respect for all defendants, if they nonetheless conscientiously strive to put into practice the legal rules that embody such respect.

On this approach, there is an important difference between a merely rule-focused conscientiousness and a conscientiousness that appreciates something of the importance of that which is expressed in the rule. The spirit of one's compliance with a rule will be quite different if one sees the rule as expressing something sublime, as opposed to seeing it simply as what must be done in order to keep the legal system working for the overall benefit of the general population.

To sustain this sense of the sublime in their daily work is no doubt difficult for the ordinary lawyer, for it is in the nature of the sublime that it resists incorporation into daily routines. And yet, where the sublime does make itself felt in the everyday, even if only indirectly and partially, it can make a profound difference indeed.

Acknowledgements

My thanks to Dr Christopher Cordner, Dr Drew Carter and Dr Craig Taylor for helpful suggestions (which I fear have been inadequately followed) on how to improve the original conference paper on which this essay is based.

Chapter 9

ON RAIMOND GAITA'S 'ASSIMILATIONIST MULTICULTURALISM'

Geoffrey Brahm Levey

I

For many years, Raimond Gaita has been an eloquent critic of the inability of successive Australian governments to recognise the common humanity of Aborigines (e.g., Gaita 1999). Yet he has also reflected warmly on the basic decency of the post-war Australia that greeted his immigrant parents and in which he grew up, a decency that, he has argued, was extended by Australia's adoption of multiculturalism in the 1970s. And he has written realistically about the fact and the value of Anglo-Australian institutions and culture in defining the nation, whilst making the vital point that love of country isn't the exclusive preserve of Anglo-Australians (Gaita 2011b).

Gaita's nuanced position is unusual today in Australian political discourse. Our political debate tends instead to be dominated by two contending and polarised positions. On the one hand, a conservative valorisation of Anglo-Australian culture and identity as rightly defining the nation and which is generally hostile to multicultural accommodation. On the other hand, we have various post-nationalists and cosmopolitans that have little time for Anglo-Australian traditions or, for that matter, any national identity, while being generally supportive of multiculturalism and the rights of minorities.

In this chapter, I want to comment both appreciatively and critically on Gaita's uncommon intervention on Australian multiculturalism. Gaita not only draws our attention to the centrality of national identity to the issues of immigrant absorption and multiculturalism, he also perceptively addresses the anxieties of those on both the right and the left of the debate. In these respects, he helpfully situates Australian multiculturalism between the stock positions that dominate (and diminish) our public discourse. At the same time, Gaita's account of what Australian multiculturalism stands for – in contrast to his effective responses to right and left perceptions of what it stands against – strikes me as overly modest and conservative. Tellingly, he describes his position as 'assimilationist multiculturalism.' It is a position, I shall suggest, that owes much to his own experience as an immigrant of the pre-multiculturalism era of the 1950s, as well as to his personal and philosophical dispositions.

II

Though there are allusions throughout several of his writings, Gaita's thoughts on Australian multiculturalism are laid out most systematically in the collection, *Essays on Muslims and Multiculturalism* (2011b), of which he also is editor.[1] Noting that he is neither an historian nor a social scientist, but a philosopher, his purpose, he says, is to 'reflect on some of the ideas that inform the belief that multiculturalism *must* undermine an attachment to nation that goes deeper than dutiful citizenship' (Gaita 2011b, 190). To this end, he first addresses conservative anxieties about multiculturalism and then leftist anxieties about national identity. I will follow suit.

Gaita begins by reminding us that diversity would have challenged Australians' conception of their national identity even in the absence of immigrants. Australia eventually had to come to terms with its indigenous peoples. The Aboriginal experience is, however, very different from that of immigrants. Aborigines were subject to forced colonisation, dispossession of their lands, and historical maltreatment by European settlers. Immigrants, on the other hand, have largely chosen, as individuals or families, to leave their home countries in order to join an established Australian society. Even if one allows for economic hardship and political 'push' factors such as instability or persecution in their home countries behind a decision to emigrate, the immigrant experience is unlike that of indigenous Australians. Australian multiculturalism policy has long struggled to bridge this divide in our diversity. Since the 1980s, the policy has been framed as applying to

---

[1] Some of Gaita's views were previously presented in the inaugural Common Good Lecture: Raimond Gaita, 'Multiculturalism and the War on Terrorism', State Library of NSW, 5 March, 2008. Disclosure: I participated in the 2006 lecture series on which *Essays on Muslims and Multiculturalism* is based and contributed a chapter to the volume.

'all Australians,' yet from the outset it has acknowledged the 'special status' of Aboriginal and Torres Strait Islander peoples and that 'it is appropriate that their distinct needs and rights be reaffirmed and accorded separate consideration' (OMA 1989, 49; Commonwealth of Australia 1999, 7). For their own part, many Aboriginal people see multiculturalism as a policy for migrants, and so identifying with it would only undercut their distinctive claims and special status (Castles 2001, 809; Scott 2000).

Gaita draws out an important corollary of this difference in Australia's diversity. The Aborigines have moral claims on the Australian state that simply do not apply in the case of immigrants. Among these claims are forms of political association that might include self-determination, and forms of political recognition that might include the allowance of customary law in certain jurisdictions. As he puts it, to 'the extent that Aboriginal leaders resisted calls to assimilation, they invited non-indigenous Australians to discuss forms of political association that would be true to the history of their dispossession' (Gaita 2011b, 191). Migrant communities do not generally seek such forms of political association and recognition, however, were they to, Gaita is right to say that their claims would have little basis: '[n]o comparable case can be made for allowing Sharia law, for example, to define for Australian Muslims a distinctive political identity' (Gaita 2011b, 194). Australians, he says, would be justifiably resentful of such claims. He also rightly points out that Australian multiculturalism provides no warrant, ideologically or in practice, for immigrants to negotiate the terms of their political association in this manner.

There is, however, an ambiguity in Gaita's analysis. The discussion subtly shifts from comparing the entitlements of immigrants and Aborigines to comparing those of immigrants, long-established religious communities, and the dominant Anglo-Australian group:

> Because immigrants come as guests who may eventually become citizens, the host country has the right, as well as a duty to its citizens, to require that immigrants do not claim for their religion a political status in the life of the nation different from the status of any other religion except the national religion, if there is one (Gaita 2011b, 194).

The problem is that claiming 'political recognition,' a 'political identity,' or 'a political status in the life of the nation' covers a multitude of possibilities, many of which are commonplace in democracies.

The United States of America is famed for its 'high wall' of separation between church and state, protected by its Constitution. Yet in New York, for example, civil courts have found ways to assist Orthodox Jews conclude a divorce proceeding where a recalcitrant spouse is otherwise able to block it under Jewish law. In France, where *laïcité* or public secularism is honoured like nowhere else, the French state in recent times has recognised certain religious bodies for the purposes of working with the government on interfaith and intercultural relations. Democracies, including Australia, often rely on church and other religious organisations for administering state welfare. Political accommodation also often takes the form of exemptions from standing law. In many cases, these exemptions predate multiculturalism by decades; for example, in New South Wales, Jews have been exempt from the laws governing animal slaughtering since the early 1920s.[2] In yet other cases, the political recognition predates even the full flowering of democracy; in England, for example, Jews and Quakers have been entitled to solemnise a state-recognised marriage according to their own customs from the time of Lord Hardwicke's Marriage Act of 1753, while Catholics and Protestant non-conformists have been able to do so since the Marriage Act of 1836 (Hamilton 1995, 43–44).

All these are examples of political and legal recognition by the majority culture of minority groups and their customs, and therefore, in some sense, of according them a 'political status' that is not necessarily uniform among other religious communities. It is unclear whether Gaita's quoted stricture is meant to apply also to these forms of political recognition and status. On the one hand, he observes that '[b]etween the political and the private realms, there is much space for many different kinds of public institutions' (Gaita 2011b, 194). So the above examples may count, in Gaita's estimation, as just such kinds of 'public institution.' On the other hand, this observation is made in reference to Rowan Williams's (2008) controversial lecture on religion and the secular state, when Archbishop of Canterbury. Gaita rejects Williams's apparent assumption that the only alternative to politically recognising religion is its privatisation and marginalisation. And yet despite the controversy his lecture provoked in Britain, Williams was not advocating political recognition or status in the sense of introducing parallel legal jurisdictions, whether of Sharia or any other religious code. Rather, his lecture considered how the secular state does already and might further make reasonable accommodations for religious conscience. As the then Lord Chief Justice (of England and Wales) Nicholas Phillips explained, there is 'no reason why Sharia principles, or any other religious

---

[2] *Prevention of Cruelty to Animals Act 1901–1953* (NSW).

CHAPTER 9

code, should not be the basis for mediation or other forms of alternative dispute resolution,' as these did not constitute a 'parallel legal system' and would never 'override English common law' (Maughan 2013).

Sharia, like Halacha in Judaism or indeed Australian law, is not one thing but a complex of laws, edicts, rival interpretations, judicial institutions and jurisprudential principles. Reasonable political accommodation typically applies to specific practices and traditions and remains ultimately subject to civil authority. This authority may be exercised judiciously; for example, some Australian banks specialise in 'Sharia compliant finance,' but the banking sector's regulator, the Australian Prudential Regulation Authority, oversees this provision. Unfortunately, civic authority sometimes also surrenders to prejudice. For example, until 2005, Catholics and Jews in Canada had been allowed to use their respective religious tribunals as alternative dispute resolution avenues; it was only when Muslims sought the same opportunity that these alternative dispute arrangements were outlawed for all.

Gaita is right, then, that multiculturalism provides no basis for immigrant and religious minorities to claim forms of political association, identity, and recognition comparable to those we might consider for indigenous groups, courtesy of their historical experience. But nor is what immigrant and religious groups might justifiably claim by way of political and legal accommodation governed simply by what such minorities have previously sought and won or by a need to protect the privileged status of a national religion. In liberal societies, reasonable accommodation has been based rather on the merits of each case and pragmatic considerations. The result thus looks more like what the British sociologist Tariq Modood (2007) calls a 'variable geometry' of provisions. Liberal multiculturalism did not initiate this process, which, as noted, has long been integral to liberal orders. It does though advance the tradition.

This is not to say that the dominant culture in Australia has no legitimate claim to its dominance. Gaita's remarks on this aspect are among the most astute ever written. Channeling John Hirst (2009), he notes that Anglo-Australians are not an immigrant group but rather those who established the institutions and political culture of the country. That this achievement came through brutal colonialism means, again, that special consideration is owed to indigenous Australians; it does not mean that Anglo-Australians are just another immigrant group among the myriad of others who have come to these shores. Reflective of his broader philosophical approach to ethics, Gaita probes what he calls 'non-theoretical multiculturalism.' He gently chides those people who worry that 'multiculturalism must, by definition, refuse to privilege the Anglo-Celtic inheritance in Australian national culture' with 'reading too much multicultural theory' and paying 'too little attention to the reality on the ground' (Gaita 2011b, 200).

What, then, is this grounded reality? Gaita highlights three aspects, though he does not identify them quite so formally. One aspect is cultural inflection. Gaita cites two of his favourite stories about Australian life. One is of an Australian soldier guarding enemy aliens, German Jewish men who had escaped Nazi Germany via Britain and been dispatched to detention camps in Australia on the *SS Dunera*. Patrolling a column of detainees marching through the desert, the soldier hands his rifle to one of them, saying, 'Here mate. Hold this while I go to have a piss.' The other story is of a senior federal minister who, on arriving late for a funeral service in Melbourne for a popular community figure, humbly chooses to sit on the steps outside the Chapel with the other latecomers rather than enter the Chapel for his reserved seat. Both stories, Gaita says, 'reveal egalitarianism inflected in recognisably Australian ways,' an attribute he sees also in the decency with which Anglo-Australians received at least white immigrants to their country (Gaita 2011b, 201).

A second aspect of the Australian reality relates to Michael Oakeshott's (1977) observation that political sensibilities are embedded in unselfconscious practices. Gaita draws on the idea to make the point that a political culture is defined partly by what is unthinkable. In Australia, for example, settling serious political conflicts through assassination is unthinkable, as is the public castration of sex offenders, stoning women for adultery, or cutting off the limbs of offenders as a means of punishment. Such norms are deep-seated and powerful. They are not, Gaita notes, the sort of thing that can be taught in schools or which reveal themselves in citizenship tests. Well, perhaps not our recent multiple-choice tests. The economist Oskar Morgenstern (1971) recounts the story of Austrian philosopher Kurt Gödel's attempt to become a United States citizen in 1946. His Princeton Institute colleague had studied up on American life and the US Constitution ahead of the interview, one day excitedly announcing to Morgenstern that he had discovered a crucial flaw in the Constitution that would enable a dictator and Fascist regime to be established in the US in a perfectly legal manner. Morgenstern assured him that this was unlikely to happen even if it were possible and, in any case, he would not be asked technical questions on the Constitution and so should put aside such issues. The day of the interview arrived, and Morgenstern and another Princeton

CHAPTER 9

Institute colleague, Albert Einstein, accompanied Gödel into the room. The first question from the examiner proceeded as follows:

Examinor [sic]: 'Now, Mr. Godel, where do you come from?'

Gödel: 'Where I come from? Austria.'

Examinor: 'What kind of government did you have in Austria?'

Gödel: 'It was a republic, but the constitution was such that it finally was changed into a dictatorship.'

Examinor: 'Oh! This is very bad. This could not happen in this country.'

Gödel: 'Oh, yes, I can prove it.'

Morgernstern comments that he and Einstein were horrified by the exchange but that, thankfully, the examiner quietened Gödel down, said 'Oh God, let's not go into this,' and ended the examination before it could get any worse for the applicant.

Citizenship interviews, then, may indeed reveal contrarian normative assumptions. Still, many norms will remain unspoken until they are violated, which, more often than not, occurs inadvertently by newcomers, who bring a different set of cultural assumptions. A good example of this was the violence exhibited, in word and deed, by some Muslims at a Sydney demonstration in September 2012, at which they were protesting against an amateurish American-made film that satirised the Prophet Muhammad. They breached a powerful social norm in Australia that migrants do not bring their homeland conflicts with them or replay their religious and national aggression here. In the event, they were instructed in that norm through the public outcry and condemnation that followed their actions, and which is likely to have impressed them much more so than their altercation with the police.

This brings us to a third aspect of Gaita's 'grounded reality,' what might be called cultural induction. Gaita here reflects on his own experience as an immigrant child growing up in Central Victoria. He notes how many readers of his celebrated book *Romulus, My Father* heard in it a distinctive voice, a voice which he attributes to the light and colours of the Central Victorian landscape and to the interactions between his immigrant parents and their Anglo-Celtic neighbours. Immigrants will perforce become inducted over time into the Australian cultural and physical landscape. But it is not a one-way process. Gaita puts the point beautifully: 'Each generation of immigrants will change the tone and resonances of the Anglo-

Celtic voice that invites them into the conversation about what it means to be Australian' (Gaita 2011b 201). He expresses the hope that this change will never be so great that what ensues will be unrecognisable to or alienate those who are 'nourished by the Anglo-Celtic pioneers' (Gaita 2011b, 201). But he also recognises that while that hope expresses an 'assimilationist ideal of multiculturalism,' the conversation must be open-ended and there are no guarantees where it might lead.

The above three aspects of Australian life 'on the ground' – cultural inflection, unthinkable practices, and cultural induction – together mean that the institutions, norms, and conventions of Anglo-Celtic Australia will likely continue their dominant place in defining the nation for generations to come.

III

This, then, is Gaita's compelling answer to conservatives who worry that multiculturalism Australian-style threatens the 'Anglo-Celtic inheritance in Australian national culture.' Though he is interested in a non-theoretical multiculturalism, it is worth noting that this position on national identity actually accords with Australian multicultural policy. From its inception, Australian multiculturalism has accepted that Anglo-Australian institutions and culture are foundational to Australian national identity. The *National Agenda for a Multicultural Australia*, for example, speaks of 'our British heritage' that helps 'to define us as Australian,' and emphasises that multiculturalism 'does not entail a rejection of Australian values, customs and beliefs' (OMA 1989). At the same time, like Gaita, Australian multiculturalism entertains an open future in which 'our evolving national character and identity' will inevitably reflect the changing composition of the Australian people (NMAC 1999). There is an acceptance that Australian national identity and culture are works-in-progress and an expectation that someday, through the culturally diverse backgrounds and everyday interactions of Australians, these things are likely to be very different from what they have been and are today.

In other respects, however, Gaita's non-theoretical multiculturalism is at odds with Australian multicultural policy, indeed, would not ordinarily be considered 'multiculturalism' at all. Where he speaks of Aboriginal claims turning on Anglo-Australians' generosity and sense of justice (Gaita 2011b, 192), he speaks of immigrant claims as calling only on their generosity. His non-theoretical multiculturalism is a matter of extending

CHAPTER 9

the level of goodwill and tolerance to immigrants rather than a matter of justice or their rights. Such an account certainly describes Australia as it transitioned from its commitment to assimilation and Anglo-conformity in the 1950s and early 1960s to something looser and more relaxed from the late 1960s through the 1970s. As Gaita notes, the 'admirable spirit' of the Anglo-Celts in the 1950s was tempered by some condescension towards 'new Australians.' While this attitude often rankled migrants, it scarcely compared with the 'murderous hatreds' many of them had endured in their European homelands. 'For that reason,' he says, 'most of the immigrants I knew accepted as a gift, rather than claimed as a right, the liberty and tolerance they found here' (Gaita 2011b, 197). Still, Australia's 'theoretically unselfconscious multiculturalism' was an improvement, in his view, since it represented 'a transformation and a deepening, by an essentially Anglo-Celtic intelligentsia ... of the tolerance I have already praised' (Gaita 2011b, 198).

Gaita suggests that most Australians have this kind of accepting and tolerant society in mind when they or others praise Australia as 'a successful multicultural nation.' Indeed, some leftist critics claim that this is all that official Australian multiculturalism itself really amounts to after almost forty years of policy effort. But if this is all that has been achieved, then Australian multiculturalism as a public philosophy and policy has fallen far short of what it was supposed to be and do. The provisions of our multiculturalism policy are very clear: they refer to the *right* of all Australians, including those not from the dominant culture, to enjoy the same liberties and opportunities, including the right to observe one's cultural background within the law. Though the policy recognises 'tolerance' as an important liberal value, it is not framed in terms of asking Anglo-Australians to show greater forbearance and generosity of spirit towards the culturally different in our community. Rather, it appeals to another 'grounded reality,' namely, Australia's liberal democratic heritage. It asserts what follows from the nation's ostensible core political values and commitments: liberty, including cultural liberty and respect; equality, including access and equity, non-discrimination, and equal opportunity; and the ability of every Australian to participate fully in the Australian community and realise their potential. These are aspects of political morality, the corollaries of liberal rights and justice; they are not about charitable giving or an enhanced generosity.

Nor is it quite right to say that the theoretically unselfconscious multi-culturalism that Gaita identifies as an improvement owed everything to Anglo-Celtic elites and 'hardly in any respect is it an immigrant achievement'

(Gaita 2011b, 198). For one thing, Anglo-Celtic elites were made to rethink their emphasis on assimilation by the increasing number of immigrants, in the late 1950s and sixties, who voted with their feet and returned to their home countries (Lopez 2000, 55). For another thing, immigrants such as Jerzy Zubrzycki, Walter Lippmann, George Zangalis, and Laksiri Jayasuriya, and the children of immigrants such as Petro Georgiou, Andrew Jakubowicz, and Al Grassby (Irish mother, Spanish father) – some activists and some conceptualisers – were instrumental in the rejection of assimilationist thinking and the development of multiculturalism in Australia.

Zubrzycki (b. 1920), who arrived in Australia from Poland in 1956 as a young sociologist, reworked the concept of cultural pluralism – advanced by the German-Jewish American thinker, Horace Kallen (1924) – for the Australian situation. Often referred to as the 'father of Australian multiculturalism,' he travelled to the United States in 1963 and met with the American sociologist Milton Gordon, author of the enormously influential book *Assimilation in American Life* (1964). Gordon delineated seven steps of the assimilation process; one of these he called 'structural assimilation,' which involved immigrants participating in the institutions of the host society without necessarily undergoing acculturation. Zubrzycki learned of Kallen's concept of cultural pluralism through Gordon's work, and accepted Gordon's criticism that while the phrase was suggestive, Kallen had failed to explain how cultural pluralism might work sociologically. In his retirement, Zubrzycki gleefully admitted that when he first presented his ideas on multiculturalism to Australian bureaucrats and politicians in the 1960s, he used Gordon's term of 'structural assimilation' instead of either 'multiculturalism' or 'cultural pluralism,' knowing full well that policymakers would see the word assimilation and rubber stamp his proposals, without realising he was actually advocating the very opposite of assimilation (Lopez 2000, 99–100). The role of immigrant Australians in recalibrating the assimilationist bent of Anglo-Australian policymakers should not be underestimated.

Gaita's 'non-theoretical multiculturalism' is assimilationist ultimately in effect as well as in terms of his perfectly legitimate personal hope that Australia will retain its predominantly Anglo-Celtic character. It is assimilationist in effect for the same reason that he thinks it is multiculturalist in effect: here, the liberties and opportunities open to immigrants and non-Anglos are tied to the goodwill and forbearance of the Anglo-Celtic majority. The fact is that generosity, while virtuous, may just as easily

CHAPTER 9

be withdrawn. 'Assimilationist multiculturalism' may well differ from traditional assimilationism in not having an assimilationist agenda. But unlike liberal multiculturalism, which defends the freedom, opportunities and participation of minorities on the basis of fundamental liberal democratic principles, the multiculturalism in 'assimilationist multiculturalism' is left entirely up to the inclination of the dominant group or its elites.

IV

So far I have considered Gaita's convincing answer to conservatives who worry that multiculturalism spells the end of Anglo-Australian institutions and culture, and his elaboration of an unselfconscious, assimilationist multiculturalism, which I find problematic. But Gaita also speaks to leftists who think that Australian national identity and attachment to the nation should be defined solely in terms of civic values and observing the rights and obligations of citizenship. He makes three powerful points. First, even if this kind of civic-cum-post-nationalist prescription were possible, it would hardly be desirable. A political community that lived according to the norms of dutiful citizenship and nothing else would make for a sterile and hollow existence. Like a Hilton hotel, being accommodating to all means being home to nobody.

But secondly, it is, on all the available evidence, doubtful that such a vision of national identity and attachment is in fact possible. Put even two people together for an extended period of time and they will begin to develop their own way of communicating with each other, their own in-jokes, their own ways of doing things. Put them together in the same place for an extended time and they will, more likely than not, grow attached to it, notwithstanding all manner of ambivalences. Or as Gaita puts it, '[i]t is just a fact of human life that many – perhaps most – people develop deep attachments to places and to institutions ... The soul needs warmth which for most people comes from being in familiar surroundings' (Gaita 2011b, 210).

We should distinguish here between spheres of national life. The sphere of formal citizenship acquisition and status does approximate the civic nationalist vision. Australia has, in recent times, largely come to exclude national-cultural prescriptions from the process of acquiring and holding Australian citizenship, with an emphasis instead – like other liberal democracies – on a commitment to respecting the laws and political institutions of the country. Affirmations of loyalty in the Pledge of Commitment as a Citizen – which all new citizens must make – are to the polity, its political institutions and norms, and to its people, and *not* to a particular national culture, the 'Australian way of life,' or to the land. This is why the Howard government's citizenship test of 2007, with its questions on cricket heroes and other Anglo-Australian icons, sparked even more controversy than it might otherwise have done. Many Australians instinctively felt that formal citizenship acquisition was not an appropriate place for propagating a particular definition of Australian identity. Where civic- and post-nationalists err is in supposing that the model of citizenship acquisition is appropriate for national life more generally. They overlook the fact that the 'denationalisation' of citizenship acquisition works only because national-cultural identity and sentiment may be expressed in other spheres of national life (Levey 2014). As Gaita observes, '[p]rotection is sought not just for the institutions of citizenship – the rule of law, democracy and so on [...] – but for those institutions infused by the spirit of a particular people, by their history, their language, their art, their poetry, their song' (Gaita 2011b, 211).

The above two considerations highlight again how cultural attachments matter and will inevitably inflect how people relate to each other and the world. Gaita's third point is that there is an even more important dimension involved here, namely, love of country. 'Even when citizenship is inflected in ways I described earlier,' he says, 'it can be cold unless nourished by love of country' (Gaita 2011b, 217). This kind of patriotism, Gaita stresses, is very different from either jingoism or aggressive nationalism. True love of country entails both a desire to be truthful and to hold one's own country to account for its deeds. A true patriot would, for example, feel shame at the wrongs suffered by Aborigines at the hands of Australian governments as well taking pride in the country's nobler pursuits. And a true patriot would bring her national leaders or soldiers to justice for crimes committed under international law. This, then, is Gaita's answer to those, typically on the left, who see only danger in talk of patriotism and love of country: 'The understandable fears that talk of love of country arouse in many people are reason for thinking hard – in ways we seldom do – about how to block the many routes love finds to jingoism and to open the routes by which jingoism can find its way to love' (Gaita 2011b, 218).

A crucial question nevertheless remains: what should be the role of government, if any, in the promotion of love of country? Though this is a vital question in the context of a discussion of multiculturalism, Gaita does not address it. His analysis is pitched rather at the level of individuals and society, not government policy. He makes it clear why immigrants, even immigrants who come with a 'vivid sense of the past evils of colonialism and racism may move beyond mere law-abiding citizenship to affection – perhaps even love – for this country' (Gaita 2011b, 218). But is it appropriate for a liberal government to be asking, let alone demanding, of its 'new' or native-born citizens that they love their country? As it happens, a recent intervention has sought to tie Australian multiculturalism to a serious, non-jingoistic patriotism not unlike Gaita's (Soutphommasane 2009), a theme picked up by Julia Gillard (2012) when Prime Minister. The British Labour Party has also toyed with embracing 'progressive patriotism' as a new mantra as it grapples with the local backlash against multiculturalism (Eaton 2012). Yet, when governments concern themselves with their citizens' love of country or, for that matter, love of anything, freedom is likely to be the first casualty. Much better that they concentrate on ensuring that all citizens, immigrants no less than the native-born, enjoy the same liberties and opportunities. Then a genuine and abiding love of country, in just Gaita's profound sense, is likely to follow.

V

Raimond Gaita's reflections on multiculturalism are challenging. They challenge the right, they challenge the left, and they also challenge aspects of liberal multiculturalism. His views bear the hallmark of four biographical details. First, his position clearly accords with his own experience as an immigrant child growing up in Central Victoria in the 1950s and sixties, when assimilationist norms prevailed and gradually ebbed into a more tolerant posture before multicultural policy was ultimately formulated along essentially liberal democratic lines. Compare, for example, the attitude and approach of another young immigrant to Australia a generation later, that of anthropologist and Gaita's Melbourne University colleague, Ghassan Hage (b. 1957). Hage arrived in Australia from Lebanon engulfed in civil war in the late 1970s. It was an Australia that was beginning to fashion multicultural policy in response to its increasing cultural diversity. Like Gaita, Hage (1998) came to see Australian multiculturalism as essentially about Anglo-Celts tolerating migrants and otherwise protecting their institutions and privileged position. But unlike Gaita who generally endorses this situation, Hage condemns it as being oppressive, discriminatory, and unjust. Where Gaita defers and accepts, Hage indignantly protests and points the finger.

If one can separate a man from his times, then a second factor informing Gaita's understanding of multiculturalism is what perhaps best can be described as his personal graciousness. One hears in his account of his parents' immigrant generation and of their and his new life in Central Victoria, his own gratitude to Australia for having taken them in and being offered a new world of opportunity. His is an attitude that does not presume to make demands on the host society, and certainly not for the host society to make itself over on his behalf.

One also detects in Gaita's discussion of multiculturalism, thirdly, something of his general and renowned approach to moral philosophy. Suspicious of philosophical abstractions and their instantiations in rights talk, he probes instead lived realities and finds instruction in human examples that move us. As he puts it, '[a]s is often the case with values that go deep, we learn from examples that we trust' (Gaita 2011b, 215). This is a large and involved topic. Suffice it to note here that it is perhaps possible to think of liberal rights as simply the codification of lessons learned from human, all-too-human experience.

Finally, Gaita's multiculturalism is nothing if not an expression of his deep love for his country. His life as a public intellectual is testimony to his serious patriotism, seeking through measured assessment – both in praise and criticism – an Australia of which we can be proud. In this, his own example is the sort of example that both moves us and strikes us as authoritative.

Chapter 10

A CRUCIBLE OF COMPASSION, A HARBINGER OF HOPE
Reflections on Child Protection and the Vulnerable Child

Dorothy Scott

My first encounter with Rai Gaita was reading *Romulus, My Father*. Like many others, I had an intense emotional response to this book. It was the powerful embodiment of love and loss in a family which moved me so deeply. The integrity and compassion of Romulus Gaita also reminded me in some ways of my own father. He came from an impoverished Welsh background and had very little formal education but he was a man of conscience and deep feelings.

Romulus, My Father also resonated with me because as a young social worker I had developed a deep affinity with, and strong protective feelings toward, women who had suffered from very serious mental illnesses following childbirth. In the 1970s I worked in a psychiatric unit in a Melbourne hospital where we pioneered the joint admission of the acutely mentally ill mother and her infant. We focused on nurturing the mother-child relationship and the mother's capacity to respond to the needs of her child. The presence of babies transformed the psychiatric unit. It became a gentler, more compassionate place.

I facilitated a support group for several years for these women and they have remained in contact for over 30 years, loving and supporting one another through periods of psychiatric illness and marked suffering. I feel compelled to say that while it may not be very obvious when they are acutely unwell, I know them to be women of character and compassion. I thus felt immense sadness as I read in *Romulus, My Father*, the account of Mrs Gaita's illness, in an era in which such treatment facilities were unavailable and in which an understanding of mental illness was so limited. Women like Mrs

Gaita were, at that time, judged very harshly for maternal acts of omission or commission, even though they were not morally responsible for such acts.

I used *Romulus, My Father* as a text for my social work students at the University of Melbourne in the years following its publication. I asked them to use the memoir as a case study for the application of the research on the factors which help a child develop resilience in the face of adversity. I specifically wanted them to understand how parental mental illness might be experienced by a child, the enormous difficulties this can create for the child but also the depth of the bond which can exist between a child and a parent with a mental illness. I wanted them to know this in their hearts. This is something which perhaps only those with the lived experience can teach.

My first written encounter with Rai Gaita, occurred a couple of years ago, when I sought permission to make reference to *Romulus, My Father* in something I was writing. While it was already on the public record, I felt very hesitant about using the material from the book as the content was so deeply personal. Rai kindly granted permission and this led to an exchange about child protection. He saw on the website of the Australian Centre for Child Protection that I had written the words 'child protection is ultimately a question of human rights.'

Raimond challenged me. 'Why is it a matter of human rights' he asked, 'and why *ultimately* so?' 'And why use rights language to do moral work?' I put up a feeble defence and then embarked on a journey of reflecting on these questions. Now I shall share my answers to these questions to date.

The conceptualisation of child protection in terms of human rights is now the prevailing orthodoxy, enshrined in the United Nations Convention on the Rights of the Child, to which Australia is a signatory. The notion of the child as a holder of human rights, as a citizen with special vulnerability whom the State is obliged to protect, even from the child's own family, has evolved over the past century, but especially in the past generation.

The scale of the child protection problem is huge. There are over 35,000 children in Australia in State care, most living with relatives or in foster families. This is double the number a decade ago. Indigenous children are almost ten times more likely to be in State care than other children. The vast majority of children in State care are there as a result of parental drug and/or alcohol abuse, and a very significant minority is there as a result of parental mental illness.

The problem is not new. The nineteenth century child rescue movement adopted a paternalistic and moralistic approach which had the effect of

CHAPTER 10

reducing the child to an object of concern rather than an agent with a voice. A child's right to be heard in relation to matters affecting them is a central part of a child rights framework. The child rescue movement advanced a moral rationale for removing children from what was seen as the contamination of their families and their impoverished social environment.

In recent times we have heard the voices of members of the Stolen Generations, the British Child Migrants and the Forgotten Australians on the painful legacy of separation. By the late twentieth century, child protection was enshrined in human rights terms, the prevailing currency of western thought, as this was seen as appealing to the highest authority. Hence my claim that child protection was *ultimately* a matter of human rights.

Perhaps we have come to use rights language generally to state what might once have been expressed in terms of morality. Rai Gaita's challenge has made me consider the relative merits of a moral framework and a child rights framework for the field of child protection.

I would like to share three of my reflections about these relative merits, before advancing a case that ultimately child protection is about, or should be about, compassion and responding to the child as an emotional being. It is also about the child as a holder of human rights and as someone who can make a moral claim on adults and the State.

1. My first reflection is based on an observation that a moral obligations framework, based on the position that all adults and institutions have a paramount moral duty of care to children, is more powerful than one based on a rights based framework.

We have witnessed in Australia and elsewhere in recent times some institutions, including powerful religious organisations, act in ways that did not protect children from physical and sexual abuse. I observed when I was in Ireland some years ago at the time of the release of their seminal report on the longstanding abuse of Irish children in church run institutions, that it was indeed seen *ultimately* as a moral failing. Thus those who did not commit criminal offences against children directly but who covered up the abuse of others and moved abusive clergy to other places where they continued to abuse children, were seen as almost as morally culpable.

The public discourse I witnessed in Ireland was not about children's rights, but about the deep betrayal of children by individuals and the church, as well as the State, which failed to hold the church accountable because of its social and political power.

2. My second reflection is that a child's rights framework does not easily address the fundamental need of children – the need to be loved.

One can legislate for standards of child-care but one cannot legislate for love or indeed, uphold a right to be loved. Does a moral framework address this problem any better than a rights framework? While one may assert that parents have a moral obligation to love their child, even those who accept such a moral obligation may not experience loving feelings for their child. That is not a hypothetical philosophical point. I have witnessed depressed mothers express deep distress and guilt about their lack of feeling for their child. One feels what one feels, regardless of what one may wish to feel. Moral obligations help to govern our behaviour and reinforce social norms in relation to responsibilities to children but cherishing children, loving children, is more than this.

Whether a moral framework is any better than a rights framework depends on how we think about morality. If we accept the perspective of Raimond Gaita, then morality may indeed be central to child protection. In the introduction to *A Common Humanity*, Raimond argues:

> Persons, rights, obligation – they are concepts at the centre of one way of thinking about morality. Human being, human fellowship, love and its requirements are concepts at the centre of another. While I favour the latter, nothing I say finally proves that I am right to do so, and nothing prevents a determined translation of the latter into the former. But if I am right about the place love plays in the constitution of our moral concepts, in my claim that talk of inalienable rights and so on is dependent on the language of love, and if love is dependent on our responses to the human form and its expressive possibilities, then my case will at least seem plausible, and perhaps even convincing (Gaita 1999, 14–15).

3. My third reflection is that a discourse on children's rights, often framed in terms of children's rights vis-à-vis the rights of their family, carries some major risks. Embedding rights, which are concepts of the public sphere into the private sphere of the family, which is based not on rights but on loyalties, may damage the fabric of the family.

In the field of child protection, the notion of children's rights vis-à-vis those of their family, is at the very core of legislation, social policy and professional practice. Most legislation in western countries upholds the right of the child to the protection of the State as paramount. However, most

CHAPTER 10

legislation also attempts to limit the powers of the State by adopting the principle that the State's intervention to protect a child should be based on 'the least restrictive option.' Thus, a child has a right to their family as well as a right to be protected from their family, and the child's right to their family and the family's right to their child must not be restricted more than is necessary to prevent the child from suffering 'significant harm.'

The problem of child protection is that what is necessary to prevent a child experiencing harm in their family, and what harm may result from statutory intervention, is extremely difficult to determine. These are not just questions that can be addressed by drawing on empirical research. They are questions about values and normative judgments which vary according to the historical and cultural context. But most of all, they are questions that must be answered for an *individual* child in a highly specific and often rapidly changing situation.

The paradox of child protection is that despite its best efforts, the State will always struggle in loco parentis for the simple reason that the structure of the State is such that it cannot perform the function of the family. The State is a cold breast and a dry nipple.

Usually it is the family, and not strangers or the State, which has the greatest capacity to meet important needs of the child, such as the need to belong, to have an identity and be loved. The State, the church or for that matter, the market, can never meet such needs. These needs can only be met through a web of enduring relationships, albeit far from satisfactorily so for some children.

However, while these needs are very important, there will be situations in which other needs of the child, including physical survival, are given greater salience. When parents deeply fail a child, such as when the child is emotionally and/or physically abandoned or is very seriously harmed as a result of neglect or abuse, the State only succeeds in securing the child's needs are met in so far as it allows others to form a deep and enduring bond with the child such that their needs for safety, love and belonging might be met.

And this is *the dilemma of child protection* – meeting some of the child's needs, for example, the need for physical safety, may entail actions which disrupt familial bonds of attachment and belonging, sometimes temporarily, sometimes permanently. These are real and agonizing dilemmas. I know for I have experienced them.

John Bowlby, whose work on parent-child attachment has been so influential, enables us to understand the difference between a child being safe and being secure. A child may be in a very unsafe place but feel secure in a parent's arms. A child may be in a very safe place but feel insecure. A child may be both unsafe and insecure, which is often the case for children who have been abused and neglected.

It is easier to make a judgment about a child's safety than it is to make a judgment about a child's security. The former is more visible than the latter, and child protection workers will usually be judged more harshly for leaving a child in an unsafe situation where they are hurt than in acting in ways that threaten a child's security. The child's safety relates to their outer world and the child's security to their inner world. The latter requires us to make a compassionate leap of imagination.

Child protection decisions must consider the outer and the inner world of the child, and the risks and the likely suffering entailed in relation to both. The response needs to be one of compassion aimed at reducing the suffering.

Thus I have come to the conclusion that while child protection is about both rights and morality, it is *ultimately* about emotion, the emotion of compassion. While compassion is a moral virtue, it is first and foremost an emotion. The word itself reflects this. For example, the Latin origin of compassion literally means 'to suffer with.' The Hebrew for compassion is rachamim, which is closely related to rechem or womb. Both of these words convey something more visceral than mental.

But it is not linguistics that leads us to recognise that compassion is essentially an emotion. Children and adults alike can feel the absence or presence of compassion in another's response to them very quickly. And the essence of deep compassion is that it is an impulse in which one feels internally *compelled* to respond to the intense suffering of another. It is not the same experience as feeling a moral obligation to another.

Raimond Gaita has often captured this in his writing. He has frequently quoted Primo Levi's concentration camp observation of the compassion of Charles for the dying, filthy and typhus infected seventeen-year-old Jewish boy, Lakmaker. 'He lifted Lakmaker from the ground *with the tenderness of a mother ...* ' (Levi, cited in Gaita 1999, 151). I have heard Rai Gaita read these words with exactly that emphasis – *'with the tenderness of a mother.'*

I do not think it is a coincidence that Levi uses this phrase to describe deep compassion, nor that Rai Gaita gives it emphasis, for the origins of compassion occur very early in our life, and are intrinsically connected to our infant experiences of attachment to a mother or mother figure. The infant is biologically predisposed to form a strong attachment to his or her primary

CHAPTER 10

caregiver but this is compromised if the psycho-social conditions are not conducive. For example, there may not be an attachment figure available in situations such as the Romanian orphanages, or a deeply depressed mother may be physically present but emotionally absent and unresponsive.

Recent research on preschool aged children highlights that children who are most securely attached to their parents are the most likely to show compassion to their peers. Attachment is central to the capacity for compassion, which involves taking the position of the other, *and* for a child's moral development. Securely attached children internalise a sense of right and wrong from those to whom they are deeply attached, which is fundamentally different from a child learning what behaviour results in reward and punishment.

There is something about the suffering of a child which evokes compassion and compels us to respond. This is very obvious in relation to one's own children – parents will go to extreme lengths to protect their children from harm and to alleviate their suffering. We do not find this surprising – it is part and parcel of the intense attachment between child and parent, so much so it is something we take for granted.

This is not confined to parents and their biological children, however. I have witnessed adults come to love children who are not of their flesh and who are so deeply damaged and their behaviour so alienating that most of us would struggle to love them. I am in awe of the source of the capacity of some foster parents I know to persist with such children and not to reject them even when provoked over and over again to do so.

Equally remarkably, we have countless examples of people risking their life to save the life of a child they do not know. As a young girl one summer I witnessed my father and other men spontaneously rush into treacherous surf to save a boy being swept out to sea. And I recall the time when my father's brother, a fireman, was lowered down a narrow, sixty foot mine shaft, the walls of which were collapsing in, to save a little girl who had fallen to the bottom. Both children survived.

Such behaviour cannot be explained in terms of the attachment between the adult and the child for they are strangers. When asked why they acted as they did, such adults usually struggle for words and speak of 'responding instinctively,' 'just doing it' and 'not thinking, just acting.' Again, the impulse sounds more visceral than mental.

Compassion is not the reserve of adults. Children too can express deep compassion, and it is divinely precious to witness this in one's own or in another's child. It is a milestone far more profound than the first step or the first word. It may be a narrower range of situations in which children can 'take the position of the other' but their empathy for the suffering of an animal or a human they can observe and understand is as authentic as that of any adult.

Returning to the vulnerable child in a child protection context, our compassion needs to be based on the child's experience and not our projection of the child's experience. That is, it is about responding with compassion *to the child as an emotional being*, and being open to what it means to *this child* to be in *this situation*.

Responding to the child as an emotional being requires an empathic recognition of the child's multiple and at times mixed emotions. I vividly recall a five year old boy who was terrified by his mother's schizophrenic delusions that people were coming into their house at night to hurt them for he believed these to be true, but he was equally fearful of being taken from her care. She was his primary figure of attachment. He was also excited and confused by her flirtatious behaviour with him. This was not secretive seductive behaviour but was done openly in front of others with no recognition that it was inappropriate. These multiple emotions capture something of the complexity of the vulnerable child as an emotional being.

Just as the evolution of the child as a holder of human rights has been emerging over the past century, so too has the notion of the child as an emotional being. This is part of the legacy of Freud. But it is not a theoretically filtered perspective on the child as an emotional being, be it of Freud or Bowlby, to which I am referring. It is the lived experience of the *individual* child as an emotional being which is the paramount consideration.

And this is the power of *Romulus, My Father*. It is not just that it is a powerful exploration of love and loss in a family. It is not just that it is a profound account of the integrity and compassion of Romulus Gaita. It is also the deeply honest and authentic way in which it enables the reader to enter the inner world of one boy, Raimond Gaita.

Anyone who can illuminate the inner world of a vulnerable child possesses a precious gift. Rai Gaita has such a gift. It is a gift he shares in his role as an ambassador, or patron, for a small charitable organization called The Mirabel Foundation. This organization provides compassionate support to children whose parents have experienced severe substance misuse and who may have died, disappeared or be in prison as a result, or who may reappear in their children's lives in unsettling and unpredictable ways. Most of these children are raised by their grandparents to whom the Mirabel Foundation gives great practical and moral support. Speaking of

CHAPTER 10

the children the Mirabel Foundation supports, Raimond Gaita was quoted in their Annual Report as saying the children needed two things – 'to be loved *and to love their parents without shame.*'

'To love their parents without shame' – what must it be like for a child to love a parent *with shame*, I wonder? Very few of us, mercifully, will ever have had to endure the painful experience of loving a parent *with shame*.

Children who harbour feelings of shame in relation to a parent they love struggle to express this because such shame is intensified by exposing it to others, *and* because it would also be an act of disloyalty to the parent they love. Loyalty is still at the heart of these children's sense of family, as fragmented as the family might be.

I found Rai Gaita's insight into this dimension of the child as an emotional being, of loving one's parents with shame, extraordinary. I had heard, over many years, people speak of how such children love their parents, and I had heard people speak of how such children feel ashamed of their parents. I had never before heard anyone articulate so powerfully and so clearly the possibility of a child loving a parent with shame.

This description resonates strongly with what I have observed in children trying to come to terms with their parent's mental illness or substance dependence. It makes me ask how we can act in ways that do not exacerbate feelings of shame in a child.

And the answer is embedded in Raimond Gaita's philosophy. We reduce the child's burden of loving with shame when we show unconditional respect to his or her parents, when we recognise their humanity, or as my fellow Quakers would say, when we respond to that of God in the other because there is that of God in all of us.

When we diminish the humanity of parents struggling, often against great odds, to nurture their children in the context of a mental illness or substance dependence, we sow shame in the hearts of their children. Children can remember these things for the rest of their lives. The memories are sealed in searing emotions.

Children also remember those who do not judge and those who act with compassion to their parents. At the very end of *Romulus, My Father*, Raimond Gaita demonstrates this when he describes the scene immediately after his father's funeral:

> When I came out of the church I saw an elderly man, standing apart, leaning on a walking stick, obviously an Australian, looking like an archetype of the men from my childhood whose character I remembered

with admiration and fondness in my eulogy. I did not recognize him. When I went towards him I saw that his eyes were filled with tears. It was Neil Mikkelsen, *the man who had been kind to my mother*, and who had fallen from the haystack when my father worked for him. 'Every word you spoke was true,' he said. 'Your father saved my life.'

His presence and his words moved me. I thought again of Frogmore and my life there with my father. I remembered my mother laughing as she talked with Mikkelsen at the chicken-wire gate (Gaita 1998, 207–08).

In an era in which the spirit of the age is one of fear and despair, Raimond Gaita speaks to our collective condition. He teaches us, not just by what he says but by who he is, that a child can be nurtured in love in the midst of great suffering, to become a most remarkable crucible of compassion and a harbinger of hope.

Ethics

Chapter 11

MORAL PHILOSOPHY IN THE MIDST OF THINGS

Christopher Cordner

The nineteenth-century German Philosopher, G.W.F. Hegel, held Philosophy to be the highest expression of what he called 'absolute spirit.' Art, Religion and Philosophy comprised that domain, and the highest of these was Philosophy. Art – including literary arts – and religion give us music, images, stories, in which the truth about ourselves and the meaning of our world is bodied forth to us. But the very richness of texture which helps give these embodiments their sense and power for us at the very same time means they cannot reveal to us with perfect clarity the truth they carry in them. This limitation, as Hegel sees it to be, is caught in the inescapability of that word 'sense' where the illuminating power of art is concerned. For Hegel the clearest understanding of things lies in a rarefied, purely rationally articulated insight beyond the reach of 'sense.' Religion can do rather better than art in this respect: it refines the sensuousness of the medium in which it gives its truth to us, but still does so with less than perfect limpidity, clarity, intellectual purity. Philosophy alone can realise that purity.

Plato has a view that is in some ways similar to this, and Rai Gaita has often meditated on aspects of it and related his own thinking to it. Hegel reminds us that the view is a recurring one, as is opposition to it, from within philosophy as well as from outside it. Repeated announcements of 'the end of metaphysics' afford one mode of such opposition. Sometimes of course what we find is not flat opposition to the view, but a teasing out of strains inherent in it.

In a way, everything I want to say can be put in the terms of this Hegelian picture of the 'hierarchy' of the modes of absolute spirit. But only in a way. Philosophy is more commonly thought of as the handmaiden of the sciences than as something needed to complete them. But, even so

A SENSE FOR HUMANITY

Hegel's view that philosophy's abstractness, with its elevation above the human lives we actually live, gives us a clearer understanding of ourselves than can be found in either art or religion, is alive and well. In its attempt to articulate our truest self-understanding philosophy aspires, according to a widely-held view, to a language at once more precise and more abstract than either the rough-hewn language of daily life or the image- and affect-laden tropes of poetry or the other arts. I want to reflect on some recurring features of Raimond Gaita's philosophical writing in relation to this stand, as we may take it to be, on what Plato famously called 'the quarrel between philosophy and poetry'.

The great Irish poet Seamus Heaney wrote two poems about Antaeus, the giant born from the earth who could not be defeated in fights because his energies were renewed by contact with the earth each time he was thrown by his antagonist. Here is one of them, titled 'Antaeus'.

> When I lie on the ground
> I rise flushed as a rose in the morning.
> In fights I arrange a fall on the ring
> To rub myself with sand
>
> That is operative
> As an elixir. I cannot be weaned
> Off the earth's long contour, her river-veins.
> Down here in my cave
>
> Girded with root and rock
> I am cradled in the dark that wombed me
> And nurtured in every artery
> Like a small hillock.
>
> Let each new hero come
> Seeking the golden apples and Atlas.
> He must wrestle with me before he pass
> Into that realm of fame
>
> Among sky-born and royal:
> He may well throw me and renew my birth
> But let him not plan, lifting me off the earth,
> My elevation, my fall.[1]

---

[1] 'Antaeus' forms part of Seamus Heaney's collection *North* 1975, 53.

CHAPTER 11

'I was thinking about what kind of poet I was,' said Heaney, 'when I wrote about Hercules and Antaeus, wondering whether I might lose my voice if I got too far off the ground.' That Hegelian metaphor of elevation or height again. One might then say, in a Hegelian tone of voice: 'fine for a *poet* to say that. But only at an elevation "above the ground" at which the poet fears the loss of his voice does the *philosopher* have anything to say at all!'

Against this, Gaita can helpfully be regarded as thinking that Heaney's question is one that every *philosopher* – or at least every philosopher who thinks about ethics – should also ask herself. Of course Heaney's question is in the first person: 'I wondered if *I* might lose my voice if I got too far off the ground.' Even so, one might plausibly think that *each* poet will – even must – put this question to him or her self. But if philosophers, also, should indeed ask the question, their responses to it may well differ not only from the already diverse response different poets will give, but also from one another. Even philosophers who agree that philosophy too should not 'get too far off the (human) ground' might differ on just where their feet lose touch with the ground, on which bits of that uneven terrain it is most important to stay close enough to, on how far one can and should sometimes rise above it, and on whether and how often one might need to 'come back down.'

Philosophy after all is reflective. In the attempt to understand ourselves and our being in the world better, more truly, more deeply, philosophising involves *reflecting* upon ourselves and our experience. Given that, there is some point in saying philosophy cannot but elevate us above the 'ground' of our non-philosophical life. But Rai Gaita has done a good deal to help us see where and how some philosophically-favoured elevations give us only the *illusion* of an illuminating perspective on our lives and selves. He has done this by himself thinking and speaking in a way that involves genuinely philosophical reflection, but of a kind that both draws upon and sustains our living not only in, but also *from*, the world.

That is admittedly a rather abstruse sentence, and I want to try to clarify what I mean by it. The English philosopher Roger Scruton described Rai's book *The Philosopher's Dog* – about our lives with animals – as 'an experiment in narrative philosophy.' Another commentator said that the book was written 'across the boundary between the philosophical and the personal'; and Simon Critchley's description of *A Common Humanity* as 'a series of ethical meditations drawn from the midst of things,' could also be applied to *The Philosopher's Dog*. In slightly different ways, these various phrases point to Gaita's work as keeping in touch with 'the ground.'

It is true to say that this is linked with the use he makes of examples (though 'narratives,' as Scruton's phrase suggests, is a better word). It's true, but saying it does not by itself take us very far. Quite a few philosophers, especially in ethics, use examples in their work, but the significant difference here is not between those who do and those who don't use examples; it is a difference in *how* they are used. We can get at that difference by seeing why 'used' is a misleading word here. Examples can be just grist for a philosophical mill whose wheels are already fixed in their movements; then the examples are merely illustrative, of a thesis or a 'theory' already determined. In Immanuel Kant's famous terms, the 'concept' is already given, and the example is subsumed under it – in an exercise of what Kant called 'determinant judgment.' When examples or narratives are used in this way, they are not elements of what Scruton means by 'narrative philosophy' nor are they constituents of 'ethical meditations drawn from the midst of things.'

Kant described a second mode of judging, which he called 'reflective' judgment. In reflective judgment, Kant said, the 'particular' is given, and a concept has to be 'found *for* it.' An example or narrative 'used' in a way that gives rise to judging in this mode, is one that – as it were – 'uses' the judger as much as he uses the example: its lessons take shape only through the response it summons from him. Rather than the example or narrative just illustrating a given concept, one's 'concept'[2] is shaped and animated by the example. The 'being' of the issue under discussion is then responsive to what the example may reveal. Let me try to be clearer about what I mean by this.

Kant himself confined the exercise of reflective judgment to the aesthetic domain, thereby entrenching a dichotomy by which moral philosophy has been badly hampered – a judgment is either 'strictly moral' or it is 'merely aesthetic.' If we resist confining the scope of reflective judgment in that way, we might see it at work throughout our morally vital engagements. The exercise of what Kant calls 'reflective' judgment is inherently more tentative, more exploratory, more open-ended, always less-than-final, and less susceptible of incorporation into a method, than that of 'determinant' judgment. Moreover, in reflective judgment the very 'being' of the judger is

---

[2] Why the scare-quotes around 'concept'? Because the expression of reflective judgment may not be a *word* at all. It may be, perhaps, the inflexions of one's body in sympathetic response to another; or if it *does* involve a word or words, perhaps an indexical term will be ineliminably involved: 'I would have you move still, still so [i.e.: "like *that*"]' as Florizel says to Perdita in singing the praises of her beauty in Shakespeare's *A Winter's Tale*. 'Concept' is thus being given a provocatively wide scope here.

CHAPTER 11

implicated. She is summoned to be present in the moment of judging, and is herself at issue – sometimes *at stake* – in the judging. Partly for this reason, it is misleading to say that we 'exercise' (active verb) reflective judgment. It is at least as true that in reflective judgment we are *exercised by* what we judge. We might for this reason speak here not of 'judging an object' but, as R.F. Holland does in a similar connection, of 'marking an encounter'. Relatedly, a generation after Kant, the English poet John Keats's describes the poetic mode as one of 'Negative Capability, that is, when a man is capable of being in uncertainties, mysteries, doubts, without any irritable reaching after fact and reason' (Keats 1968, 53). This marks a kind of creative receptiveness closely akin to Kantian reflective judgment. Again, the attitude – an inadequate word, but I cannot find a better one – need not be confined to 'poetry.'

It would be instructive to stay longer with Kant's idea. But I mention it here just to help orient us to something distinctive of Gaita's moral philosophising. Moral judgment is commonly understood as determinant judgment (and typically distinguished as *moral* judgment by its subject matter). Gaita would not deny that moral judgment can *sometimes* be thus 'determinant,' but (I suggest) thinking of it as originally and typically closer to what Kant calls 'reflective' judgment – and so to a kind of receptive responsiveness that it is rather misleading to call 'judgment' at all – brings us much closer to Gaita's main themes.[3]

These two sentences from Iris Murdoch make a very similar double point: 'The central concept of morality is 'the individual' thought of as knowable by love' (Murdoch 1970, 30). But, she also says, it is not always like this: 'Often … we are just "anybody" doing what is proper or making simple choices for ordinary public reasons' (Murdoch 1970, 43). In the latter case (where the choices need not in fact be 'simple' or the reasons 'ordinary') choosing and doing express roughly what Kant meant by determinant judgment. Roughly, we see our situation as an instance of this or that relevant universal (this or that 'principle'), and we act accordingly: I receive my bill and I pay it; I hand in the expensive camera I find on the bus stop; I lend a hand when my neighbour asks. But this situation, says Murdoch, is the one 'which some [read "many!"] philosophers have chosen exclusively to analyse.' Her point is not that they have focused only on 'simple' situations (though at the time she wrote this

---

[3] I hope this helps to suggest that on Gaita's view, our *moral thinking itself* is fundamentally narrativistic. The point is not just that if and when we introduce specific examples 'into' the discussion of a moral issue we should 'use' them reflectively rather than determinantly. The deeper point is that our own moral responsiveness is itself inherently narrativistic (or narratival), in the sort of way I've described.

was largely true), but that they read moral thinking as always and essentially *like that*, whereas for Murdoch, moral thinking must be seen against the background of the 'darker, less fully conscious, less steadily rational' image crystallised in the first of the two sentences I quoted. 'Attention' is a key term in Murdoch's exploration of love. Attention is not (as quite a few of her interpreters mistakenly assume)[4] a matter of scrutinizing a person or object to determine as many of their 'properties' as possible – thus tying attention to 'determinant' judgment. Attending (*'really* looking') involves being present to another, open – without defensiveness – to how one might unpredictably be called in response. (The meaning of 'attendant' as one who is present at an event or who waits on a person is in play here, though of course in a sense extended beyond mere physical presence.) The 'individual' is 'given,' and one finds oneself summoned in response – here, again, are terms akin to Kant's reflective judgment.

I spoke of something distinctive in Gaita's *philosophising*, rather than just in moral judgment as he understands it. For Gaita, appreciating moral judgment as having the kind of character I've briefly suggested will show in the mode of one's philosophical reflection upon it. That is to say: the mode of one's philosophising – and not just the content of the philosophical propositions one affirms – must to some degree be informed by the character of what is to be appreciated. 'Narrative philosophy,' 'meditations drawn from the midst of things' – themselves expressed in a way that shares something of that more tentative, exploratory, open-ended, always less-than-final character of reflective judgment – are then needed to 'capture' the reality of our moral thinking and responsiveness.

We could turn to many passages in Gaita's philosophy to help illuminate what is at issue here. With Kant's contrast providing guidance, I shall fasten on one specific moment of Gaita's thinking that (I hope) helps to draw out more clearly what Scruton and Critchley are pointing to in their descriptions of Gaita's work. Here is a marvellous passage from *The Philosopher's Dog*:

---

4   For example, Elijah Millgram: 'Murdoch took it that seeing what's really in front of you will lead to ever greater conceptual idiosyncrasies, because your concepts have to be tailored to the particularities and foibles of the different people you are trying to perceive carefully' (Millgram 2004, 511); Julia Driver (on Murdoch's example of M and D): 'It gives us an example of moral reflection, and how it works. Attention to detail gets us further at the truth. But we have to approach such cases with mental descriptions that are general, and then search for more detail.' ('"For every Foot its own Shoe": Method and Moral Theory in the Philosophy of Iris Murdoch', in Broackes, 2012, 302); Bridget Clarke: 'To attend to something is to … perceive it in its unbounded particularity and complexity and so as it truly is' ("Iris Murdoch and the Prospects for Critical Moral Perception", in Broackes 2012, 236).

CHAPTER 11

Bees have always inspired affection in human beings, because they give honey, because they are symbols of industriousness, and because there has been for a long time acknowledgment of their extraordinary 'social' life. Ants inspire a kind of respect because they have some of the same qualities – they are industrious and they too interact in complex ways – but they do not, I think, awaken affection. In our imagination we elaborate on the association of bees with flowers and warm days, and because they die when they sting we readily forgive them the harm they cause us, even though we know they can be deadly when they swarm.

Perhaps that is why my father consented to their stings, never wearing protective clothing when he caught a swarming hive in a nearby tree or when he took the racks from the hives. ... When I asked him why he refused [to don protective clothing], he said that he did not think of them as enemies against which he needed to protect himself. I did not fully understand his answer. Nor I suspect did he. But it had to do with, and was certainly of a piece with, his tender compassion for them.

Sometimes on cold mornings he found bees lying on the grass outside the hive, to all appearances quite dead. He would collect them in the palm of his hand and take them into the kitchen where he placed them on the table. Then he would take an electric bulb and move it to and fro, fifteen or so centimetres above them, so they would be warmed by it but not harmed by a concentration of heat on any part of them. When I first saw him do this I was moved by his attentive tenderness and entranced by its results. Gradually signs of life appeared. Legs twitched so slightly that one wondered whether it had really happened, and then more surely so that I knew that the bees had been restored to life by this gentle miracle-worker. Soon they tried to turn right side up, and when they succeeded, often with a little help from us, my father brushed them from the table with the side of an open hand into the cupped palm of the other, as one does breadcrumbs, but gently, and we took them outside where they flew away ...

Tender though he was to his bees, my father hated flies. If one came into the kitchen, which happened frequently enough, he would not rest until he had killed it. He became quite expert at catching them. He would sneak up on one and, with a sideways sweep of his open hand, palm upwards, catch it and instantly close his fist. People can become obsessive with things that irritate them, even when they are inanimate, like dust or leaves falling in the garden in autumn. But for my father the flies were not just an irritant: they were an enemy to be vanquished and he killed them with appropriate satisfaction. Though he was a wise and thoughtful man, I'm sure it never occurred to him to wonder whether there was some tension between his attitude to his bees and his attitude to flies.

My father's attitude to his bees moved me and transformed my sense of the insect world. Over the years I reflected on it, but not because it alerted me to new facts about bees, nor because it made me wonder whether the facts I knew required me to bring my conduct towards insects under principles I had hitherto applied only to my conduct towards animals. He taught me what compassion for an insect could be and what behaviour to them could mean. He taught me by his example, but I do not think of his example as having introduced me to something I could assess independently of the authority with which it moved me (Gaita 2002, 131–33).

Interestingly, Gaita does not say either that his father *should* have wondered whether his attitudes the bees and flies were in tension, or that he was quite right not to do so. Peter Singer would not remain thus silent. Singer quotes Jeremy Bentham saying: 'The question [of the moral considerability of creatures] is not, Can they *reason*? nor Can they *talk*? but, *Can they suffer?*' (Singer 1993, 57). And the seriousness of the wrong done to a creature whose suffering is not 'take[n] … into consideration' (Singer 1993, 57) is determined by the degree of its suffering. Bees and flies would seem to be at much the same level as far as capacity for suffering is concerned. Since 'the principle of equality requires that [a being's] suffering be counted equally with the like suffering … of any other being' (Singer 1993, 57), Romulus Gaita's failure to take account of the suffering of the flies at his hands shows him, given his concern for the bees, contravening that principle. Singer does not say what justifies the 'principle of equality,' but he seems to think it a requirement of logical consistency in thinking. Violating it then shows logical *in*consistency.

Singer's philosophical discourse here takes place at a level of abstraction from – or elevation above – the 'ground' of Gaita's narrative. On Singer's outlook, Gaita's description of the background to his father's care for bees – one that resonates with us reading it – is irrelevant to how anyone 'ought to' respond to the bees, as the background to his father's treatment of flies is irrelevant to how we should respond to them. We get to nothing 'morally

CHAPTER 11

true' in our responses unless and until we elevate ourselves above all of that merely human dross.

But the contrast to be drawn with Gaita here is not confined to Singer, or even consequentialism more broadly. I highlight Singer here just because Gaita's story is peculiarly apt in connection with Singer's views, since the direct implications of what Singer has written – about 'levels of capacity to suffer pain' – so bluntly confront and adversely judge what Gaita shows us of his father's radically different responses to the bees and to flies. But the example also invites closely related contrasts with Kant, with Aristotle, and with many contemporary moral philosophers. Rather than explore these, though, I want to tease out a bit more from Gaita's story about his father and the bees and flies. As I noted, Gaita says only that he is sure it never occurred to his father to wonder whether there was some tension between his attitude to his bees and his attitude to flies, while Peter Singer would identify logical tension – inconsistency indeed – in Romulus. If Gaita does not himself think his father should have wondered about that, why does he not? And is he right not to think it?

As I read him, Gaita does *not* think his father 'should have' wondered about this. A few pages later, he reflects on a passage he quotes from Pablo Casals, expressing his gratitude for 'the miracle of nature,' the wonderful beauty of the world. And Gaita says: 'It is impossible to imagine [Casals] rising from the piano and casually crushing some insects or plucking the wings off flies. Can we imagine him catching flies in his hand and killing them with sweet satisfaction? About that, I have no opinion' (Gaita 2002, 139). This tantalizing reflection clearly refers back to his father's habit of doing just that. The contrast drawn here is between crushing insects casually, or perhaps cruelly delighting in plucking the wings off flies, on the one hand, and on the other hand taking satisfaction in killing flies 'because they were not just an irritant, even a gross irritant, but an enemy to be vanquished' (Gaita 2002, 133). That latter is the meaning Gaita thinks is to be found in his father's killing of flies: there is a kind of contest with a resourceful and relentless enemy, where success in one's well-planned guerrilla tactics – 'sneak[ing] up on one and, with a sideways sweep of his open hand, palm upwards, catch[ing] it and instantly clos[ing] his fist' (Gaita 2002, 133) – carries its own 'sweet satisfaction'. This is a very different thing from taking pleasure in simple or casual cruelty (which is not to say no further moral questions can arise about it).

There is simply no inconsistency or logical tension between helping one's friends and fighting with, even killing, one's enemies. So far as Romulus's engagements with the bees and the flies exemplify (something like) those contrasting relations, he need recognise no tension or inconsistency between them.

Of course moral questions about whether one should treat these others as enemies, and if so whether and when and in what ways that might warrant killing them, can still arise. And one may imagine this to be so for Romulus and the flies too. We can take it, surely, that Romulus's treating the flies as an enemy carries within it his answer to those questions: flies are an 'enemy' because, for example, by contrast with the bees they are (roughly) dirty, unproductive transmitters of disease, constantly and brazenly engaged in their own guerrilla sorties on our food. Fly-spray, perhaps, might have got rid of the flies just as well as Romulus's manual dexterity did. Gaita does not say what his father's attitude to fly-spray was (if the doors and windows were open it would probably not have been much use anyway), but whatever satisfaction he might have felt from freeing the house of flies that way would not – *could not* – have been the satisfaction he took in what he actually did. Perhaps he might have thought using fly-spray mean-spirited.

That last speculation, especially, might be thought to put our imaginations under some stretch here, but it is worth being clear why this might be so. It is not because there is anything silly in the very idea of something like having to confront one's enemy in a way that is not morally evasive or inhuman. Recently there has been much discussion of the ethics of drone warfare – putting oneself in a position where one can kill the enemy while completely avoiding any exposure of one's own troops. It is far from a silly thought that this might be a mean-spirited, disrespectful, even contemptuous attitude, and that fighting this way is morally wrong; and something analogous then might possibly come into play in connection with the use of fly-spray. If our imagination is under strain here it is not because it is silly to think of there being ethical dimensions of how one faces one's enemy. It is rather because thinking of flies under that aspect at all *already* puts our imaginations under some strain.

Even this last point, though, is more complex than it might seem. Romulus's attitude towards his bees shows that he spontaneously responds to them as his fellow creatures. But in a way his 'sweet satisfaction' in killing flies manifests something like that same spontaneous responsiveness. For only a fellow creature can *be* an enemy – however much we may sometimes 'demonise' others sometimes in order to hold them in place, so to speak, as 'enemies.' Indeed, perhaps the demonising is necessary only with regard to those to whom we *do* spontaneously respond as 'fellow creatures.' *Romulus's* imagination is not strained in regarding the flies as 'enemies,' just *because* he spontaneously takes them to be his fellow creatures.

Recall Gaita saying about Casals: 'It is impossible to imagine him rising from the piano and casually crushing some insects or plucking the wings off flies. Can we imagine him catching flies in his hand and killing them with sweet satisfaction? About that, I have no opinion' (Gaita 2002, 139). Gaita's thought here seems to be along these lines: 'I cannot imagine one who feels and lives in the world in the way Casals also ponders casually crushing insects or wantonly plucking the wings off flies. But killing them in a spirit of engagement with an enemy considered to be a worthy foe? That is a different thing; here the possibilities are less clear.' But the reason they are less clear is *not* that there is some perfectly *general* difficulty with the consistency of Romulus's attitudes. I've already addressed *that* point by noting that there is no inconsistency in killing enemies while helping friends.[5] The possibilities are less clear here for the very specific reason that imaginatively thus engaging with flies as 'an enemy to be vanquished' is already stretching things a bit. Only a *bit*, mind you – I remember myself responding when young in a similar way, though even then perhaps with an inchoate sense of there being something a *bit* strange in doing so. So that if someone else were present, for instance, the thing could pretty naturally become a matter of some humour, which would not happen were 'real' enemies being engaged.[6] This ambivalence (if that is the right word) is, I think, the source of Gaita's 'I have no opinion' about whether we could imagine Casals killing flies 'with sweet satisfaction.'

Gaita shows us into a distinctive way of thinking about our moral relation to (in this case) insects. Among other things, he enables us to see why we should resist supposing that Romulus's attitudes *must* be described as 'inconsistent' or in logical tension with one another. Equally, though, Gaita does not say that it must therefore be a *mistake* to describe them that way (i.e., as 'inconsistent').[7] Is that just an oversight, or perhaps evasiveness, on Gaita's

---

[5] As I hope I have already made clear, there are of course often *other* powerful, even decisive, moral considerations against killing one's enemies.

[6] Gaita himself implicitly acknowledges some imaginative strain here when, after telling us that Romulus said he 'did not think of [his bees] as his enemies', Gaita says 'I did not understand exactly what he meant and I suspect he did not either.'

[7] Perhaps if Romulus had got to the point of wondering if there was a (logical) tension between his attitude to the bees and the flies, this would mean he was *already* beyond the 'engaged' attitude with which Romulus actually 'lived with' bees and flies, and so already on the brink of concluding that there *was* a tension, and of moving to resolve it. There is a very important point here, which Sartre expressed (and exaggerated) by

part? Surely the attitudes either are, or are not, logically inconsistent with one another? But I don't think Gaita believes the matter is so simple. Consider here a pair of attitudes towards animals (rather than insects) that Gaita also ponders: deep compassion for animals and readiness to kill them to be eaten. Gaita says that the fact that there are people whose compassion for animals makes it morally impossible for them to kill an animal for food does not 'show up' his father, who *did* kill animals for food while also throughout his life showing deep compassion for animals. Again, this does *not* mean Gaita is saying that someone who found eating animals incompatible (inconsistent) with his compassion for them is mistaken. But he *is* insisting that it cannot flatly be said that readiness to eat animals and having genuine compassion for them are inconsistent attitudes. Gaita's view here is crystallised in his saying: 'we sometimes find something morally impossible for us, but do not think that people who find it possible are thereby mistaken.' Many philosophers – nearly all – do not think that is coherent. In fact I agree with Gaita here: the assumption that moral convictions are *necessarily universalizable* is to be rejected.[8] Persuading others is of course another matter, but an appreciation of the narrative dimension of moral thinking – where the kind of meaning one finds in one's living relatedness to the world is what is most fundamentally at issue – does perhaps put some pressure on that assumption of universalizability. To put that point slightly differently: if one supposes that moral thinking is a matter of arriving at the correct moral principles, one will more naturally be disposed to assume a requirement of universalizability. How, after all, could a *principle* be 'valid' for me but not for you or vice versa? But the assumption perhaps does not look quite so compelling within a narrative conception of ethical responsiveness.[9]

Romulus's example can be put alongside the work of David Attenborough. These are not the same, since Romulus's gentle compassion for the bees is

---

saying 'quand je delibere, les jeux sont faits.' He meant that 'deliberating on possible reasons' is not a morally neutral activity. That one is thus deliberating means one's situation is now constituted by an 'issue to be resolved' in a way that it was not before one found it necessary to deliberate. *And*: this is not necessarily a moral improvement. To put that another way: one can sometimes say *both* that a person might correctly identify – and even correctly resolve - a tension, *and* that prior to her wondering if there was such a tension, there *wasn't* one. But there are difficult issues here, whose exploration is for another time.

[8] See Gaita, 2004b, 105–113.

[9] Although he does not speak of 'narrative', Craig Taylor's discussions of several examples in his book *Moralism* also I think dovetail with, and help to take further, these brief remarks here about universalizability. See especially his discussion of J.M. Coetzee's novel *Disgrace*, in Taylor (2012, 118–30).

CHAPTER 11

integral to his example, whereas Attenborough narrates film footage. But like Romulus, Attenborough's work enables those who see it to come into a different living relation to many different creatures, including various insects. Though we do learn 'new facts' from his work, it does not *only* give us 'information.' It enables us imaginatively to find our footing with the lives of these creatures, seeing *this* as a 'fight,' *that* as a spiders' 'dance,' this as a 'courtship ritual,' and so on. The scare quotes indicate the imaginative extension involved in our coming to see things in these terms. These extensions are themselves *expressions* of our fellowship with these creatures: that fellowship is realised – *enacted*, one could say – in the narratives into which we find ourselves woven with these creatures when we make sense of their behaviour in these terms.

There are complexities here. I hinted earlier that stories – narratives – are not necessarily the site of what I called 'reflective judgment.' As many philosophers have noted, there are ever-present moral dangers of *fixing* others in our stories, simply giving them an already-determined role. This is equivalent to judging 'determinantly' in Kant's terms. Such a story may not be a bad one, and the role may even be (so to speak) written 'for the other's benefit.' But still there is a difference from a narrative in whose unfolding the roles are so to speak always allowed to be in the process of creative realisation. To 'see' these insects' behaviour as a 'dance,' for example, is thereby to find the possibilities of dance creatively extended, and so even one's *own* possibilities as a potential dancer likewise extended. As in Kantian reflective judgment, here the very 'being' of the 'judger' (the witness of Attenborough's film, or of the bees under Romulus's gentle care) is creatively changed in his receptiveness to what he witnesses.

The examples just given are in (relatively) minor key, as it were, and deliberately so. It is important to see that the philosophical terms here do not apply *only* to existentially and morally dramatic or profound transformations. That said, though, we should not under-estimate the potential impact even of such 'witness' as I have just been describing: 'My father's attitude to his bees moved me and transformed my sense of the insect world.'

As hinted two paragraphs ago, the mere fact that one's orientation is cast in narrative terms *of course* does not constitute one as ethically 'sound.' Stories can be challenged, criticised, revised, in any number of ways, and often *need* to be challenged. But one key point of Gaita's outlook is that *this* is where real ethical transformation takes place – in this contestation within and between our narratives, which Gaita more often calls contestation of *meaning*. This contestation takes place at the site of the narratives themselves

– that is, 'on the ground' of our lived engagement with the world and its creatures. It is not deferred to a site of elevation above all that, which we ascend to and from which we then return to restructure our meanings from outside them:

> My father's attitude to his bees moved me and transformed my sense of the insect world. Over the years I reflected on it, but not because it alerted me to new facts about bees, nor because it made me wonder whether the facts I knew required me to bring my conduct towards insects under principles I had hitherto applied only to my conduct towards animals. He taught me what compassion for an insect could be and what behaviour to them could mean. He taught me by his example, but I do not think of his example as having introduced me to something I could assess independently of the authority with which it moved me (Gaita 2002, 133).

By reflecting on just one episode from *The Philosopher's Dog* I've tried to convey some sense of what Roger Scruton calls Gaita's 'narrative philosophy', including a sense of it as both drawing upon and sustaining our living, like Antaeus, *from* the world. I want to end with some brief remarks on one further question that I think naturally arises here. Suppose one is persuaded that Gaita does offer us a distinctive and important kind of practice of moral philosophy: is there then a question about the place, in the professionalised academy, of this practice of philosophy, that does not arise for 'traditional' philosophy? In briefly engaging with that question, I also want to locate it in a wider question about the implications for philosophy of its professionalisation within the Academy.

In a way that wider question was launched by Plato's founding of the Academy, moving philosophy off the street, where Socrates had practised it. One might think that it is just silly, though, after so many centuries of academic practice of Philosophy, to moot the concern that the discipline is threatened by having its home in the academy. Or if the suggestion *is* made, the reason for it may lie in specific concerns about for example recent pressures on academics to publish as much as universities expect them to. Certainly that expectation *is* a danger to philosophy, and perhaps a greater danger to it than to most, perhaps all, other disciplines. But that is not my focus here.

Both the bent of Gaita's critique of extant moral philosophy and the character of his own philosophical practice mean that Gaita's work has been a constant exploring of what philosophy is, and a testing of the

CHAPTER 11

boundaries between it and other kinds of writing. Perhaps the best work in philosophy always constitutes its own specific answer to the question of what philosophy is. Certainly revisiting the question is ever an important task for philosophy. Over 2000 years ago Plato spoke of the 'quarrel' between poetry and philosophy as he sought to shape a personal and cultural space for the practice of philosophy. That space was not secure then and it is not secure now. This is not because 'what philosophy is' is perfectly clear, and there is just a question of whether our (or any) culture will continue to value it. Philosophy is unique among disciplines because the question of just what is involved in philosophising is always a contested one. 'What philosophy is' is *never* simply clear.

It is difficult for a professionalised discipline to sustain an appreciation of that truth. The pressure is always towards fixing and institutionalising the practice of the discipline. Of course really good philosophical work has been done in the philosophical academy, and this will continue to happen. But the 'never-givenness' of what philosophy is means, I think, that philosophy is always in tension with the academy to a greater extent than other disciplines are. That is generally true, but there is a still sharper question about how easily or well moral philosophy in the mode that characterises Rai's work fits into that context. It isn't an accident that Rai has published so little in the main philosophical journals, or that he has not been more discussed there. There is I think an interesting parallel between his work and that of Iris Murdoch in the latter respect. Her work has drawn a great deal of praise from many philosophers, but (until very recently) relatively little academic philosophical discussion. For reasons partly similar and partly dissimilar from those that apply to Gaita, Murdoch's work also ill-fits the professionalised context.

In Gaita's case, the reason can be put this way. I hope my earlier discussion helps show why Gaita thinks that many important things in moral philosophy can be said only when its language is closer to poetry than it has traditionally been acknowledged to be. 'Closer to', not the same as, and not aping poetry either. The closeness involves, among other things, seeking to use – or perhaps a better way of putting it, opening oneself to be used by – language 'at full stretch.' But that is perhaps a relatively 'formal' point, as it were. In relation to Gaita's work, the point gets more content when we say that his philosophy is porous to the spirit infusing *Romulus, My Father*, his remarkable book about the man at the centre of the long passage I quoted earlier. In different ways his books *Good and Evil*, *A Common Humanity* and *The Philosopher's Dog* – the heart of his philosophical work – all resonate with that spirit. It is hard to think of other work in contemporary moral philosophy about which one could say something of that *kind* – that it is work whose philosophical content also expresses the distinctive vitality of a rich, complexly human way of being alive *in*, and *to*, the world. And that gives point to saying that Gaita's writings in moral philosophy give us not just different arguments for various views, but also something much rarer: a different philosophical voice, philosophy in a different register, philosophy which is indeed *in one way* 'closer to poetry.'

But poetry is a practice whose home cannot, I think, be in the academy, as painting and sculpture and dance and theatre cannot have their homes there – even if there may be university departments which in various ways engage with the practice of these things, most recently of course 'departments of creative writing.' To the extent that it is 'closer to poetry', then, the mode of philosophical practice that Gaita's work embodies is one that is in even greater tension with the commitments and pressures of the academy than is philosophy in its more traditional modes. Of course, tension is not necessarily something that we are better off without.

Chapter 12

MORAL THOUGHT AND ETHICAL INDIVIDUALITY

Craig Taylor

What does moral thought involve? On what we might call the standard view (at least in analytic philosophy) we can say that such thought should lead either: to true propositions like, for example, 'it is wrong not to help someone who is suffering if you can;' or to imperative statements such as 'you ought to help someone who is suffering if you can.' This view depends more broadly on a particular account of what thought is. As Raimond Gaita puts the point here,

> The assumption is that thought is truth-valued and stands in logical relations to other thoughts. The primary terms of critical appraisal, then, are 'true', 'false' and the names of the various modes of valid inference (Gaita 2004b, 265).

In various works, but most explicitly in his *Good and Evil: An Absolute Conception*, cited above, Gaita has argued that this view fails to capture the nature of moral thought and discounts many of the critical concepts that are involved in thinking well or badly on a given occasion about some moral matter. Gaita is, of course, not the only philosopher to challenge the standard view I have just alluded to. In different ways a number of philosophers, including notably Stanley Cavell, Cora Diamond, Iris Murdoch and more recently Alice Crary, have challenged this view of what moral thought is basically like. While it would take some time to explain what these thinkers in making this challenge have in common we might say briefly, and roughly, that they share a view according to which the development of certain human sensitivities or emotional capacities is essential to moral thought leading to moral understanding. In this essay however I will examine Gaita's own distinctive contribution to this debate.

A SENSE FOR HUMANITY

The first and most striking thing to note about Gaita conception of moral thought is his account of what is involved simply in having something to say on a moral matter:

> We say of some people that they 'have something to say' on moral or spiritual matters, but we do not mean that they have information to impart or a theory to propound. We mean that they speak with an individual voice, but not because they know something that few people know ... To have something to say is to be 'present' in what we say and to those whom we are speaking, and that means that what we say must, at the crux, be taken on trust. It must be taken on trust, not because contingently there are no means of checking it but because what is said is not extractable from the manner of its disclosure. In matters of value we often learn by our being moved, and our being moved is not merely the dramatic occasion of our introduction to a proposition which can be assessed according to critical categories, whose grammar excludes our being moved as being extraneous to the cognitive content (Gaita 2004b, 268).

The two points that I want to focus on from this passage are, firstly the importance of being 'present' in what we say, and secondly, and in connection to the first point, the idea that the meaning of what we say may not be 'extractable from the manner of its disclosure.' By focussing on these two ideas I hope to explain by the end of the chapter something of what it means, as Gaita says, to 'speak with an individual voice.' To start with the second point, the idea that the content of some moral thought which we are imparting to another cannot be characterised independently of the how that thought is expressed by us to another would be rejected outright by many philosophers. For the point here is not, as a teacher in any field knows, that the manner of delivery of some point can make it difficult for someone to see the point. Rather, it is that we cannot recognise what it is that another is trying to convey to us independently of being moved in specific ways by what they say, and that to be moved in the appropriate ways here itself depends upon the way in which that person is expressing themselves. This brings us to the first point; that we need to be present in what we say. For the power to move another in the requisite ways here depends, I think Gaita would say, on being present in what we say to them. So what is it to be present in what we say to another? I cannot hope to do complete justice to that idea here, in many ways much of Gatia's *Good and Evil* is an answer to

CHAPTER 12

that question. Here I can only begin to characterise this important idea and its relation to Gaita's conception of moral thought.

One might begin to understand what Gaita means by being present in one's speech by considering a kind of speech that is altogether lacking in such presence. I suggested above that the power to move someone through one's speech depends on the way in which a person expresses themselves. But the power involved here is not the power of mere rhetorical skill. Indeed Gaita develops his account of what is involved in being present in one's speech precisely by contrasting this kind of speech with that of the orator. Thus Gaita observes that Socrates in Plato's *Gorgias* 'criticises the orators for pandering to the souls of their audience' (Gaita 2004b, 273). What is needed if someone is to really learn anything morally from what we say, as Socrates suggests and Gaita notes, is that that we are able to converse with them. But, as Gaita goes on to say, the orator, and he has in mind here Gorgias's student Polus, 'speaks to the crowd and thus to no one in particular' (Gaita 2004b, 273). To speak to someone, to someone in particular, and thus to converse with them, then requires Gaita says that one 'be a proper respondent to another's call to seriousness' (Gaita 2004b, 273). Polus is not a proper respondent here because he does not take his potential partner in conversation seriously in the sense that there is nothing that such a partner might say to *him* that might move him to new understanding. Thus to be present in what we say is not to *project* oneself, to use for example the force of one's personality to bring others around to one's view. Rather, it is in an important sense to *offer* oneself to one's partner in conversation. Thus being present in what one says is not merely to mean what one says or even be prepared to stand by it, it is also to be prepared to revise it; to be prepared be moved and changed by what one's partner in conversation may have to convey to us.

One can say then that being present in what one says makes certain ultimately emotional demands on us. Thus Gaita's point is in part to contrast moral thought and understanding as he envisages it with what might be said by or conveyed to a mere rational agent. A particular example Gaita gives here involves contrasting the way in which sentimentality may affect the judgement of a biologist about some aspect of his field as opposed to someone expressing an explicitly moral thought. According to Gaita, if for example we detect sentimentality in the claims of the biologist about animals, then that is relevant only to the extent that it leads such a biologist to make false claims about animals. But in the case of some moral thought or conviction,

Gaita's example is of a person's decision to light a candle each year for a dead dog, 'sentimentality is not ... the cause of what primarily is wrong with such a thought [as was the case with the biologist]: it *is* what is primarily what is wrong with it' (Gaita 2004b, 269). Gaita's point here is that the concept of sentimentality marks out a *mode* of a thoughts failure as opposed to the *cause* of its failure. Concepts like sentimentality, along with cliché, jadedness and many others are part of that extended critical vocabulary through which Gaita suggests we characterise what it is to think badly, for thought to go wrong, in moral matters. However one might now ask: what exactly is wrong with a person's thought here if it is not that it leads them to assert something that is contrary to the facts, something false? What do we mean when we say that a person's thought fails by being sentimental if that is not that it leads them (causes them) to claim something that is false? Gaita suggestion is that we understand what it means for a person's thought to fail through sentimentality by contrasting it with thought that is not sentimental; it is through such thought that we gain a sense of why sentimentality is the kind of failure of moral thought and understanding that it is. As Gaita puts the point, 'Sentimentality needs to be shown up by example' (Gaita 2004b, 270).

But of course sentimentality is just one of the modes through which our moral thought may fail. More broadly, a central theme of Gaita's philosophical work is to draw out the variety of ways in which philosophy that adheres to something like the standard view I have sketched fails to capture much of what human life is like and what is morally significant in it. Particular, and recurring, concerns of Gaita here have been that philosophy that adheres to something like the standard view of moral thought cannot make adequate sense of the nature and significance of love in human life, or the individual preciousness of each human being, or connected with these things how we should understand the demands of justice. To give an extreme illustration of the kind of failure of moral thought that Gaita is concerned with, consider the following passage from philosopher Richard Brandt:

> If one wants to fall out of love ... one can take steps to associate the image of the beloved with thoughts of displeasing attributes or events involving her. This reflection will have the desired effect, and it is rational criticism if the beliefs are true/justified (Brandt 1996, 55).

This piece of advice from Brandt is offered to a person pained by 'imagining ... a tender moment' (Brandt 1996, 55) with someone whose love they have

CHAPTER 12

lost. Brandt, I suggest, radically mis-describes and so underestimates the place of love in human life and what he calls 'rational criticism' is really far from it. But Brandt's reflections here follow naturally from his view that love is really just one other of so many desires a person may have. What Brandt has no sense of, but what Gaita wants to defend, is the idea that love can be a mode of access to reality, to the reality here of the beloved. And if we dismiss that admittedly difficult idea we can perhaps understand Brandt's remark; the reality that concerns us now is simply the unfortunate fact of a desire that we cannot satisfy and some fortunate countervailing fact about, say, what our beloved's breath smells like first thing in the morning.

I concede the above example is extreme and that such things as love, human preciousness and justice are difficult for any of us, philosophers included, to make sense of. Further, and to be fair, many of the thinkers who defend what I have called the standard view are: firstly, serious and sincere in their efforts to try to make sense of human preciousness, justice or even love; and secondly, alert to the ways in which sentimentality, cliché, jadedness, cynicism and many other broadly emotional shortcomings can lead a person in their moral thought and judgement into error. In order to better see Gaita's general point against the standard view it is important to consider again what it is to fail to be present in what one says, for it is precisely in the kind of failure of responsiveness to others that this involves that the distinction between thinking well and badly that Gaita is highlighting, and which goes beyond the standard view, becomes apparent.

I have noted Gaita's suggestion that to be present in what one says to another is 'to be a proper respondent to another's call to seriousness.' But how should we understand this call to seriousness; what is it to be serious here? Obviously many of the thinkers that Gaita is explicitly critically of, and here I have in mind in particular many contemporary Kantians and utilitarians, are in an obvious sense very serious, and particularly *about morality*. Thus a utilitarian out of concern for the suffering of others may make enormous financial sacrifices to help those suffering and in need, or he may campaign tirelessly for those millions of people living lives that are more horrible, more destitute, than we can imagine. What more could we require of a person here, what is it beyond this that is really required to be a proper respondent to another's call to seriousness? Consider here another example, one I hope that illustrates what it is to be called to seriousness in the way Gaita is suggesting by another.

Prince Myshkin

Think of Prince Myshkin, or 'prince' as he is called, in Fyodor Dostoyevsky's *The Idiot* (Dostoyevsky [1868] 2004). The prince we immediately recognise is a kind of innocent; suffering from epilepsy, which earns him the appellation 'idiot', he has spent much of his young life in relative isolation away from society and his homeland, Russia. On his return to St Petersburg it is clear that he is humble, compassionate, always assuming the best of others and immediately forgiving them their transgressions even as they exploit him for their own gain. For it is also clear that the society to which the prince has returned is deeply corrupt. On the face of it the prince is the very paradigm of moral seriousness while those rounds him are the opposite, vain, self-deceiving, selfish narcissists and scoundrels. All the same, by the end of the novel it becomes clear that what the prince counts as moral seriousness has had catastrophic consequences for those most dear to him, and so we may come to wonder whether the prince really understands what serious moral thought really requires of him.

On his return to Russia, the prince is loved by, and in different ways he loves, two women. First, and after only seeing her photograph, he loves Nastasya Filippovna, a great beauty who as a child had been groomed by her guardian Totsky to be his young concubine. But the prince is not entranced by Nastasya's beauty so much as by the suffering he detects in her face, suffering caused by the violation of her innocence by Totsky. So the prince loves her out of compassion for what she has endured. Determined to save Nastasya from a disastrous marriage to the passionate but also violent Rogozhin the prince offers to marry her. But Nastasya, though she loves the prince, runs away from him unwilling to let him sacrifice himself for her sake. Later the prince falls in love with Aglaya Ivanovna, the youngest and still immature daughter of Lizaveta Prokofyevna a supposed distant relation to the prince. Not wanting the prince to ruin his life through his compassionate love for her, Nastasya eventually tries to promote his marriage instead to Aglaya. But Aglaya is young, inexperienced and consequently madly jealous of the older and more sophisticated Nastasya, and so drags the prince along with her to see Nastasya so as to reassure herself that the prince loves her more than her rival. Nastasya, though she knows she can compel the prince to marry her, is prepared to give him up to Aglaya. But Aglaya's hatred for her during their meeting is so intense that something in Nastasya snaps and she declares hysterically that she could command the prince to marry her if she wished. As both women stare at the prince in expectation he is silent until he can

CHAPTER 12

endure the sight of Nastasya's suffering no longer and he pleads to Aglaya 'How can you do this? I mean, she is ... so unhappy!' (Dostoyevsky [1868] 2004, 666) The prince seeing how much suffering these words have caused Aglaya eventually goes to her, but his momentary hesitation is too much for the young girl to bear and she rushes from the room humiliated.

At this stage at the end of the novel the narrator has given up any attempt to interpret events and this tasks falls to Yevgeny Pavlovich who is a friend of Aglaya's family and her one time suitor. In this affair as Yevgeny sees it the prince has mistaken, particularly in the case of Nastasya, 'an enormous, rushing mass of cerebral convictions ... for genuine, natural and spontaneous convictions' (Dostoyevsky [1868] 2004, 676). Turning specifically to the meeting between Nastasya and Aglaya Yevgeny goes on,

> 'But for the sake of compassion ... was it justifiable to disgrace another girl, one who was high-minded and pure, to degrade her in those [Nastasya's] arrogant, those hate-filled eyes? But to what lengths will compassion take you after that? ... And was it justifiable, since you loved the girl, to degrade her like that in front of her rival, to turn your back on her for the sake of the other, in front of the others eyes, and after you'd made her an honest proposal? ... And I mean, you did make her a proposal, you made it to her in front of her parents and her sisters!' ...
>
> 'Yes, yes, you are right, oh, I do feel that I'm to blame,' said the prince in inexpressible anguish.
>
> 'But is that sufficient?' exclaimed Yevgeny Pavlovich in indignation. 'Is it enough simply to exclaim: "Oh, I'm to blame!" You're to blame yet you persist! And where then was your heart, that "Christian" heart of yours? I mean, you saw her face at that moment: well, was she suffering less than the *other*, than *your* other, her rival in love? How could you see that and allow it? How?' (Dostoyevsky [1868] 2004, 677–78).

Yevgeny's challenge to the prince presents I think a striking example of what it is to be called to seriousness as Gaita suggests. Moreover it is a call the prince is unable to meet; the prince's failure to be a proper respondent to Yevgeny's call to seriousness shows us something of what thought in this context really demands of us, something of what it is to be present in what one has to say to another and how moral understanding may depend on this.

I have noted Gaita's suggestion that what may show a person's thought to be sentimental is thought that is not sentimental. What I want to suggest similarly in the above case is that the particular failure of thought we see in the prince is revealed through Yevgeny's challenge to him. This is not to say that Yevgeny merely points out that the prince's compassion is misplaced, and thus the *cause* of his moral failure here. Rather, Yevgeny's challenge and his thought about the prince's situation shows up the failure in the prince's thought here in much the same kind of way that non-sentimental thought show up thought that is sentimental. Thus what the prince thinks of as compassion is really a parody of compassion. Compassion makes no sense as the prince understands it; for you cannot love someone in the sense that the prince is loved by Aglaya and Nastasya, and that they hope to be loved by him, out of compassion. When the prince appeals to Yevgeny that Aglaya will understand his decision to marry her rival Yevgeny replies 'No, Prince, she won't understand! Aglaya Ivanovna loved like a woman, like a human being, and not like … an abstract spirit. Do you know what, my poor Prince? It's highly likely that you never loved either the one or the other!' (Dostoyevsky [1868] 2004, 680). When Yevgeny asks 'But to what lengths will compassion take you after that?' he is asking the prince to think about the way in which he *responds* to those around him and how that does not cause but rather constitutes his failure to see what life requires of him. Thus to meet Yevgeny's challenge, to understand what Yevgeny is trying to convey to him, it is not enough simply for the prince to say 'I'm to blame', beyond that he must be moved by Yevgeny's words to respond differently in his relations to those around him. But that is exactly what is lacking, as Yevgeny says 'You're to blame yet you persist!'

To further explain the point here, part of Yevgeny's, and our, exasperation with the prince is the fact that Yevgeny's words, as we might say, simply wash over him. This is moreover by no means uncharacteristic of the prince in his relations to others. In this connection a striking feature of the prince in his relations to others is his failure to take offence or even defend himself. While at first we may think this is a sign of almost saintly goodness in the end it appears contemptible, since it amounts at many points to a failure to take what others say seriously in the sense that I, following Gaita, have been concerned with. For insofar as recognising what someone has to say to you involves being moved in certain ways by what they have to say, the fact that the prince is unmoved by those around him indicates that he cannot see that they have anything to say to him. In his conversation with Yevgeny all he can see is that things have turned out badly and that he is to blame (whatever that means); he has no conception of what Yevgeny is trying to convey to him about what this situation demanded of him.

CHAPTER 12

In the end the prince's universal equanimity, if I can put it that way, far from being laudable is shocking. A striking example here occurs earlier in the novel when the prince informs Aglaya that the consumptive boy Ippolit has tried to kill himself. Ippolit has read a written 'confession' to the prince and a group of his friends and associates before trying unsuccessfully to shoot himself, a confession that he wants delivered to Aglaya who he is infatuated with. As the prince relates it, Ippolit 'probably wanted us all to surround him and tell him that we love and respect him very much, and wanted us to implore him to remain alive' (Dostoyevsky [1868] 2004, 497). When Aglaya says that she understands what Ippolit had in mind, that when she was younger she had thought of poisoning herself, writing a letter about it, and imagining her parents weeping over her coffin, the prince smiles then laughs. To which Aglaya replies,

> I really don't feel like joking with you ... I will see Ippolit; please let him know. But as for you, I think you behave very badly, because it's very ill-mannered to examine and judge a man's soul in the way that you judge Ippolit. You have no tenderness: only truth, and so you're not fair (Dostoyevsky [1868] 2004, 497–98).

For all his supposed moral seriousness, and despite the fact that what he says about the boy is perfectly true, there is something quite chilling in the matter of fact way the prince talks about Ippolit. Aglaya is right; the prince is not being fair. But in what sense is he not being fair? If one thinks that moral thought is ultimately about reaching true propositions or imperative statements then it is hard to see how we can make sense of that. What is missing in the prince here can only be characterised by appealing to the kind of responsiveness to others that he so clearly lacks, a kind of responsiveness that is internal to understanding what others have to say to him. What Aglaya has to say, though many philosophers would baulk at this, is exactly right. The prince has only truth but no tenderness and he is unfair precisely for that reason. For it is only through tenderness and related capacities of response to others that we can most fully recognise what they may demand of us and what it is to be fair to them.

Conclusion

I have tried to explain something of what it is, and why it should be important, that a person be, as Gaita suggests, present in what they say to another. What I hope the example of Prince Myshkin also helps to capture is what it means, as Gaita also says in the passage I quoted earlier, 'to speak with an individual voice.' To be present in what one says and thus to converse with another is, I think Gaita would say, for one's individuality to be manifest in what one says. If it is difficult to get a sense of why that should be important, it is a help to think again of the prince, and particularly Yevgeny's claim that he mistakes 'an enormous, rushing mass of cerebral convictions … for genuine, natural and spontaneous convictions.' Yevgeny's point here is in part I think that the prince's 'mass of cerebral convictions' lack a kind of essential connection with the prince's life. But then what exactly does it mean to say, as this implies, that the content of real conviction may depend in an essential way on the individual life of the person who holds it? Surely the conviction, its content, is one thing, the individual life of the person who holds it another. But crucially that is exactly what Gaita wants to question, thus he suggests that ethical understanding is often seeing something through what someone has made of it in their particular, individual, life. But we need to be clear about what that means, as Gaita says,

> seeing 'what he made of it' is not seeing to what practical purpose he put it in his life. It is seeing what he made of himself through it, or rather the two – his making something of himself and his making something of it – are interdependent. The ethical, and the individuality of which I am speaking, mutually determine one another (Gaita 2004b, 281).

Gaita's point here is that if in my relations with another I come to see something that I have not seen before it will be because of the way in which what I see is determined by, and itself has determined, the individual life, the individuality, of that other. When Yevgeny asks the prince at the end of the long passage I have quoted how *he* could allow Aglaya's humiliation the import of that is not – as the prince supposes in immediately admitting blame – 'you ought not to have done what you have done.' Yevgeny's question is more directly and honestly to ask the prince *to account for himself.* How he accounts for himself, including both what he makes of his decisions and actions and what they may then reveal about the moral contours of human life and the ethical possibilities that that may indicate, will determine our own thought and judgement about this situation.

Of course the idea that our ethical thought about some situation might depend on what is revealed through what an individual human being has made of their life and that situation flies in the face of the standard view of moral thought according to which the morally salient features of any situation are there be discovered by anyone so long as they are capable of

CHAPTER 12

disinterested rational inquiry. Nevertheless against the appeal – to many – of such a view one needs to consider how it is the ethical possibilities, as I just put it, come into view in our attempts to understand the moral contours of human life. What Gaita invites us to consider is that they may come into view essentially through the lives of particular individual human beings. As Gaita puts the point, '[u]nderstanding in ethical matters is ... the expression of a life' (Gaita 2004b, 281).

Chapter 13

THE POWER OF NEGATIVE THINKING
Remorse and Blame

Miranda Fricker

There aren't many laughs in philosophy, and philosophical jokes are not usually funny, not even to philosophers. But just occasionally philosophy can share in a particular mechanism of humour that real jokes often trade in; and that is to make explicit something that is deeply true, and which the audience has somehow always known, but has never before brought to consciousness. When I first read the Preface to the second edition of *Good and Evil: An Absolute Conception* (which, as the title signals, is not a work of comedy) one of its passages made me laugh out loud so decidedly that the moment is forever imprinted on my mind.

So much so that since then I have rarely missed an opportunity to quote it to students, and I don't want to miss the opportunity to quote it again now, sharing the brilliance of Rai's critique of moral philosophy and its power to show one what one always knew, but (for my part at least) was never quite able to make explicit in thought. Deliciously to me, then, as now, he effectively pokes fun at the moral philosophical tradition that we philosophers in the English-speaking tradition are trained in: that of *moral theory* – the enterprise of attempting to codify moral thinking so that morality may be revealed as organised according to some set of fundamental principles, or (better still!) just one supreme principle, with moral value conceived variously as conducive to human flourishing, or respect for rational agency, or the maximization of aggregate happiness. Here, then, is the passage from *Good and Evil* that cheers me up no end every time I read it. Just now I described Rai as 'poking fun' of the moral theoretical tradition, but really it is more accurate to say that, with gentle relish, he helplessly observes the self-inflicted absurdity of that tradition:

CHAPTER 13

> When we ask what makes a principle a moral principle ... an obligation a moral obligation — then I think we should seek at least some part of the answer in the kind of elaboration we give when we express most seriously our sense of what it means to wrong someone. Nowhere is that sense more sober than in lucid remorse. 'My God what have I done?'... But now, if one puts in the mouth of the remorseful person many of the philosophical accounts ... we get a parody.
>
> ... 'My God what have I done? I have ruined my best chances of flourishing.' 'My God what have I done? I have violated rational nature in another.' 'My God what have I done? I have diminished the stock of happiness' (Gaita 2004b, xxi).

When – to take a canonical example – the tragically ill-fated Oedipus discovered just what *he* had done, so that he came to know the terrible significance of his actions, what was on his tormented mind was nothing remotely resembling any of these things. What racked his conscience was that he had married his mother and killed his father; and it was these immediately morally contentful thoughts that led him to dash out his own eyes for shame. This kind of contentful reaction to wrongdoing tends to be lost on much of moral theory, for it tends to lose this imminent perspective on its own subject matter as soon as it sets to work on it. We might say that moral theory gives us only maps of the land – contours, relations, and boundaries, when what we'd hoped for among other things from moral philosophy was a contentful appreciation of the features of the landscape of a kind that might actually help us see it better. Don't get me wrong: we need maps, but they assist only one dimension of understanding. The quotation from *Good and Evil* exposes the moral theorist's sleight of hand, and it brings to consciousness the absurdity of a moral philosophical tradition that is so exclusively a product of the cartographer's mindset. This dominant paradigm for moral philosophy does not represent all that moral philosophy can, or should, be.

There are many historical reasons for the disappointing narrowness of moral philosophy taken as a whole, but one that specially interests me, and which I aim to focus on here, is the very conception of morality that philosophy tends to start with. It is a conception which assumes that the domain of moral responsibility or accountability is co-extensive with the domain of moral praise and blame. Rai has called this a 'moralistic conception of morality' (Gaita 1998, xvii) and he's surely right. There are many kinds of moralism, but let me first present the kind that Rai is concerned with, and which he calls 'judgementalism.' We can introduce the idea by recalling his discussion of the terrible case of Mary Bell, who at the age of 11 killed two other children, and whose story is told by Gitta Sereny in her book *Cries Unheard*. Rai observes that having read Sereny's account of the horrors of Mary's childhood, few would fail to be diverted from the default stance of readiness to blame the wrong-doer, or evil-doer as one might well put it. He observes that most would surely withhold blame once they knew the background. He says:

> The judgment they would withhold is judgement of the sort implied by what we now call judgementalism – judgement that would *blame* her (bearing in mind all the connotations of that word), that would encourage one to point a finger at her and to turn one's back on her. But a preparedness to see (and in that sense to judge) a situation in a severe moral light while at the same time refusing to blame strikes some people as incoherent. That, I think, is the effect of a moralistic conception of morality (Gaita 1998, xvii).

Blame is indeed not a *necessary* feature of severe moral judgement. A conception of morality – or of moral responsibility – which cannot comprehend serious negative moral judgement of someone's deeds without the application of blame is indeed a moralistic conception. For there is a kind of holding responsible – holding someone *answerable*, as we so suggestively say – which, according to Rai, does not require blame at all. He continues:

> Nearly everyone is vulnerable to the tendency to believe that severe moral appreciation must run together with blame. But there are voices in our culture that speak of different possibilities. Sophocles' *Oedipus the King* shows how moral severity may take the form of pity. The chorus does not blame Oedipus for the evil he did on account of ignorance for which he was not culpable. It pities the evil-doer he became and that informs the quality of the pity it feels at the terrible spectacle of a man who has lost a kingdom, whose wife/mother has hanged herself, who has blinded himself and is exiled. Its severe pity holds him fast in serious moral response – it holds him *responsible to* the evil-doer he has become – insisting that he face the full meaning of it (Gaita 1998, xvii; Gaita 2011a, 86–87).

This continues the thought that there can be contexts of wrongdoing – such as that of Oedipus – which reveal that the attitude of blame is more limited than the attitude of holding responsible, and even judging

CHAPTER 13

severely. In this, Rai is in broad agreement with another humanistically minded moral philosopher whom he discusses in this connection, namely Bernard Williams, who wrote about Oedipus in a similar vein, and who emphasised the place of luck in influencing the question of whether blame is appropriate. He talked of 'agent-regret' to describe cases in which luck intervenes to determine the consequences of a person's actions in a way that makes blame inappropriate. In Williams's example, a lorry driver is driving responsibly, but a child runs into the road and is killed. Even though the child is killed through no fault of the driver's, Williams affirms that the driver may entirely coherently and rationally suffer terrible feelings of guilt and moral regret, in a way that may scar his life ethically, and which may prompt him to try to make amends or in some other way honour his responsibility for what he, through no fault of his own, has done. (That the pained regret he feels is indeed *moral* regret is chiefly substantiated in the fact that such attempts to make amends are in order.) This idea of agent-regret goes against the grain of much moral theory, whose blame oriented conception of responsibility means it lacks resources to construe the driver's moral suffering as a genuinely moral response, and tends instead to sympathetically pathologise it as an understandable emotional reaction. Agent-regret signals the sometimes profound ethical significance in our lives of those things we cause through our actions, even when it is no fault of our own that we have caused them. One can feel moral regret, guilt and shame in respect of such actions. Remorse too on Rai's conception (though not Williams's). Yet *blame* would be out of order. Blame essentially involves *finding fault* with someone for an action or omission, and in a case where bad moral luck has intervened in this way, there is precisely no fault.

This kind of bad moral luck (whether that of Oedipus, or of the lorry driver) generates the possibility of blameless wrongdoing, and so reveals that we can be responsible for actions even when blame is out of order. Failure to see this is to entertain what Rai rightly calls 'a moralistic conception of morality.' But now let me address what I find philosophically perplexing in the quotation in which he makes the point. His characterization of blame there, as elsewhere in his writing, is such that to blame someone is characteristically 'to point a finger at her and to turn one's back on her.' I don't want to over-invest his remarks with philosophical commitment, so let me say hypothetically that if there is an implication here that blame *essentially* or even typically involves these things, then I want to make a case for a different view – a more internally differentiated view of blame. I do agree that blaming someone essentially involves 'accusing' them of some wrongdoing, and in that sense requires a certain 'pointing of the finger', but I would not agree that it must involve pointing the finger long enough to wag it judgementally, let alone that finding fault with them for their wrongdoing entailed shunning or turning one's back. All these are marks of a judgemental style of blame indeed, but I think it crucial that we see how *distinct* a style of blame that is. The stance of finger wagging or shunning is an unpleasant stance at the best of times, as is turning one's back on another person, bearing a grudge, or closing down relations by refusing to talk to them. These things are part of severing relations with another, which is a way of giving up on any continued positive relationship with them. Blame can sometimes take this form, but it need not.

Let's think about *Romulus, My Father* in this connection. As depicted, Romulus didn't go in for blame of the finger wagging type (or at least, if he had done so, it would have been thoroughly out of character). Rather, it is the voice of severe pity (reminiscent of the Chorus in *Oedipus Rex*) that Rai depicts his father as characteristically adopting in the face of others' wrongdoing, even on occasions when blame would *not* have been inappropriate, in that luck had not intervened in any exculpatory way. Rai describes his father's moral outlook in the following terms:

> Even his most severe judgments were made in many tones. If he called you an incorrigible liar he might do it angrily, scathingly, sorrowfully or, strange as it might sound, matter-of-factly, but never in a tone that suggested he would turn his back on you. You were always welcome at his table, to eat and more importantly to talk; always to talk (Gaita 1998, 179).

I understand this kind of moral seriousness as centrally involving an ongoingly *communicative* stance towards the wrongdoer, a continuing to hold them in dialogue – for what else besides dialogue could possibly sustain the idea of holding them *answerable* to one's charges? Let one make the charge, and so invite them to make their answer. But (here's my point) I think to do this *is* to blame. It is to find fault with someone for what they've done or failed to do; and this, especially when it is second-personally expressed, entails an accusation, a certain pointing of the finger. However it is a distinctively *communicative* style of blame, and one which – precisely in virtue of that commitment to ongoing open two-way communication with a wrongdoer who remains 'welcome at one's table' – is surely not judgemental, not moralistic.

Now I admit that in *After Romulus* Rai says something which perhaps reveals that while he has roughly the same conception of blame as I do, anchored in an attitude of 'finding fault', he regards even that as extrinsic to the business of holding someone responsible for what they've done. He says this:

> I learnt [from my father] that we can free ourselves from the moralistic conception of responsibility that ties being morally responsible to being praiseworthy or blameworthy if we see that to hold someone responsible means, essentially, to require of them a lucid response to the moral significance of what they did. It means that they and we must not evade that significance, *but it does not, necessarily, mean that we find fault with them, or accuse them or judge them to be blameworthy* (Gaita 2011a, 87–88, emphasis added).

So now, *pace* cases of moral luck, I must register a difference of view, or at least a difference in how best to put things: first, blaming someone needn't take the form of finger wagging, shunning, or excommunication; and relatedly, *holding someone in lucid response to the wrong they have done* is, in my view, *not* possible without at least some minimal finding fault with them in the manner of blame. When Romulus says to someone that they are an 'incorrigible liar' (to continue with Rai's example) he surely finds fault, though in the non-moralistic spirit of one who states a fact, inviting the other to respond, to answer for himself in the light of this charge. What could this be other than to find fault, and so to blame? I see no reason to deny this, and good reason to assert it, for how else could one hold another to a lucid response to their deeds but by holding them to the fact that they have been, precisely, at fault for acting that way? What's crucial, and what we learn from Rai's account of his father, is that finding fault in this way can be done in a non-moralistic tone – that is, without finger wagging or threat of excommunication, or grudge bearing, or adopting an air of moral high ground. The emphasis in this style of blame can be on how to acknowledge the wrong and move on, or make good; and the medium is conversation. This style of blame is distinctly communicative – we might call it *Communicative Blame*.

What I've argued, then, is that the stance of moral severity towards another, even as they remain welcome at one's table to talk, should not be understood as a refusal of blame *per se*, but rather *a refusal of one kind of blame in particular* – namely, the non-communicative, finger-wagging kind of blame. That style of blame is indeed a quite generally non-compulsory moral response to wrongdoing, and even most of the time a rather unpleasant kind, which we might well do without. It is too close to the mean-spirited style of moral response that Nietzsche describes as *ressentiment* – an inward-looking resentfulness prone to stagnation and grudge bearing, or which generates at best a mean-spirited retributive aspiration. This we could surely do without. But I want to argue that Communicative Blame – where one goes in for a primarily second-personal expression of the fact that one finds fault with the other person for something they've done or failed to do – is in fact a mainspring of moral consciousness. Further, I want to argue that it is the necessary partner to remorse, which Rai so convincingly argues should be at the heart of moral philosophy, determining the sphere of wrongdoing. My overall claim, then, shall be that if remorse should be at the heart of moral philosophy – and it should – then so should Communicative Blame.

Styles of blame

Let me explore the mechanism of what I'm calling Communicative Blame. I am reminded of a recent piece by Susan Wolf, which is a response to Tim Scanlon's account of blame (Scanlon 2008), in which she contrasts what she calls 'blame Italian style' with his emotionally retentive characterisation of blame as a *rupture in a relationship* which is made by someone withdrawing friendly, co-operative, or other solicitous relations in response to wrongdoing (Wolf 2011). Blame Italian style is, by contrast, a positive style of blame, and one that typically involves the second-personal expression of some anger, and which Wolf depicts as an essential part of her rewarding, happy family life. As she says: 'The angry emotions do not seem to me to be especially associated with a disposition to withdraw from the object of the emotion. Rather than get some distance between you and the person you're angry with, you might as likely want to "get in his face"' (Wolf 2011, 338). Angry blame is only one kind of Communicative Blame, inasmuch as communicating resentment needn't be angry as such. But it is important to bear in mind the positive, honest, communicative spirit of angry blame as an essential part of one kind of shared moral life in which people – in this case family members – hold each other responsible and make demands of each other as part of how they sustain their ongoing loving relationships. This possibility is particularly worth remembering when we are trying to distinguish moralistic from non-moralistic styles of blame. Angry blame has none of the marks of moralism, such as an attitude of personal rejection, a tendency towards ex-communication, or degeneration into *ressentiment*. It can just be a noisier way of keeping ourselves in each other's midst, as Rai puts it, always 'welcome at the table', but where the dialogue over dinner may sometimes have quite a bit of attitudinal heat.

CHAPTER 13

I believe the context of loving family relations in Wolf's scenario for angry blame is profoundly suggestive for how we locate different styles of blame within our understanding of moral life and of goodness. Love is that most fundamental form of human attachment which, quite apart from anything else, is the psychological precondition of the universalized impartial form of itself which Rai describes as the capacity for Goodness with a capital G – the kind of goodness exhibited by the nun in the psychiatric hospital, by whom anyone, no matter how afflicted, is cared for without condescension. This point about love as a precursor to moral consciousness is made in more than one place by Rai, and by other philosophers too. In an essay called 'Love as Moral Emotion', for instance, David Velleman says that the kind of sympathetic understanding we naturally have in relation to those we love tends also to awaken us to the reality of the suffering of others:

> My own experience is that, although I may be insensitive to suffering until I see it in people I love, I cannot then remain insensitive to it in their fellow sufferers. The sympathy that I feel for my wife's difficulties at work, or my children's difficulties at school, naturally extends to their coworkers and classmates (Velleman 2006, 108).

That love should be a morally enabling and moral educative emotion in this way is a beautiful thing, and I think we need to notice that Communicative Blame, even of the angry kind, surely occupies a central place in explaining exactly how love enables our moral sense. Susan Wolf's anger at her daughter's raiding her closet yet again to borrow clothes without permission, and her daughter's experience of being on the receiving end of that angry blame exemplifies an essential aspect of the enabling process. The daughter's love for her mother near-guarantees that her mother's blame has a certain negative impact on her. Not *merely* an emotional impact in some psychologically reductive sense, for sure, but rather an emotional impact of a cognitively loaded kind which awakens her to the reality of the way she has acted against her mother. The daughter's love, then, guarantees that she will be moved in some measure by her mother's blame, and as we shall see, the blamed party's being moved is essential to the mechanism of Communicative Blame as I understand it.

I am suggesting that Wolf's idea of angry blame, understood as a central form of Communicative Blame, is a proper part of how personal loving attachments educate the sentiments so that our moral consciousness grows outwards, ultimately to be capable of assuming an impartial form. But one might detect a tension here between angry blame and Goodness with a capital G so long as that is conceived in terms of 'saintly love.' Rai never says that blame is anathema to 'saintly love', however it must be said that our normal sense of the saintly ideal certainly doesn't involve 'getting in the face' of the wrongdoer. It involves things like meekness, selflessness, and turning the other cheek. This reveals, I think, that the concept of the *saintly* risks significantly misleading us about what we need to say about Goodness with a capital G (even while it may remain central to what we need to say about our post-Christian cultural forms of such Goodness.) It seems to me that the concept of the saintly is distinctly narrower than the concept of Goodness with a capital G, in that the saintly is only one of its possible cultural formations. The historical-cultural specificity of our post-Christian idea of 'saintly love' – and so its contingency as a form of Goodness – reveals itself most clearly when it comes to the question of blame. I do not believe there is any incompatibility between Goodness with a capital G and sometimes 'getting in the face' of a wrongdoer; but I do sense a certain comedic potential in the idea of a saintly nun 'getting in the face' of a wrongdoer. Indeed one recognises this scenario as a familiar trope of comedy in movies from *The Sound of Music* to *Sister Act II*. There is no equivalent joke automatically available in relation to other less selfless ideals of what it is to be Good with a capital G. On the contrary, one can readily imagine situations in which that is exactly what one would hope such a person would do – when sticking up for someone who is being bullied, for instance, perhaps sticking up for herself in the face of a bully.

Let me summarise the conception of Communicative Blame I am proposing, and of which I take Wolf's angry blame to be a central case (though anger is not necessarily involved in Communicative Blame *per se*). The point of Communicative Blame (we might say its illocutionary point) is to make the wrongdoer aware of the wrong she has done you, with a view to her coming to understand her own motives and actions more fully and in a moral light. This kind of blame is a transformative mechanism in human relations, which enables us to communicate harm done, in a way that brings awareness to the wrongdoer and might prompt them to make amends. It is forward-looking, and psycho-socially dynamic. But this is still somewhat under-described. We must ask what exactly *is* it that the blamed party is supposed to come to recognise? If she is to be successfully transformed in any measure, the answer must be that blame brings her to recognise *the harm that she has done and what it means that she has done it*. We can capture both thoughts by saying that she needs to be brought to confront the *moral significance* of what she has done, and this can only be a matter of her feeling *remorse*. When someone goes in for Communicative Blame, the illocutionary point of their speech act is precisely to prompt the blamed party into remorse – into what Rai describes as a 'shocked and bewildered realisation of what it means to wrong them' (Gaita 1999, 34). And so my proposal is that we conceive of remorse and blame as correlative moral responses, essential partners in the ongoing development of our moral consciousness.

Indeed we might express the essential partnership of these two moral emotions, blame and remorse, still more tightly. We might say that the cognitive content of each is *the wrong done*, but that in the two cases it is felt – suffered – from the different points of view of subject and object. Let me adapt Rai's forms of expression to help me make the point: while remorse is the pained acknowledgement of *the harm one has done*, communicative blame is the pained acknowledgement of *the harm that has been done to one*. If remorse may be captured in the bewildered question (to which there is no answer) 'How could I have hurt you?', blame is captured in the similarly bewildered question 'How could you hurt me?' These are shocked responses to the moral reality of a wrong done, as perceived from one or the other point of view of subject and object. Remorse and blame are two sides of the same coin.

Forms of moralism as forms of inappropriate blame

This conception of communicative blame and remorse as partner moral responses allows us to see more clearly what makes for a moralistic style of blame. If to blame is to find fault, by way of a speech act whose illocutionary point is that one's interlocutor is brought to remorseful awareness of the moral significance of the harm that they have done, and with the perlocutionary aim of changing their behaviour, then blame will look at best redundant if there is no sense in finding fault, or no chance of either getting someone to recognise the harm they have done, or getting them to change their attitudes. Let's recall for a moment the cases of Oedipus and the lorry driver, each of which illustrated a different kind of moral bad luck. We can see, quite generally, that where luck intervenes so that a harm done is not the fault of the agent, then it would obviously be inappropriate to find fault by blaming them – for *ex hypothesi* there is no relevant fault to be found.

Let me look once again to *Romulus, My Father*. Rai writes:

> My father never blamed [Mitru] for the affair with my mother. He blamed her (in the sense that he saw her as its primary cause) and,

because he saw it as an expression of her promiscuous nature, he pitied Mitru, believing he was caught in something he could not control, which would cause him considerable pain and perhaps consume him (Gaita 1998, 84).

We are told that Romulus didn't blame Mitru, but the passage implies too that he didn't blame Christine in anything but the minimal sense of her being the primary cause of the affair. She is represented as having a promiscuous nature, and our knowledge of her mental illness and its connection with promiscuity also adds to our sense of Christine as someone in relation to whom there was simply no chance of changing her attitudes or behaviour. Insofar as her promiscuity was in her nature, or in other features of her make-up such that she could not be brought to a proper understanding of the harm she had done, and/or which stemmed from character traits that wouldn't shift, there could be little point in blame. And so, one speculates, perhaps Romulus instinctively knew that blame had no pointful role to play. I would like to think that the brief outline I've offered of Communicative Blame helps us understand a moral outlook, where one refuses blame in this way, wherever the communicative aim could not be achieved.

Let's take stock. I have argued that there are various styles of blame, and that Communicative Blame is necessary to the stance of holding someone responsible for their actions – necessary, that is (in Rai's terms), to holding them in lucid moral response to what they've done. And I've argued that the illocutionary point of Communicative Blame is to inspire remorse in the blamed party, in which case it's not just remorse that should be at the heart of moral philosophy, but also its prior partner response, Communicative Blame. All this has generated the possibility of making sense of the non-blaming moral outlook of Romulus in relation to the point of Communicative Blame, and its pointlessness in certain cases. But while I think this is the right backdrop against which to understand Romulus's refusal of blame, it is not enough to say that he withheld blame whenever he recognised its pointlessness – though he surely did that (Rai reports that he saw Christine's behaviour as a 'helpless case'). Rather, the moral outlook that Romulus is described as living by may be significantly further away from our normal blame responses than I have so far allowed, and the earlier remarks about how bad moral luck renders blame out of order might help us make sense of this possibility. For there is a certain latitude of choice in quite where we draw the line of moral luck. A flexibility, that is, in which actions we regard as sufficiently subject to luck, or subject to it

CHAPTER 13

in the right way, to render our actions non-blameworthy. Our lorry driver and Oedipus were both subject to a tragic kind of bad moral luck. But there is a perspective on human beings, their drives, compulsions, wills, and actions which effectively represents us permanently under the aspect of moral luck. Insofar as Romulus really did sometimes withhold even Communicative Blame when others would have gone ahead, I wonder if the *generalised* aspect of moral luck is one way to understand his outlook? Rai describes his father's conception of human beings in a way that is very suggestive in this regard, as all 'fellow mortals, victims of fate and destined for suffering' (Gaita 1998, 122), and this is a levelling conception, where we are all represented as 'helpless cases', tossed around on the seas of fate so that there is never more than a very limited point in regarding us as the authors of our actions in the sense requisite for blame. From this ultimately charitable perspective we are like actors, our lives largely a matter of being landed with this or that good or bad part, and where the cosmic contingency of it all puts the entire hubbub of human behaviours in a certain tragi-comic perspective. At the end of the day, a sense of pathos for who we are and what we make of it is most of what we are left with.

And so, ultimately, I want to leave things somewhat open-ended. I have tried to rehabilitate one style of blame by attending to its communicative and transformative possibilities. And I've urged that there might be room for it even in the non-moralistic, non-judgemental outlook of someone like Romulus. But I also want to leave room for another possibility, a possibility in how we might understand the non-blaming tendencies of Romulus, and indeed what any cultural form of Goodness with a capital G might involve: it is the possibility of a moral outlook which more often than most shifts the moral focus away from the busy interactive details of everyday human accountability, to reveal instead the broader contours of human beings considered as ultimately all 'helpless cases' more or less, all protagonists in a drama not altogether of our making. There is a transcendent charity in that, and a moral poetry too. We should leave room for it.

AFTERWORD
Anne Manne and Raimond Gaita in Conversation

What follows are three questions by my dear friend Anne Manne and my answers to them. Anne and I agreed that she would write her questions and that I would write my answers. I always felt her presence in my answers.

Anne sent ten questions. Because she is one of my best readers, her quesions are penetrating and challenging in ways that do not allow me to separate my work from my life. Foolishly I thought it would be easy to respond to them. Instead it proved very difficult. I wrote thirty-thousand words in my first attempt. When I tried again, I wrote another twenty-six thousand, without even looking at my first attempt. With apologies, I offer the reader around fourteen thousand.

My struggle to write something worthwhile and honest took me to the point where either the book would be held up, or I would fail to deliver. To prevent the latter at a time when Craig and Melinda were overwhelmed with work, I sought editorial help from Alison Arnold. She came to the rescue immediately. I am very grateful.

Now is the time to express my very deep gratitude to Craig, firstly for organising the conference at which versions of the essays in this collection were first presented and secondly for editing the book. In the modern university these are thankless tasks so we have more than the usual reasons to be thankful for those, who like Craig, selflessly give so much of themselves when they take them on. At the conference one of the contributors said to me, 'This is why I became an academic,' though (or was it because?) a significant number of the contributors are not academics.

Contributors have told me how grateful they are to have been edited by Melinda.

Raimond Gaita

Q.1

Anne Manne:
Rai, I would like to begin with your own words: 'The philosopher Plato said that those who love and seek wisdom are clinging in recollection to things they once saw.' I wonder if you could talk about those words in connection with your father and your memoir about him, *Romulus, My Father*; truly a book to wonder over.

Raimond Gaita:
I've referred many times to that passage from Plato's *Phaedrus*, usually when I have written of the wondrous goodness of works of saintly love towards people who suffer radical and often incurable affliction. Love gives the gift of humanity to people whose humanity has become invisible or barely visible even to themselves. Simone Weil says that it sees what is invisible. Not all love does that. The love I have written about and to which I have been bound in a kind of witness, reveals something so wondrous – so unnatural to reason, so radically *unreasonable* – that a sense of its reality becomes attenuated and sometimes even deserts those who have witnessed it. That is why they *cling* in recollection. But though Plato believes that philosophers (lovers of wisdom) are clinging in recollection to something wondrous, and though he called it 'the Good,' Chris Cordner has convinced me (in an essay in another collection) that the Good should not be conflated with the kind of Goodness revealed by saintly love. I was misled by Simone Weil.

Later in that passage in *Romulus, My Father* I say: 'On many occasions in my life I have had the need to say, and thankfully have been able to say: I know what a good workman is; I know what an honest man is; I know what friendship is; I know because I remember these things in the person of my father, in the person of his friend Hora, and in the example of their friendship.' These are not examples of wondrous goodness. Indeed they might seem prosaic by comparison with what I spoke about just a moment ago. For my father and Hora, however, honesty was a more pervasive and deeper virtue than a refusal ever to cheat or deceive and different from even the most scrupulous truthfulness. In the book, I borrowed a phrase from someone I identified only as an English philosopher. He was R. F. (Roy) Holland, who, to my great good fortune, supervised my PhD. Later we became friends. In a fine essay called 'Is Goodness a Mystery?' Holland criticised accounts of the virtues that focus on how difficult it is to conceive

AFTERWORD

of any form of social life that does not value them. In regard to truthfulness he said that alongside the kind of truthfulness necessary for any society, and even when 'in view of the advanced state of commerce, say, the standard might have to be very precise or very subtle ... there could co-exist for at least some people in the society, a concern with truth of an altogether different character, in which *not to falsify* became a spiritual demeanour. Where then could this spirit come from?'

That evidently goes beyond and is deeper than saying that truthfulness can be valued for its own sake rather than only for what it can deliver to individuals or a society. There are forms of the latter – even scrupulous forms of it that might exist in a strict academic professionalism, for example – that one would never dream of describing as a spiritual demeanour. But truthfulness as the 'spiritual demeanour not to falsify' entered the lives of my father and Hora like, to adapt Wallace Stevens, a thread through a needle; everything they did was stitched with its colour. That is why, when he was asked to sign a copy of *Romulus, My Father* at its launch, Hora wrote: 'Romulus Gaita was the most honest man I have known.' It was the highest praise he could have accorded his dearest friend. It marked their friendship through and through, which is why it has been an inspiration to me. But it also characterised my father's work. He was, I say in *Romulus, My Father*, 'so at ease with his materials and always so respectful of their nature that they seemed in friendship with him, as though consenting to his touch rather than subjugated by him.' From him I developed a respect for inanimate objects, especially for the mountains I climbed. I felt I had to climb with grace, fully lucid about the dangers, as an expression of respect for the mountains and of gratitude for what they gave to those who climbed them with love. I always found talk of 'conquering the mountain' distasteful and hubristic.

My father and Hora were unnervingly morally intense and could be severe, though they were not judgmental. They were fiercely disdainful of the opportunities we take to look down on others. Nothing mattered more to them than to live decently, and when I say nothing I mean nothing. I likened their sense of the importance of morality to Socrates' affirmation that it is better to suffer evil than to do it. When I was first appointed to a lectureship in the Philosophy Department at King's College London (which was then one of five philosophy departments in the federal University of London), most of mainstream British and American moral philosophers in the analytical tradition were suspicious of the intensity shown by people like my father and Hora (as they were of Socrates, Plato, Wittgenstein, preferring Aristotle and Hume). Some found it distasteful, believing it to be simplistic, moralistic, judgmental and puritanical. I knew they were wrong because my father and Hora were not like that.

Sophisticated urbanity has attractions beyond the pleasures of condescending to moral intensity. The charm, brilliance, subtlety and sophistication of Bernard Williams made them evident to British and, to some extent, American philosophers during much of my academic life. David Wiggins, who was subtle with a vengeance, was also influential at the time I wrote *Good and Evil: An Absolute Conception* (which along with much else I have written could have been subtitled *Against Urbanity*). He says of Hume: 'Hume's theory partakes copiously of the benevolence and good humour of its author, whom many of his readers might confidently choose ... for a cheerful and trustworthy companion in a shipwreck.' Cora Diamond, on the other hand, reports Dorothea Krook as complaining that, 'Hume's approach to morality is ... shallow, trivial, low, frivolous, unserious, unsolid, unreal, lacking any sense of the higher, lacking any genuine sense of evil. Hume's cheerfulness is the complacent comfortableness of the eighteenth-century clubman; reading Hume is like being asphyxiated in a sea of cotton wool.' I don't know that I would dare go so far, but I see her point and understand her frustration. She might have said much the same of Aristotle.

Cora Diamond quotes Krook in a fine essay called 'Moral Differences and Distances: Some Questions.' She says that differences such as those between Krook and admirers of Hume (she does not mention Wiggins) are differences of temperament. I wouldn't put it that way, but they are differences of sensibility and are, as she points out, more interesting than differences in moral judgments about this or that, which are the differences moral philosophers tend to focus on. I'm sure that the former are connected to psychological factors and to the demise of religion. In regard to the latter, adapting an Eastern European joke that Communism was the longest and most painful route between capitalism and capitalism, Bernard Williams said that Christianity was the longest and most painful route between atheism and atheism. The demise of religion, he suggested, explained why philosophers took so naturally to the ancient Greeks, though, really, it was to Aristotle rather than to Plato. Williams gave reflective philosophical attention, rare amongst moral philosophers, to Greek tragedy. It resulted in his best book, *Shame and Necessity*, which, interestingly, hardly mentions philosophers, and when it does is seldom friendly to them. There he argues that an account of ethical necessity (he called it practical necessity) as it appears so often in Greek tragedy, together with a psychoanalytical account of the importance of shame and the destructive nature of guilt, would reveal why something deeply inner could present an outer authority quite different from familial, social or political authority, or the disguised force of brute power.

I have always agreed with the anti-moralistic drift of Williams' work and also with his attack on what he called the 'thin characterless moral agent.' But I had already learnt from my father and Hora, although in a very different tone, to be suspicious of the moralistic distortions that philosophers build into their accounts of the very idea of morality. And I have taken guilt to be (most of the time) the condition we acknowledge in remorse when remorse is not corrupted. It often *is* corrupted, as Nietzsche reminds us with corrosive brilliance, but when it is not it represents one of the most sober moments of the moral life – that moment when a wrongdoer understands fully, perhaps even for the first time, what it means to have wronged someone. To be sure, remorse will be different in different ethical conceptions or traditions, but in the tradition to which Williams is hostile, it is, at its truest, a realisation through wronging someone of how precious that person is and all other human beings are. If we scoff at remorse, mindful only of its pathologies, or complacently declare it to have no constructive purpose, we will lose touch with the most sublime aspect of a tradition to which we are now ambivalent, if not hostile, heirs. What we will lose used to be expressed in the affirmation that every human being is sacred. Kant expressed it as the unconditional respect owed to the inalienable dignity of every person. Keeping a distance from Christianity and also from Kant's pious attempt to render it tractable to reason, I expressed it by speaking of the inalienable preciousness of every human being.

Respect for that tradition has prompted me to satirise the urbanity that condescends to it; fear that our modes of expressing it will go dead on us has prompted me often to cast my work as a form of cultural reclamation; and the fear of falling away from it myself has made me cling in recollection to what the lives of some men and women revealed to me. I was therefore very lucky to meet Roy Holland when I first went to England in 1972 and, later, Peter Winch. They were, in their very different ways, morally intense and, inseparably from that, intense about philosophy. That was, at least in part, due to the example and profound influence of Rush Rhees, with whom they worked for some years in the fifties at the University of Wales at Swansea. Rhees had been a student of Wittgenstein.

You will see, I think, why I have accorded such importance in my work to learning from example. Often we see the value of something only when people take it into their lives, deepen it and are deepened by it. Sometimes we see that something is precious only in the light of someone's love for it. Roy Holland's love of Plato had a deep effect on me. As, rather differently, did his love of England. The latter influenced my work, especially when I wrote on reconciliation and collective responsibility, on multiculturalism, on the common good and on Israel and Palestine, distinguishing real love of country from its false semblance, jingoism. But that is a topic for another time.

People have often said that they hear a distinctive voice in my writing. I knew that from my early years in London. I'm sure it was formed by my country boyhood in the landscape of Central Victoria, growing up with my father and Hora and haunted by my mother who lived with us only occasionally, but always intensely, before she killed herself when I was 12. Though I loved London I was sometimes anxious, living such a different kind of life so far from the people and landscape that had nourished what is distinctive in my work, that I would lose it.

Perhaps I can explain what I feared to lose and why I 'clung in recollection' to it in order to resist a tendency by most of the best moral philosophers of the time to identify intensity with a dour moralism, if I comment on this passage from *Romulus, My Father*.

> Riding the motorbike that summer, through the hot yellow grasslands of central Victoria and around the expansive waters of Cairn Curran, wearing only shorts and sandals, crystallised in me a sense of freedom that I possessed earlier, but never so fully, and which I always associate with that time in the country. I felt I could do anything provided I was respectful of others. The law and other kinds of regulations seemed only rules of thumb, regulative ideals, to be interpreted by individuals according to circumstances and constrained by goodwill and commonsense. From my father and from Hora I had already acquired a sense that only morality was absolute because some of its demands were non-negotiable. But I was too young to be troubled by that. I was eleven years old, riding my father's motorbike to collect the mail and visit friends, yet no one was troubled by this breach of the law. It left me with a sad, haunting image of a freedom, impossible now to realise, and which even then the world could barely afford.

Later, at a more sombre moment, I describe my response to seeing my father for the first time in a mental hospital:

AFTERWORD

Life at Frogmore, in that landscape and under that light, nourished the sense, given to me by my father and Hora, of the contrast between the malleable laws and conventions made by human beings to reconcile and suit their many interests, and the uncompromising authority of morality, always the judge, never merely the servant of our interests.

Evidently, I could not have thought of morality in those terms when I was eleven years old, but even then I sensed from the example of my father and Hora that it mattered to them differently from anything else. For them it was not just the most important value, overriding all others: its importance was different in kind from anything else, even – this became apparent to me by the time my father went mad – from all the misfortunes they had seen and suffered.

Those passages are two of many that show that only a philosopher could have written *Romulus, My Father* and, indeed, a philosopher of a certain kind. When I say that morality is always the judge never merely the servant of interests, I mean that morality judges not only the means by which we realise our interests and purposes but also which interests and purposes we can decently make our own. If our purpose is to flourish, then morality judges not only the means we seek to do it, but also what kind of flourishing we could decently desire. If our purpose is the social good, then morality judges not only the means we deploy to achieve it, but also what kind of social good we could decently enjoy. That is why I say that morality is sui generis.

I hope that the first passage makes evident that what I called 'the absolute' demands of morality were not at all oppressive to me. To the contrary I absorbed, however inchoately, that conception of morality together with a joyous, sensuous and anarchic appreciation of my country boyhood. It was no accident that when I was a student I fell in love with Albert Camus' lyrical essays on Algerian summers, which express more beautifully than his bad philosophical writings, a sundrenched, tragic humanism. Or, that when I wanted to celebrate Hora and our life at Frogmore in *After Romulus*, I called the essay, 'A Summer Coloured Humanism'.

Q.2

Anne:
In a column in *Quadrant* through the 1990s you wrote a series of remarkable essays, informed by the philosophical work in *Good and Evil*, but where

readers were able to see you thinking in a supple and more accessible way for the general reader, about contemporary moral and political issues: the Mabo decision regarding native title and the injustices done to indigenous people in Australia, for example. Those essays had an arresting title: 'Turnings of Attention.' I remember reflecting at the time that it is not so usual a phenomenon that we rise to what is required of us, and absolutely and fully swing our attention deeply, openly and without some nibbling distortion, to another human being, that we hear her as she needs to be heard. Those turnings of attention, sometimes sudden and unexpected in the wider community, seem always to be at the centre of those moments of moral quickening in history, when we suddenly see injustice that has been ever before us, yet to which we have formerly been blind. Relatedly, without that moral effort of attention and a phrase Simone Weil spoke of in relation to love, 'this pure disinterested attention,' any human being and a human community can be guilty of what W. E. H. Stanner called 'sightlessness,' such as that which forms the basis of the 'Great Australian Silence' on the question of white Australia's treatment of indigenous people. Those essays formed the basis of *A Common Humanity: Thinking about Love and Truth and Justice.* In it you have a passage that I found quite profound in the application to many forms of injustice, and the striving of equality movements like feminism and the anti-racist movement to overturn those injustices. This is the passage:

> It can hardly be doubted that the world is a better place for it even though foolish things have been said and done in its name and even though unjust accusations of racism have actually contributed to racism. Like feminism, to which it has been both aligned and compared, it has expressed a concern for equality that cannot adequately be captured in talk of equal access to goods and opportunities. Treat me as a person, see me fully as a human being, as fully your equal, without condescension – these are not demands for things whose value lies in the degree to which they enable one to get other things. These are calls to justice conceived as equality of respect, calls to become part of a constituency within which claims for equity of access to goods and opportunities may appropriately be pressed. It is justice of the kind often called social justice because of its insistence that our state and civic institutions should, to the degree that is humanly possible, reveal rather than obscure the full humanity of our fellow citizens.

I wonder if you could talk a bit about *A Common Humanity* and also about this distinction between 'equal opportunities' and justice, the kind of deep-order equality you are speaking of here. Also is this why 'rights talk' can be inadequate?

Rai:
I called the column 'Turnings of Attention' because I wanted to redirect my readers to possibilities that had been ignored and often obscured as the poisonous culture wars dulled imaginations, stifled any charitable impulse to see what is true in something we think to be largely false or to explore, justly, the cultural sources and deeper variations of the beliefs to which we are opposed. But I didn't want to add possibilities to the battlefield. I didn't want to get on the battlefield. I wanted to explore other terrains.

At the time I was unfriendly to what was called practical ethics – not just to the practice, but also to the idea of it. It struck me as ironical that there should be a professional academic journal called *Philosophy and Public Affairs* that made no real attempt to speak beyond the academy. Philosophy's engagement with public life, I thought, should be in the organs of public life, even if, like *Quadrant*, *Meanjin* or *Arena* (there were no bloggers then) they are the organs of public intellectual life. Mostly when people ask whether philosophers should be encouraged to become publically engaged they think of academic philosophers. The answer to their question should therefore depend on an assessment of the state of the discipline and also of the public intellectual culture.

Elizabeth Anscombe, who was often fierce about these matters, wrote a paper in which she asked whether Oxford moral philosophy corrupted the youth. She answered that though consequentialism had corrupted moral philosophy, that was an expression of the times. Since most students were, in the pejorative sense, children of their times they would not be corrupted by their teachers, not much, at any rate. Consequentialism is the theory that, in the end, only the consequences of what we do matters morally. My point is not that she was right, but that hers is the kind of point we ought to engage with. If the discipline is in decline, especially if universities are also in decline, making it difficult for academics to be critically reflective rather than merely appearing so, then both might become enriched by engagement with the intellectual life beyond them. Whether we have reason to hope for that will, as Anscombe's point brings out, depend on our confidence in the culture. If that confidence is misplaced, the academy will bring the worst of itself to that culture and impoverish it even further, by, for example, in the case of philosophers whose skill in argument often frightens people, imposing on public discussion a narrow conception of what counts as legitimate persuasion, or of the relations between understanding and emotion or between art, science and philosophy.

If Robert Manne had not asked me to write a column for *Quadrant* when he became the editor, I might never have written for an audience beyond the academy. Although academics at the University of Melbourne, when I was an undergraduate in the sixties, had a strong sense of obligation to participate in public discussion, I had little inclination to do so during the twenty years that I spent in England before I wrote for *Quadrant*. Rob changed that. I am deeply grateful to him, especially since he came under constant and sometimes hostile criticism for keeping me on as a columnist.

I wrote over fifty columns for him. (I say 'for him,' because it would never have occurred to me to write for *Quadrant* had he not been the editor, even if I had been inclined to write for a non-academic audience). A fair amount of material from them, revised, went into *A Common Humanity*. Although much of what I wrote in those columns was informed by ideas expressed in *Good and Evil: An Absolute Conception* (note the indefinite article), I was not simply applying those ideas to more practical concerns. I was, as you say, rethinking them in the light of such concerns, though I'm glad that I listened to a dear, mutual friend, Denis Grundy, when he advised me never to write on public policy. Writing the columns over a six-year period enabled me (as I see it) to deepen and extend those ideas. That is most evident in the way that I developed the concept that gives the title to the book, *A Common Humanity*.

Many people think that if only we could see all the peoples of the earth as sharing a common humanity then we would have the basis for a universal morality and for the universal aspirations of international criminal law. There is good reason to believe that, but the conception of humanity that would be realised, indeed is expressed in, that hope is ethically inflected. Whatever its connections may be to the fact that human beings are members of the species Homo sapiens, the failure to see someone as fully human, or as a fellow human being, is not a failure to see them as members of the species.

In an essay on racism in *A Common Humanity*, I argue that we misunderstand certain forms of racism – usually those based on skin colour – if we focus on the empirical stereotypes with which racists attempt to justify their attitudes, or if, realising them to be mere rationalisations, focus on the psychological or social reasons of why people are racists. I said we will better understand how such racists see the victims of their denigration if we reflect on why we could not see the full range of human expressiveness in a face that looked to us like the *Black and White Minstrel Show*'s caricature of

AFTERWORD

an Afro-American face. If, as Wittgenstein said, the human face is the best picture of the human soul, then faces like that cannot picture souls that have any depth.

That took me to what is, perhaps, my most important point: that racists do not see the victims of their denigration as shallow. Instead, they see them as existing outside the conceptual space in which attributions of depth and shallowness make sense. To judge someone to be shallow you have to believe they are the kind of being who could, at least in principle, rise to the demands of something deeper, just as if you accuse someone of irrationality, you must think them open to rise to the demands of reason. But that, I argued, is what this kind of racist finds inconceivable. In the same way some extreme misogynists do not think they can learn anything important from women, not because they think women are incorrigibly irrational, but because they do not see women as existing in a conceptual space in which the call to be rational, to think logically, even makes sense.

I have, though, never been happy with making that point by speaking of a *conceptual space*. It does not capture the importance of language to our understanding of what is at issue. Racists are blind to the *meaning* of what their victims do and suffer. I'm thinking of meaning as we intend it when we reprimand someone by saying, 'You don't know what it means to grieve. You are always so self-absorbed.' Or, 'You don't know what it means to love, because you are always intoxicated by your infatuations.' Or, as a remorseful person might mean it when she says that only now does she realise the full meaning of what she has done.

Explorations of such meanings can deepen without limit and are in idioms that unite form and content. Yet it goes deep, not only in philosophy, but more generally in the discursive tradition of the West, to believe that anything of cognitive substance should be extracted from its form in a natural language, especially if that form is infused with feeling, and examined in a style-free, tone-free zone. If you think that is an exaggeration, then this, probably apocryphal, story told by Bernard Williams might encourage you to change your mind. It is about two philosophers who are writing a book together. One tells the other, 'First let's get the content right. Then you can add the style.'

Against this I argue that when we discuss how to live, we will be true to our subject matter and its historical depth only if we develop an account of what it is to try to see things as they are rather than as they appear, of what it means to be persuaded legitimately of something, and of what it means really to orient our thoughts to truth, that shows thinking and feeling, form and cognitive content, to be inseparable. We will then have a richer conception of the discursive than the one assumed by Williams' philosophers, who are representative not only of philosophers, but also of a pervasive conception of the connection between reason and feeling, content and style that goes deep in Western intellectual history.

I have called the cognitive realm in which head and heart, style and content are inseparable the 'realm of meaning' because it is where we discuss what it means to love or grieve truthfully and why it matters; what it means to suffer wrong and what it means to do it. It is where we elaborate questions about how to live and develop tentative, or not so tentative, answers to them, where we argue about whether the psychotherapist Viktor Frankl was right to say that for most people meaning matters more than happiness. It is what I meant when I referred to the conceptual space from which racists exclude those whom they denigrate. Since writing *A Common Humanity* I have also come to think that it is in that cognitive, discursive realm that we should discuss the jurisprudence of international criminal law. That implies that the universality to which such law aspires will be more like the universality of great literature, which may speak to all the peoples of the earth, but always as translated from one natural language into another, than the universality of science or metaphysics.

I hope that it is now evident why it is not rhetoric to say that to overcome racism is to acknowledge the full humanity of peoples whose humanity had been only partially visible. Believing that the application, if not the theory (derived from Lockean notions of property), of *terra nullius* was based on such racism, on an incapacity to see that indigenous peoples could have relations of any real depth to the land and therefore could not be dispossessed in anything like the way that is implied by the ordinary moral connotations of this word, I argued that the High Court judgment in Mabo was nothing less than the acknowledgement of the full humanity of our indigenous peoples. Only if one failed to see this could one deride the judgment as 'merely symbolic,' serious though the failings of native title legislation have been. Justice was done, but not because the indigenous peoples were treated fairly or because they were given access to goods and opportunities previously denied them. True and important though that is, these forms of justice belong to a different plane from the justice that is the recognition of their humanity.

Simone Weil expressed this beautifully when she writes:

> The just must be thanked for being just, because justice is so beautiful
> a thing ... Any other gratitude is servile and even animal. The only

difference between the man who witnesses an act of justice and the man who receives a material advantage from it is that in such circumstances the beauty of justice is only a spectacle for the first, while for the second it is the object of a contact and even a kind of nourishment.

That, I think, is why many people in all parts of the world wept tears of joy when Barack Obama was inaugurated President of the United States. I think of Mabo rather like I think of Obama's election to the presidency. Nothing Obama does or fails to do can take away from the wonderful fact that America now has a black president. Of course, it's a baleful comment on our history that we should think it that wonderful, but it doesn't diminish the joy, just makes it bittersweet. For a generation like mine, raised watching films in which blacks were portrayed as brutish and ridiculous, or reading Tarzan comics, what began in the sixties was a revolutionary change in sensibility.

Stanner was right. We were sightless. He (though not only he, of course) gave us sight and hearing when he taught us that the culture of Australia's indigenous peoples possessed 'all the beauty of song, mime, dance and art of which human beings are capable.' That enabled us to acknowledge in black cultures an ever-deepening responsiveness to the defining facts of the human condition – our mortality, our sexuality, and our vulnerability to misfortune – and therefore to see them as cultures from which we could learn. Like us they love rather than just 'love,' grieve rather than just 'grieve.' Like us they are unique and irreplaceable.

I'm glad that you mentioned Simone Weil. When I came to compile a bibliography for *A Common Humanity*, I realised that I had quoted her more than anyone else. I shall quote her again to answer your question about rights. But first I want to observe that the word 'rights' hardly ever – if ever – appears in *A Common Humanity* though I wrote about justice, about genocide, about racism, about collective responsibility and reconciliation, freedom of speech and other topics whose discussion is often dominated by talk of rights. I know that does not mean that I did not rely on the concept, but it makes a prima facie case for saying that I didn't.

In her essay 'Human Personality,' Weil is critical of the importance we attach to the concept of rights when we try to explain what it means to wrong someone, or when we try to protect people from wrongs, or when we try to awaken someone to a full understanding of a wrong done. The wrongs she has in mind are moral wrongs. Because her focus is on the moral dimension of the wrong done when we say a right has been violated, to the exclusion of its legal and political dimensions – or, perhaps better, because she thinks that the moral dimension of a wrong done when a right is violated exhausts its legal and moral dimensions – her discussion is lopsided, and also unfair. But because the moral dimensions of the violations she is thinking of are so fundamental, I will also focus on them. She writes:

> If you say to someone who has ears to hear: 'What you are doing to me is not just,' you may touch and waken at its source the spirit of attention and love. But it is not the same with words like 'I have the right ...' or 'you have no right to ...' They evoke a latent war and awaken the spirit of contention. To place the notion of rights at the centre of social conflicts is to inhibit any possible impulse of charity on both sides.
>
> Relying almost exclusively on this notion, it becomes impossible to keep one's eyes on the real problem. If someone tries to browbeat a farmer to sell his eggs at a moderate price, the farmer can say: 'I have the right to keep my eggs if I don't get a good enough price.' But if a young girl is being forced into a brothel she will not talk about her rights. In such a situation the word would sound ludicrously inadequate.

The rhetorical comparison of talk of rights with a farmer haggling over the price of his eggs is deeply unfair, but the point Weil goes on to make survives that, I believe. The reason she says it would be ludicrously inadequate for the girl to protest that her rights had been violated is not because it would be pointless to do so, although of course it would be. It is because she believes that the concept of rights is of itself inadequate to an understanding of the terribleness of what the girl suffers. That is one reason why Weil says the concept of rights is a 'mediocre' one. The moral force of an appeal to rights depends upon elaborations of the kind to which we gesture when we say, incredulously, 'Don't you understand what it means to suffer this kind of humiliation?' or which a person who is seriously remorseful would seek in order to understand fully what she did. Were it not for its reliance on such elaborations, the relatively bare appeal to rights would indeed seem absurd. Imagine if, at the moment of a bitter remorse, the perpetrator of the evil against the girl were to say, 'My God! What have I done? I violated her human rights.' And though the moral dimension is, as I said earlier, not the only ethical dimension within the concept of a right, it is the primary one in this kind of case. Indeed it is so in all cases where the concept of a violation comes first to mind, as it does when we think of rape, torture, and other forms of cruel and degrading treatment. I choose these examples because

AFTERWORD

they are not only crimes against a person but, when committed as an act of warfare, are crimes against humanity.

I hope that I will not be misunderstood about this. The battles for what we call 'human rights' have been amongst the noblest in Western history. God only knows where we would have been had we not fought and won so many of them. But one aspect of our commitment to human rights – and Weil saw this more clearly than anyone I have read – rests on an illusion, one that is reinforced by the way we talk about Dignity, with a capital 'D,' or of inalienable dignity. Though there is a Catholic natural law tradition that speaks of the Dignity of the Human Person, the way we speak of it owes more to Kant. Like almost everything moving in Kant, it is in a heroic register. But some people suffer affliction so terrible, either through natural causes or because of human cruelty, affliction that crushes their spirits so completely, the idea that they could rescue their Dignity by crying for their rights is as absurd as it is to imagine that the girl being dragged into the brothel could do it. They have, Weil says, 'sunk into a state of dumb and ceaseless lamentation.'

I saw people like that when, as a student, I worked over a summer vacation in a mental hospital in a ward where some patients had been for more than twenty years. They were heavily medicated and rightly, at the time, regarded as incurable. The nursing staff treated them brutishly; many of the psychiatrists were not much better. When they soiled themselves, as some often did, they were dragged to a shower, forced to undress and washed down with a mop, sometimes still partially clothed.

At that hospital five or so psychiatrists insisted that those patients be treated humanely. It cost them to do so. The nursing staff mocked them as fools. So, probably, did many of their colleagues. One of them said to me that even those patients possessed inalienable dignity. I did not understand what he meant, but the gentle intensity with which he spoke moved me. One day a nun came. When I saw her move among the patients I knew I had encountered something wondrous. The inflections of her demeanour and the way she spoke revealed that even those fine psychiatrists had condescended to the patients.

I tell the story and try to elaborate its significance in what I chose to be the opening chapter of *A Common Humanity*. I did that to set the tone for much of the book. I wanted to take the reader to a place where she could see why people might speak of 'Goodness' in a way that invites a capital 'G,' why they might connect it with talk of the inalienable preciousness of all human beings, a preciousness revealed to us — and I say this as someone who is not religious — in the works of saintly love.

Ever since I first wrote about her in *A Common Humanity*, I have tried to express adequately the difference between her and the psychiatrists, most recently in *After Romulus*. The difference does not lie in their respective virtues: I admired the psychiatrists for their compassion, their preparedness to suffer ridicule, their tireless hard work and more. But when I reflected on the nun, I realised she dropped out of the picture. I did not reflect on her and her qualities: I reflected on what her behaviour revealed. It was that, rather than any of her virtues, that seemed wondrous.

What did her behaviour reveal? Here I stumble. I have said it revealed that even those patients who had lost everything that gives meaning to our lives were 'fully our equals.' I said she revealed the 'full humanity' of people whose affliction had made their humanity invisible. But when I try to explain what I mean by these expressions, I can only say that she showed a compassion that was without condescension and that I cannot deny the wondrousness of it and what it revealed. My problem is not that it all seems circular. That is true of all the ethically inflected ways of speaking of our humanity. When we say, 'You can't treat a person like that. She's a human being!' we sometimes take reference to her humanity to function like a reference to a person's bad temper, such as when we say, 'Be careful what you say, he has a violent temper.' But we are, in the first example, not offering an explanation. We are trying to make someone acknowledge what they know: that it is part of our understanding of what it is to be a human being that we do not treat people like that. So my problem is not a logical one, namely that it seems circular to say that she revealed their full humanity. During the course of our history people like her, people who have done the work of saints and given us a language of love in which to record it, have also given us a new and mysterious understanding of what it is to recognise another person's full humanity and the full humanity in ourselves.

On one occasion when I spoke of the nun, someone said to me that she seemed just like his mum. I suspect she wasn't like his mum, but I knew someone who worked at the hospital who probably was. A couple of times each week the patients went to occupational therapy. One of the therapists often congratulated them if they had worked well or sometimes if they worked at all. I heard her praise a patient by saying that on that day he had made twelve clothes pegs whereas the previous week he had made only five. She was a kind woman who said this with openhearted generosity, but her tone betrayed a benign condescension. Or, perhaps more accurately,

AFTERWORD

her tone made it clear that she would have found it literally unintelligible that kindness that was truthfully responsive to their condition could be different.

What makes me stumble is my inability to find a better way to express the nun's demeanour towards the patients than that she behaved towards them without a trace of condescension. This makes it look as though I saw her in the light of an idealised egalitarianism, whereas really I want to say that egalitarianism, its ideals and our failures to rise to them, are the wrong concepts to bring to an attempt to understand the nun. When I first wrote about her I said she 'showed up' those fine psychiatrists. Marina Barabas asked me if I really wanted to say that. I realised that I didn't. The gap between her and the psychiatrists was not of a kind that should have made them feel ashamed in the way that those who condescend to others because of their superior prestige, fame, wealth or intelligence should. I am not critical of the psychiatrists and the occupational therapist. No conception of virtue, of what is natural or reasonable, could require that they should have acted differently. The occupational therapist, as I said, behaved with a benign condescension because she found it unintelligible that compassion for such patients could be other than condescending if it were unsentimental and truthful.

The reason I would not criticise the psychiatrists or the occupational therapist is not because the nun's behaviour was supererogatory, beyond and above the call of duty. We learn from supererogatory acts what human beings are capable of. Sometimes what we learn astonishes us but supererogatory deeds are perfectly intelligible to those who know they cannot perform them. They are, to exaggerate only a little, moral *feats* that leave us awestruck. Heroic deeds are their paradigm. We can dream that we might be heroes. We might be Walter Mittys, but there is no conceptual difficulty in imagining what in fact we haven't the slightest chance of doing. I don't say flatly that we cannot hope to be able to behave like the nun, but the difficulty is not, as it is when we imagine ourselves as heroes, of seriously believing we could ever possess a virtue to such an exemplary degree. The difficulty lies in conceiving exactly what we imagine ourselves to be able to do. To think of the nun as the agent of supererogatory deeds is to think of her as a superwoman of compassion. But the nurses, the warm-hearted social worker, the noble psychiatrists and the nun are not on a continuum of virtue, with her much further along than even the psychiatrists. The nun's love is mysterious because, like other works of saintly love towards the afflicted, it calls us to affirm, to bear witness to, something that is deeply foreign to reason and even more to reasonableness. Hardly anyone can behave as the nun did, but the reason is different in kind from the reasons that explain why few people can be heroes.

I've now tried to say more than I should have in this interview. I've again failed to heed Wittgenstein's warning that in philosophy the hardest thing is to know when to stop. I'll therefore return to your question about rights and say that my point, Anne, as you know, is not to say that all we need is love. Nor is it to suggest that we try to banish talk of human rights. That's not possible. Nor is it desirable. But I think that Weil was right to insist that if we are to respond truthfully to affliction, it is imperative that we disengage the way we talk of human rights from the illusion that even the most radically afflicted – those who, as Weil puts it, have been 'struck one of those blows that leaves a human being writhing on the ground like a half-crushed worm' – retain a Dignity that their degradation cannot take from them.

Only saints can see, and their love reveal to us, the full humanity of such people by revealing that they are inalienably precious. That is why Weil said that compassion for the afflicted is 'a more astounding miracle than walking on water, healing the sick or raising the dead.' When the concept of rights is underpinned by a heroically inflected conception of inalienable dignity, it dulls our sensibility to the very thing we want to assert as surviving radical degradation, and obscures our vision to what the love of saints would otherwise enable us to see. At the same time that it dulls our vision, it encourages us to believe, innocently, as it did the psychiatrist who spoke to me of the inalienable dignity of the patients and worked tirelessly to improve their welfare, that we are able to respond fully to the humanity of the afflicted, to see their full humanity in their affliction, when we don't and can't. This does not mean that we should not speak of the inalienable dignity of such people: it means that, when we do, we should resist its heroic inflections, and see it as part of the language of love that is inspired and nourished by the works of saintly love.

There is a practical moral to this: in our political and public institutions – prisons, detention centres for asylum seekers, mental hospitals, aged care homes for example – we should never permit conditions that would so undermine people's ordinary, alienable dignity, that only a saint could see the full humanity in them.

* * *

AFTERWORD

I had intended not to say anything about the relation of my thought to religion, especially to Christianity, but even as I was writing this I was made aware, by comment on my work in a philosophical journal, of how often I am taken to be a closet Christian. So I will say something in the hope that it will prevent misunderstanding, or at least misattribution of religious beliefs to me.

When I speak of the works of saintly love, I have in mind compassion for the afflicted of the kind shown by the nun, as those who witnessed it have expressed it historically, usually in Christian terms. There are other religions, of course, which inspired such wondrous deeds, but in the West, it was mainly their Christian expression in ritual, music, painting and poetry, that grew and nourished a language of love. But what has grown in one place can take root elsewhere, provided it has food to nourish it; what we learn to say in one language, we can try to say in another. Obviously it is a serious question what will sustain the language of love outside of religious practices. I do not take the need to answer it lightly, but I will not try to do it here. I will, however, say here that I cannot see how religious doctrine, especially if it is a system of metaphysics, renders intelligible the idea that we could rightly respond to people whose degradation is complete and irreversible with a compassion that shows no trace of condescension. If someone were to reply that religious people believe every human being is sacred, I would say that we need an account of how it became intelligible to us – by hearing or reading doctrine or metaphysics – that the concept of the sacred, or that we are God's children, should have included the idea that we could respond to those of God's children who have been reduced to such a state, with anything other than a benign, perhaps even loving, condescension. Or, that we should not cast out some of God's children, as He cast out the fallen angels, if they committed the most terrible deeds. I do not believe that this can be made acceptable to Reason, still less to a developed reasonableness. I am not religious – I wish to make that clear - but if I were, I would agree with those who say that God's love is gratuitous and mysterious. We should not think of it as something that enables us to explain anything that would otherwise be dark to reason. We should sing hymns of praise and gratitude to it.

There is something else that I must say, given how often I praise Simone Weil. She was repugnantly hostile to Judaism. It is hard to know what her attitude to Judaism would have been if she had lived to read thinkers like Martin Buber or Yeshayahu Leibowtiz. The latter condemned the idolatry she takes to be at the heart of Judaism, and its political consequences, as fiercely as she did and as an expression of the same love of justice, but he did it because he thought it was a corruption of Judaism. What she said about Judaism was and remains a boon to anti-Semitism. Many readers – certainly most Jews – will justifiably find her unrelenting hostility repugnant. Because she expressed it during the most terrible years of the Holocaust, when the Vichy Government participated with alacrity in the Nazi extermination of French Jews, they will also find it unforgivable.

This pains me, though it does not diminish my gratitude that she could write so truthfully about affliction. The Holocaust has affected my sensibility profoundly. I was born in Germany to a German mother and have a German family I love. I have a Jewish wife, step children and step grandchildren. Hardly a day passes when I am not at some level aware that in the lifetime of my parents most of the nations of Europe were glad to see Jews exterminated like vermin unfit to live on this earth. Centuries of Christian anti-Semitism made that possible. For that reason I could not be further from being a closet Christian. To become a Christian would feel to me like a betrayal of the Jewish part of my family.

Q.3

Anne:
I'd like now to press you a little on your relation to psychology. One day walking with you in the landscape of your childhood, you said something that stayed with me. We were looking over a field belonging to the Lillies: a great expanse of white stubble stretching out before us, under a roiling purple sky with dark clouds scudding across, threatening rain. As we stood there, near the ruins of your boyhood home, Frogmore, you spoke of something your father said to you, with great intensity, about mental illness: 'That is the worst sickness, the sickness of the mind.' I think he is right, for in physical illness, the spirit and the soul of the person is not, of necessity, distorted in the way that it can be with mental illness. What we now call mental illness, and you call madness, in the adults around you that you depended on was a deep part of your childhood. And yet, although you began at university studying psychology, you soon turned away from it to moral philosophy. Your stance is not simply a question of being more interested in one way of looking at the world, but more an antipathy. It is the reasons for that antipathy which I am interested in drawing out here. You deliberately eschewed describing your mother's life in terms of mental illness, as manic depression, in *Romulus, My Father*. And one of your next big projects is to write about psychology and – correct me if I

AFTERWORD

am wrong – the inadequacy of its concepts. And yet, treatments born of the psychological paradigm and our as yet rudimentary neuroscience, manage to save lives – medications like lithium for manic depression, for example, or antipsychotics for those suffering from schizophrenia. There is nothing easy or pleasant about such treatments but, put simply, they can save lives. And for all we can justly mock bad therapy – we could also mock bad philosophy – there is surely something humane in the kind of deep listening to another human being that the best therapists offer. Indeed, to use another of your phrases, 'Turnings of Attention,' that is, at its best, what is hoped to be given in the therapeutic situation is the deepest attentiveness to a person's 'never listened to story.' You see that in the HBO series *In Treatment*, where a kind of Platonic therapist, listens, struggles to hear the resonances of the soul he is sitting with and provides illuminations from psychology, while – I thought this was an inspired and reality-based touch – his own motivations and soul remain frustratingly opaque to him.

I suppose I partly wonder how much of your aversion is due to the era in which you began to study, when psychology was astonishingly crude, behaviourist and reductionist. (And of course it can still be all three.) It was the 'Rats and Stats era.' I notice Bernard Avishai, in *Promiscuous*, also talks about the explosive nature of Phillip Roth's writing on sexuality in that era, so it wasn't just in Australia. Yet behaviourism has long since given way to much richer contributions from psychoanalysis, attachment theory, cognitive science, understandings about emotion and their relationship to reason, and so on. I have also heard you make the same point I would about Freud and the project of psychoanalysis: that in his understanding that madness is not an 'Otherness' residing in freaks unlike ourselves, the way we used to stigmatise the mentally ill as sharply and irrevocably different from 'the normal,' he made us see that all those who suffer from mental illness are on a continuum with those who are not currently 'ill.' This means Freud's project was partly about getting people to see our common humanity, to use one of your phrases, with people who are neurotic or psychotic: that these are only more extreme, lasting states of what we all experience.

Let me put this another way. Philosophy is the effortful attention to the concepts we use when thinking, to make them more precise, to think well about thinking. Yet the best of those working in the psychological paradigm are, like philosophers, thinking about thinking. Because it is in distortions of thought – how we think about someone, or about other people, about ourselves and our world and our relation to it, that we can find the sources of injustice, self-deception, cruelty, dehumanisation and so on.

So psychology at its best is another kind of effortful attention to the way the mind works, a window through which to look for understanding – notwithstanding that it is not the only window and that it does some things better than others. Psychoanalysis draws attention to the obscure or opaque nature of our consciousness and our intentions – we are not always who we think we are. It is sometimes called 'depth psychology' because it attempts to excavate those aspects, to bring us closer to reality by forging an awareness of ourselves without illusion.

In my own work I am deeply interested in the psychological paradigm, without ever finding it to be 'everything.' It can never be 'everything' because I am interested in the vivacity of everybody in their particularity, their absolute uniqueness, the queer vitality of life precisely because of those qualities that has me turn to poets or novelists again and again. Yet I am also deeply interested in psychoanalysis, theory and research in attachment, and neuroscience because I am also a person interested in finding the underlying patterns of things. For example the way, as the outstanding Melbourne psychoanalyst, Clara 'Mama' Geroe – who treated her patients with such tenderness – once said: that life can be lived in the light – or shadow – of those first love relationships. As indeed your life as a philosopher, and as a person, has been in the light of those first relationships, deeply shaped by spirits you encountered as a child. But some people live in their shadow, in the darkest place. As one of Geroe's former patients once said to me with anguish, 'It is so hard to go forward in life when you are always looking back.' And for some people, as Freud said:

> A thing which has not been understood inevitably reappears; like an unlaid ghost, it cannot rest until the mystery has been resolved and the spell broken.

Rai:
I'll first say something about medication. You are right, of course. Medication has made it possible for people to live something like a normal life, and sometimes a great deal more than that. I often wonder how my mother's life would have gone if she had the medication now available to people who suffer from manic depression. I don't think, however, that there are quick conclusions to be drawn from that – nor, I am sure, do you – about what concepts should enter an account (I put it that way because causation is a tricky concept here) of the development of a psychotic form of mental illness in a person. In *Romulus, My Father*, for example, I say that my father's descent

AFTERWORD

into madness was in part a function of his sense of the reality of good and evil. I don't think it would be adequate to an account of the role that sense played in his madness to say only that, in his circumstances, his beliefs about good and evil *triggered* something whose essential nature can be understood independently of the concepts of good and evil as they had been available to him in his culture and what he made of that cultural inheritance. One cannot understand these concepts without a high degree of inwardness with them, which cannot be that far from taking them seriously. Psychology will be different, I think, in a culture in which such concepts are alive, in which they have a full speaking part in our life with language. If that is true, it makes a difference to what it can mean to say that a psychiatrist needn't share the moral beliefs of his patients because he needs only to attribute those beliefs to them to explain their condition, or how they respond to therapy, and to guide his behaviour in therapy. If that is true, ethical concepts, sui generis, of the kind I have elaborated throughout our discussion, must enter an account of what the Platonic therapist does when he listens attentively to his patients.

My father was talking about Vacek, a friend who was mentally ill, when he was moved to say, 'There is no sickness worse than mental sickness.' I do not know whether he had a premonition of his own fall into madness, but he understood the terror of mental illness long before he succumbed to it. The time when he conveyed this to me is among the most vivid of my childhood memories. This is how I describe it in *Romulus, My Father*:

> I have seldom seen such affliction as I saw my father suffer in those last years in Frogmore, and I only saw it again when I worked as a student in psychiatric hospitals. He understood it before he became its victim. Some years before, while we were traveling on the motorbike, he talked about Vacek and said, 'There is no sickness worse than mental sickness.'
>
> I remember his words clearly. I remember the exact point where we were on the road. Most of all, I remember his strong, bare, sun-darkened arms on either side of me as I sat on the petrol tank. For me to remember his words and our surroundings so vividly, the authority with which he spoke them must have impressed me deeply. The sight of his muscular arms protected me against their terrible meaning.

From the time of my boyhood I have had a deep sense of the terror of madness, especially as I saw it in my father eyes when he went mad.

I am, though, ambivalent about using the word 'mad.' I understand entirely why people are resistant, even hostile, to its use, believing that it denigrates those who suffer from what, of course, is an illness. But we must be careful in how we describe it as an illness. People sometimes say that mental illness is an illness just like any other illness. They mean to emphasise that it *is* an illness. They could say, 'It's an illness, you know, not a failing of character, not anything to be ashamed of.' Of course, I sympathise with this. But it is perhaps mistaken to say, flatly, against that, against the claim that it is an illness like any other, that it is the *worst* illness. That can distract attention from, or dull our awareness to, the significance of the fact that it is an illness that denies those who suffer it the ability to be lucid about it, to know what attitude to take to it. To oversimplify a little, to make the point clear: you cannot trust your mind to tell you whether you have lost your mind. This matters as much as I am saying, of course, only to people who care that they live their life with a degree of lucidity about the things that are most important to them – for some that means to rise to the gift of their humanity, even to the gift of life. For others, none of this matters much. They would probably say the worst illness is a protracted and painful fatal illness. They might argue about whether heart disease, cancer or suicidal depression is the worst illness, as though they were on a line from bad to worst. Therapists cannot be neutral about this disagreement. They have to know in their bones why someone like my father said what he did. But to know it that way is to place an ethical value on lucidity.

I studied psychology for two years of a double major because I wanted to understand human beings in the hope, of course, that I would understand what happened during much of my childhood. It is true that I turned away from psychology to philosophy because I was hostile to behaviourism and the generally scientistic orientation of the psychology department, knowing that they could not deliver what I wanted. At the end of my second year I wrote an essay called 'Man or Methodolatry' (the title speaks for itself). Frank Knopfelmacher, who gave brilliant lectures critical of behaviourism and was sympathetic to what the Europeans called *Verstehen* psychology, marked it. He called me to his office and said, 'You are not an empirical psychologist, are you, Gaita?' He urged me to study philosophy. When I told him that I had no desire to study philosophy, that I wanted to help change psychology into a humane study, he told me he had already made an appointment for me to see the professor of philosophy. I kept the appointment. It changed my life.

At that time two friends and I had started a magazine called *Threshold*, in which we advanced the claims of 'humanistic' psychologists who were resistant to scientism – Abraham Maslow, the less (it seemed to us) dogmatic psychoanalytically oriented psychologists Erich Fromm and Karen Horney,

AFTERWORD

and the existential psychologists Rollo May and Ludwig Binswanger. Much of this was what was then called, and you call, depth psychology. I even read quite a lot of Karl Jaspers' 922-page (counting the index) *General Psychopathology*.

Knopfelmacher was perhaps prescient when he said that I wasn't interested in empirical psychology, rather than saying only that I wasn't interested in its scientistic variations. The psychologists who then inspired me *were* empirical psychologists, though some like Binswanger and Jaspers were also philosophers, but he sensed – though I didn't see it myself until years later – that scientism in psychology was not what troubled me most. I enrolled in philosophy and became absorbed in conceptual issues in psychology – in philosophical psychology, as the subject was called. I took *Threshold* with me and focused its criticism on the more tedious dimensions of analytical philosophy, urging analytical philosophers to be open-minded towards continental philosophers like Sartre and Maurice Merleau-Ponty. I wrote my MA on whether reasons for actions were causes of actions – a natural topic for someone who had resisted scientism in psychology. At the time I had no interest in moral philosophy as an academic discipline; it seemed facile. I developed an interest in it only when I read Iris Murdoch's *The Sovereignty of Good* and then the work of R. F. Holland, who supervised my PhD, but only after I had begun it in the philosophy of logic.

A failure to be interested in empirical psychology continued until relatively recently. I suppose that calls for an explanation, though all I will say is that there are many reasons for it, and that some are more personal than I would discuss here. In *After Romulus*, in the essay 'An Unassuageable Longing,' I wrote as personally as I am ever likely to. It was, as you know, Anne, very hard for me. I doubt I would have written it were it not for you, nor would I have found a voice as trusting of my readers. But it is evident from that essay, especially from its opening pages, that I know how little we understand ourselves and how powerfully unconscious factors motivate our deeds and our false understandings of what is deepest in us.

Since my student days I have believed that an adequate psychology requires an account of the self, of how it builds and sometimes disintegrates, an understanding of the unconscious, which must include a theory of its interpretation. I said as much in *A Common Humanity* and also in *The Philosopher's Dog*. Yet, I confess that I am suspicious of most interpretations or, at best, I shrug my shoulders. I suppose that is revealing, as is the fact that I strongly resisted philosophical and psychological forms of reductionism long before I had coherent reasons to support that resistance. What did I feel

I would lose? Many things – many *kinds* of things – I suspect. By the time I reached university, Greek tragedy had more effect on me than anything else I read. It helped me understand my life, the way people could be broken yet mysteriously not diminished by their suffering, and that I needed to protect that understanding from what I studied in psychology and later in moral philosophy. That is why I wrote *Romulus, My Father* in the style that I did, unconsciously to be sure because I wrote the first draft in three turbulent weeks without really understanding what I was doing. The most evident sign of that is that I set out to write a book about my father yet spent almost the whole of the first week writing about my mother. When I finished the book I thought of it as a kind of tragic poem. That is the reason for – the complete reason, I believe – why I did not revise it as a longer, more psychologically probing, memoir.

In *After Romulus* I said that I believe it is impossible to understand my mother's deep sensuality without understanding her romanticism and the way it informed, and was perhaps informed by, the heightened sexuality that is a common feature of manic depression. That illustrates an emphasis in my work: how an adequate account of what it means to be a human being, of what it means to rise to the demands of our humanity, must include an understanding of how the self can be transformed by contact with values sui generis, of the ways our sense of the independent reality of other people is morally conditioned. The world looks very different to someone who believes that, as you put it, and quoting Simone Weil, 'respect is owed to the human being as such, and has no degree,' than it does to someone who doesn't believe that or never even had an inkling of it. Or, to put it as Kant did (from whom Weil derived that way of expressing it, though she was more often inclined to speak of what is revealed to love): the world looks very different to someone who affirms that every human being possesses an inalienable dignity to which is owed unconditional respect (not esteem which, of course, is conditional and admits of degrees) than it does to someone who does not believe it. The virtues, love and compassion will look different. The same is true of the kind of empathy needed for the 'attentive listening' of the therapist you praise. Therapy will be different for those who offer and who receive it according to whether it is infused with a deep sense the inalienable preciousness (or the inalienable dignity), of every human being. Even the understanding of the moral significance of The Golden Rule – that one should always treat others as one would wish them to treat oneself – which many people take to be the basic precept of morality and to capture the essence of the biblical command to love one's neighbour, will be different.

AFTERWORD

But no theory of human nature can take us unaided to these ethical ideas. To the contrary, it is these ethical ideas that transform our understanding of human nature.

In *After Romulus*, I talked about the way my father found it impossible to turn his back on my mother's need. I said that this should not have been construed as a psychological force, as something that he might wish to overcome, or that someone else might urge him to try to overcome. Hora was sometimes impatient with my father over this because he had little sympathy for my mother. He might sometimes have thought my father a fool as, in fact, a lot of his compatriots did – and a shameless fool at that, paying the rent of a man who had cuckolded him – but it would never have occurred to Hora to urge my father to try to do what he said he could not do when he said he could not turn away from my mother's need. To make the point clear, I said that had Hora done so, he would have betrayed a failure of understanding. The same failure would see someone respond to Martin Luther when he said, 'Here I stand. I can do no other,' with a comment that perhaps he should try, because it might not be as hard as he thinks.

In my work more generally I have argued, developing thoughts from Peter Winch and Simone Weil – indeed Peter Winch on Simone Weil – that the kind of impossibility my father expressed is partly constitutive of and partly expressive of, our sense of the reality of another human being. Kant thought of ethical necessity as limited to a very special kind of obligation. My father had a strong sense of his obligations to my mother, indeed, still considered her to be his wife, but it was not that sense of obligation that motivated him. He was motivated by compassion, but it was an ethically necessitated compassion and, as such, expressed his understanding – or better, was a *form* of his understanding – of what it meant for my mother and Mitru, her lover (and my father's friend, even so) to suffer as they did. Iris Murdoch said that an aspiration to moral clear-sightedness is an aspiration that the world becomes compulsively present to our will. She meant, I think, that we should come to see the world in such a way that we are motivated, in the right circumstances, by this kind of ethical necessity. In this she was influenced by Weil, who said the purest motives are the ones that prompt a person truthfully to ask, 'What else can I do?'

Theorists whom I regard as reductionists try to argue that this sense of necessity and impossibility is itself to be explained by a psychology of the self, of its modes of integration. Crudely, their point is that insofar as it is genuinely impossible, rather than a hyperbolical and careless expression of a sense of obligation, it voices a fear of psychic disintegration. This would be explained, according to this way of thinking, by a psychology of what we call moral identity that made no necessary reference to moral concepts.

Against that, I would say that the self becomes transformed by contact with a sense of others as that distinctive kind of limit to the will that shows itself when someone says, 'I cannot do this,' and which is interdependent with the idea that this person, like every other, is inalienably precious, or possesses inalienable dignity. The reason I say it is interdependent with that idea rather than that it is based on it, is because though it is tempting to say, 'I cannot do this *because* this person, like every other, is inalienably precious,' in fact, for a person to be such a limit to the will *is part of what it means* to say that he or she is inalienably precious. Or, to put in another way: the way our moral values and the necessities and impossibilities intrinsic to them matter to us is not explained by a morally neutral psychology of identity; the constitution of our moral identity is, in irreducible part, explained by our contact with values and impossibilities and necessities that are sui generis. The same is true, as I said earlier, of ethically inflected ways of speaking of human beings, as we do when we speak of seeing or failing to see someone as fully human. These ways of speaking of human beings do not provide reasons (in any uncomplicated or simple sense) for not being able to act in this or that way. That one cannot act in this way – cannot refuse someone a burial, for example – is part of what it means to see someone as a human being.

When I contrasted ethical impossibility with psychological impossibility – with anything that we could be asked to try to overcome, even if that means gradually, with a strategy or therapy, for example – I did not mean to imply that psychology had nothing to say about it. It might, especially about its early development. But it will not show it to be really the same kind of impossibility as the kind I identified as 'psychological.' Ethical necessities are, as I said earlier, modalities sui generis: they transform our understanding of the mutually constitutive sense of self and other, of what Martin Buber called the transformative sense of coming to see another as Thou, and myself as I to her Thou. I mention Buber because he influenced the 'humanistic psychology' that attracted me as a student, and is, I know, the kind that attracts you.

In much of my work I have emphasised that to acknowledge fully the reality of another human being is to see them as someone who can be wronged. I emphasise 'fully,' because I believe this understanding waxes and wanes and is often weak in us. That is why I have written so often of remorse as a bewildered realisation, or remembrance, of what it means to wrong someone. What have I done? How could I have done it? I suggested in my answer to

AFTERWORD

your first question that we should take these lamentations as expressing the realisation of what it means to have wronged someone, rather than simply the emotional reaction to having done so. The person wronged suffers not only the physical and psychological harm caused to them, but also the fact of having been wronged, a fact that is an irreducible source of torment to her and that could inspire pity in an onlooker – pity different from and not reducible to that felt for the physical and psychological harms. Remorse also expresses the horrified realisation of how terrible it is to have become that wrongdoer. That too, as Socrates said when he said that evildoers are *necessarily* miserable and pitiable, can be the focus of pity for the wrongdoer independently of any further consequence of his wrongdoing.

Think, for example, of a mother who sorrows for two of her children, one of who murdered the other. She sorrows for the son who is wronged, for the loss of his life, of course, but also because of the wrong he suffered, which is compounded by the fact that it was his brother who killed him. She also sorrows for the murderer that her other son became, not because he will be imprisoned or suffer other consequences of that sort, or because he suffers the pains of remorse, which he does not. Her sorrow focuses on the significance of his having become a murderer, and it is deepened by the fact that it appears not to matter to him. If he should become remorseful, then the pain of it would be the form of understanding what he is by virtue of what he did and was all along even though he had not even an inkling of it. The murderer, his victim and their mother come into contact with a value different in kind from anything we would include in psychology of human nature that was not itself morally informed.

These are all matters I have emphasised in my work. They are all part of its anti-reductionist impulses. But I have also emphasised that these ethical matters, though sui generis, are embedded in the natural conditions of a human life. That is why I emphasised – in *A Common Humanity* and even more so in *The Philosopher's Dog* – the importance to our understanding of the forms of the ethical, especially of morality, of the concept of a human being rather than the concept of a person or rational being. It is why I placed weight on a sense of a common humanity – rather than on a constituency of persons or rational beings united by their principles – and that the relevant sense of a common humanity depends on seeing all the peoples of the earth, different though their cultures may be, as striving for lucidity about what it means to be a mortal being, defined by sexuality, at every moment vulnerable to misfortune. In *The Philosopher's Dog*, I emphasised the importance of our creatureliness to our sense of our humanity. But in emphasising our creatureliness, I opposed the natural inclination to think that it is the sciences that will deepen our understanding of our creaturely nature and of what we have in common with other animals. I argued that science will best help us to deepen our understanding of what it means for us to be living things if it resists the temptation to look upon art as advancing that understanding only because it provides imaginative hypotheses that could, ideally, be extracted from their artistic form and presented to scientists and scientifically friendly philosophers to adjudicate their cognitive value. In that book I emphasised the importance of attending to what scientists are inclined to regard as mere surfaces — that we and some animals have faces, eyes to look into, that we are of flesh and blood and seek comfort from the warmth of other bodies.

In the projected book that you mention, I want to develop all that. I have spent long enough arguing the anti-reductionist case. I want now to deepen it by attending to what I may have wrongly taken to be expressions of reductionism. Essential to that development will be an assessment of what psychology, perhaps aided by evolutionary theory and neuroscience, can teach about the ethical circumstances of our lives, including the ethical contexts of psychotherapy.

I was educated in a philosophical tradition — though I always stood at a critical distance from it — that drew sharp distinctions between philosophical inquiry, which it deemed to be essentially conceptual, and scientific or other forms of empirical enquiry. I don't accept that sharp distinction. My attitude is partly to say, 'Let us see what science, including psychology, can deliver.' But, of course, what you think science has delivered will depend on your sense of what it has set out to illuminate and explain. If at the start you have a reductionist, or just a simplistic, understanding of the forms of the ethical, especially of morality you will not be alert to reductionism in science. As I have sometimes put it, if you have a crude enough idea of what it is to act for another then even ants will look altruistic.

A few years ago I was involved in a colloquium on forgiveness with one of Britain's top neuroscientists. It seemed as though two thousand years of reflection about it had passed him by. I feel the same when I read some evolutionary theory about compassion or altruism and think of the hundreds of years of discussion, reflection and debate on what it can mean to act for the sake of another, to have a sense of the reality of another.

My point is not that the neuroscientist had a limited understanding of the number and variety of hypotheses that the history of art and humane studies had made available to him. My point is — and it is the burden of my case in *The Philosopher's Dog* — that a deepened understanding of forgiveness,

AFTERWORD

of love and so on, must be sought in the realm of meaning, a distinctive cognitive realm, where, as I said earlier, form and content are inseparable. This is a realm in which the criticism that a claim is sentimental, or shows a tin ear for irony, or reveals a vulnerability to pathos – categories more often associated with literary judgment – should not be treated as though it merely directed us to a cause of a cognitive impairment of a kind that could be described independently of our vulnerability to such afflictions. If that were so, the claims that are criticised in such terms could be expressed, as Williams' philosophers think all cognitive claims should be expressed, in a language for which style mattered only for adornment or clarity. Your book *Motherhood* is a marvellous example of how to avoid these pitfalls, of how to get it right.

I also think that psychology has nothing to offer on the gap, as I characterised it, between the nun and the psychiatrists and the occupational therapist. Or, to our affirmation – to the extent that we feel compelled to make it – that we owe justice to every human being no matter how terrible their deeds or their characters, for their sake as human beings, rather than because we are afraid of the slippery slopes that open up if we come to regard someone as outside the constituency of a common humanity.

LIST OF CONTRIBUTORS

J.M. Coetzee was born in South Africa in 1940 and educated in South Africa and the United States. He has published thirteen works of fiction, as well as criticism and translations. Among awards he has won are the Booker Prize (twice) and, in 2003, the Nobel Prize for Literature. He lives in Adelaide.

Christopher Cordner teaches Philosophy at the University of Melbourne. His main area of philosophical interest is ethics. He is the author of *Ethical Encounter*, and of many articles in philosophical journals, as well as the editor of *Philosophy, Ethics and a Common Humanity: Essays in Honour of Raimond Gaita*.

Nick Drake wrote the screenplay for the film of *Romulus, My Father* (directed by Richard Roxburgh, starring Eric Bana), which won Best Film at the AFI awards. His poetry collections include *The Man in the White Suit* (winner of Waterstone's Best First Collection) and most recently *The Farewell Glacier*, a collection which grew out of a journey to the Arctic. He wrote the libretto for the opera *Between Worlds* (composer Tansy Davies), which will be produced at English National Opera in 2015, and he is adapting *White Mughals* by William Dalrymple for Ralph Fiennes to direct.

Miranda Fricker is Professor of Philosophy at the University of Sheffield. She is the author of *Epistemic Injustice: Power and the Ethics of Knowing*. She co-edited *The Cambridge Companion to Feminism in Philosophy* with Jennifer Hornsby; and she is co-author of *Reading Ethics*, written with Sam Guttenplan. Her main areas of interest are ethics, social epistemology, virtue epistemology, and those areas of feminist philosophy that focus on issues of power, social identity, and epistemic authority.

Barry Hill has won Premier's Awards for poetry, the essay, non-fiction and history. He is possibly best known for the biography *Broken Song: TGH Strehlow and Aboriginal Possession* which John Mulvaney described as 'one of the great Australian books.' He was post-doctoral fellow at the University of Melbourne in 2005–6 and Poetry Editor for *The Australian* between 1998 and 2008. His most recent poems, *Naked Clay: Drawing from Lucian Freud*, was short-listed for the UK's 2012 Forward Prize.

LIST OF CONTRIBUTORS

Geoffrey Brahm Levey is an Australian Research Council Future Fellow and Associate Professor in Political Science at the University of New South Wales. He was the foundation director of the UNSW Program in Jewish Studies. His publications include *Political Theory and Australian Multiculturalism* (as editor), *Secularism, Religion and Multicultural Citizenship* (edited with Tariq Modood) and *Jews and Australian Politics* (edited with Philip Mendes).

Anne Manne is a Melbourne writer who has been a columnist for *The Australian* and *The Age*, and has written many essays for *The Monthly* and other publications. The author of *Motherhood: How Should We Care for Our Children* (2005), *Love and Money: The Family and the Free Market* (2008), the memoir *So This Is Life: Scenes from a Country Childhood* (2009), her new book is *The Life of I: The New Culture of Narcissism*, Melbourne University Press, 2014.

Robert Manne is Emeritus Professor of Politics and Vice-Chancellor's Fellow at La Trobe University. Manne has written or edited twenty books including *The Petrov Affair*, *The Culture of Forgetting*, *In Denial: The Stolen Generations and the Right*, *Left, Right, Left*, *Making Trouble* and *Bad News*. His books and essays have won numerous awards. Between 1987 and 2004 he was a columnist on public affairs for both Fairfax and the Murdoch press and a regular commentator on ABC radio. Manne is a Fellow of the Academy of the Social Sciences in Australia.

Alex Miller's eleventh novel, *Coal Creek*, was published to wide critical acclaim in 2013. Alex is twice winner of the Miles Franklin Literary Award and an overall winner of the Commonwealth Writers Prize. He is also a recipient of the prestigious Melbourne Prize for Literature and numerous other awards, including The Manning Clark Award for an outstanding contribution to Australian cultural life. Alex lives with his wife Stephanie in the Victorian country town of Castlemaine, where he writes full-time.

Brigitta Olubas is Associate Professor of English at the University of New South Wales, President of ASAL (the Association for the Study of Australian Literature) and editor of the Association's scholarly journal *JASAL*. She has published widely in the fields of Australian literary and visual culture, including most recently, *Shirley Hazzard: Literary Expatriate and Cosmopolitan Humanist*, based on her Australian Research Council Discovery-funded research, and *Remembering Patrick White: Contemporary Critical Essays* (editor).

Helen Pringle is in the Faculty of Arts and Social Sciences at the University of New South Wales. Her research has been widely recognised by awards from Princeton University, the Fulbright Foundation, the Australian Federation of University Women, and the Universities of Adelaide, Wollongong and NSW. Her main fields of expertise are human rights, ethics in public life, and political theory.

Emeritus Professor **Dorothy Scott** OAM was the Foundation Chair and Director of the Australian Centre for Child Protection at the University of South Australia. She is also an honorary Professorial Fellow in Social Work at the University of Melbourne.

Gerry Simpson holds the Kenneth Bailey Chair of Law at Melbourne Law School, the University of Melbourne, where he is Director of the Asia Pacific Centre for Military Law, and Convenor of The Global Justice Studio. He is a Visiting Professor of Public International Law at the London School of Economics, where he held a Chair until 2009, and is currently an AFP/Open Society Fellow (based in Tbilisi, Georgia). He is the author of *Great Powers and Outlaw States* (awarded the American Society of International Law's annual prize for Pre-eminent Contribution to Creative Legal Scholarship in 2005 and translated into several languages).

Craig Taylor teaches Philosophy at Flinders University. He is the author of *Sympathy: A Philosophical Analysis*, *Moralism: A Study of a Vice* and numerous scholarly articles, as well as co-editor of *Hume and the Enlightenment*.

Steven Tudor is a senior lecturer in the Law School at La Trobe University, with an academic background in both Philosophy and Law. His research interests include the intersections of emotions, ethics and law. In addition to various articles in academic journals, his publications include *Remorse: Psychological and Jurisprudential Perspectives*, co-authored with Dr Michael Proeve, and *Compassion and Remorse*.

BIBLIOGRAPHY

Aelred of Rievaulx. 2010. *Spiritual Friendship*, edited by Marsha L. Dutton and translated by Lawrence C. Braceland. Collegeville, Minn: Liturgical Press.

Akhmatova, Anna. 1992. *Complete Poems*, translated by Judith Hemschemeyer. 2nd ed. Boston: Zephyr Press.

Al-Ghazali. 1976. *On the Duties of Brotherhood*, translated by Muhtar Holland. Woodstock: Overlook Press.

Arendt, Hannah. 1965. *Eichmann in Jerusalem: A Report on the Banality of Evil*. Revised ed. Harmondsworth: Penguin Books.

Barthes, Roland. 2010. *Mourning Diary*, New York: Hill and Wang.

Bielenberg, Christabel. [1968] 2011. *The Past is Myself* with *The Road Ahead*. London: Corgi Books.

Benedict XVI. 2005. Encyclical Letter, *Deus caritas est*. Accessed 8 October 2013. http://www.vatican.va/holy_father/benedict_xvi/encyclicals/documents/hf_ben-xvi_enc_20051225_deus-caritas-est_en.html.

Blanchot, Maurice. 1997. *Friendship*, translated by Elizabeth Rottenberg. Stanford: Stanford University Press.

Blair, Tony. 2004. Speech delivered at Sedgefield (5 March).

Bloom, Harold. 2002. *Genius: A Mosaic of One Hundred Exemplary Creative Minds*. New York: Warner.

Brandt, Richard B. 1996. *Facts, Values, and Morality*. Cambridge: Cambridge University Press.

Broackes, Justin, ed. 2012. *Iris Murdoch, Philosopher*. Oxford: Oxford University Press.

Bull, Hedley. 2002. *The Anarchical Society: A Study of Order in World Politics*. New York: Columbia University Press.

Castles, Stephen. 2001. 'Multiculturalism in Australia'. In *The Australian People: An Encyclopedia of the Nation, its People and their Origins*, edited by James Jupp. Cambridge: Cambridge University Press, 807–811.

Catullus, Gaius Valerius. 1978. *The Poems of Catullus*, translated by Frederic Raphael and Kenneth McLeish. London: J. Cape.

Cicero, Marcus Tullius. 1887. *De Amicitia (On Friendship)*, translated by Andrew P. Peabody. Boston: Little, Brown, and Company.

—— 1913. *On Duties (De Officiis)*, translated by Walter Miller. Cambridge: Harvard University Press.

Cocking, Dean, and Jeanette Kennett. 2000. 'Friendship and Moral Danger'. *Journal of Philosophy* 97 (5): 278–296.

Commonwealth of Australia. 1999. *A New Agenda for Multicultural Australia*. Canberra: AGPS.

Critchley, Simon. 2006. 'Forgetfulness Must: Politics and Filiation in Blanchot and Derrida'. *Parallax* 12 (2): 12–22.

Derrida, Jacques. 2005. *The Politics of Friendship*, translated by George Collins. London: Verso.

———2001. *The Work of Mourning*, edited by Pascale-Anne Brault and Michael Naas. Chicago: University of Chicago Press.

———1994. *Spectres of Marx: The State of the Debt, the Work of Mourning and the New International*. London and New York: Routledge.

Dogen. 1985. *Moon in a Dewdrop: Writings of Zen Master Dogen*, edited by Kazuaki Tanahashi. San Francisco: North Point Press.

Dostoyevsky, Fyodor. [1868] 2004. *The Idiot*, translated with notes by David McDuff. London: Penguin.

Duff, R.A. 2009. *Answering for Crime: Responsibility and Liability in the Criminal Law*. Oxford: Hart Publishing.

Eaton, George. 2012. 'Meet Miliband's new guru: Tim Soutphommasane'. *New Statesman*. Accessed 8 August, www.newstatesman.com/blogs/politics/2012/08/meet-milibands-new-guru-tim-soutphommasane.

Fiske, Adele. 1965. 'Paradisus Homo Amicus.' *Speculum* 40 (3): 426–459.

Gaita, Raimond. 1998. *Romulus, My Father*. Melbourne: Text Publishing.

———1999. *A Common Humanity: Thinking About Love and Truth and Justice*. Melbourne: Text Publishing.

———2002. *The Philosopher's Dog*, Melbourne: Text Publishing.

———2004a. 'Breach of Trust: Truth, Morality and Politics'. *Quarterly Essay* 16: 1–68.

———2004b. *Good and Evil: An Absolute Conception*, 2nd edition. London: Routledge.

———2007. 'Romulus, My Father: From Book to Screenplay to Film'. In Nick Drake. *Romulus, My Father: Screenplay*. Sydney: Currency Press, vii–xxiv.

———2008. 'The Pedagogical Power of Love.' Accessed 28 January 2014, http://alumni.cfsnc.org/page.cfm?p=636

———2011a. *After Romulus*. Melbourne: Text Publishing.

———2011b. 'Multiculturalism, Love of Country and Responses to Terrorism'. In *Essays on Muslims and Multiculturalism*, edited by Raimond Gaita. Melbourne: Text Publishing, 187–220.

Gillard, Julia. 2012. 'Introductory Remarks by Prime Minister of Australia, the Hon Julia Gillard MP', Australian Multicultural Council Lecture, Parliament House, Canberra, 9 September.

Gordon, Milton. 1964. *Assimilation in American Life*. Oxford: Oxford University Press.

Grahame, Kenneth. 1908. *The Wind in the Willows*. New York: Charles Scribner's Sons.

Hage, Ghassan. 1998. *White Nation: Fantasies of White Supremacy in a Multicultural Society*. Sydney: Pluto Press.

Hamilton, Carolyn. 1995. *Family, Law and Religion*. London: Sweet and Maxwell.

Han-Shan. 2013. *Cold Mountain Poems*, translated by Gary Snyder. Berkeley, CA: Counterpoint.

Harrison, Robert. 1994. *The Dominion of the Dead*. Chicago: University of Chicago Press.

Heaney, Seamus. 1975. *North*. London: Faber.

Hill, Barry. 2008. *As We Draw Ourselves*, Parkville, Vic: Five Islands Press.

Hirst, John. 2009. *Sense and Nonsense in Australian History*. Melbourne: Black Inc.

Hobbes, Thomas. [1651] 1996. *Leviathan*, edited by Richard Tuck. Cambridge: Cambridge University Press.

BIBLIOGRAPHY

Holmes, Richard. 1974. *Shelley: The Pursuit*. London: Weidenfeld and Nicolson.

Jones, Gail. 2006. 'A Dreaming, A Sauntering: Reimagining Critical Paradigms'. *JASAL* 5. Accessed 28 January 2014, http://www.nla.gov.au/openpublish/index.php/jasal/article/viewArticle/95.

Kallen, Horace. 1924. *Culture and Democracy in the United States*. New York: Boni and Liveright.

Kant, Immanuel. [1785] 1997. *Groundwork of the Metaphysics of Morals*, translated and edited by Mary Gregor. Cambridge: Cambridge University Press.

——[1790] 1952. *The Critique of Judgement*, translated by J.C. Meredith. Oxford: Clarendon Press.

——[1795] 1983. *Perpetual Peace*. Indianapolis, IN: Hackett.

——[1797] 1991. *The Metaphysics of Morals*, translated by Mary Gregor. Cambridge: Cambridge University Press.

Keats, John. 1968. *Letters*, selected by Frederick Page. Oxford: Oxford University Press.

Kierkegaard, Søren. [1843] 1985. *Fear and Trembling*, translated by Alastair Hannay. Harmondsworth: Penguin.

Koskenniemi, Martti. 2006. *From Apology to Utopia: The Structure of Legal Argument*. Cambridge: Cambridge University Press.

——2012a. 'International Law in the World of Ideas'. In *The Cambridge Companion to International Law*, edited by James Crawford and Martti Koskenniemi. Cambridge: Cambridge University Press, 47–63.

——2012b. 'Law, Teleology and International Relations: An Essay in Counterdisciplinarity.' *International Relations* 26 (1): 3–34.

The Lankavatara Sutra: A Zen Text. 2012. Translation and commentary by Red Pine. Berkeley, CA: Counterpoint.

Le Carré, John. 1986. *A Perfect Spy*. New York: Knopf.

Levey, Geoffrey Brahm. 2014. 'Liberal Nationalism and the Australian Citizenship Tests'. *Citizenship Studies* 18: 2 (2014): 175–189.

Lewis, C.S. 1960. *The Four Loves*. New York: Harcourt, Brace.

Lopez, Mark. 2000. *The Origins of Multiculturalism in Australian Politics 1945–75*. Melbourne: Melbourne University Press.

Mann, Thomas. 1960. *Magic Mountain*, translated by Helen Tracy Lowe-Porter. Harmondsworth: Penguin.

Marrus, Michael R. 1997. *The Nuremberg War Crimes Trials 1945–1946: A Documentary History*. New York: Bedford/St. Martin's.

Maughan, Philip. 2013. 'Rowan Williams: Sharia Law Question "Still Pertinent"'. *The New Statesman*. Accessed 5 June: www.newstatesman.com/politics/2013/06/rowan-williams-sharia-law-question-still-pertinent.

Millgram, Elijah. 2004. 'Kantian Crystallizations.' Ethics 114: 3 (2004): 511–513.

——2005. *Ethics Done Right*. Cambridge: Cambridge University Press.

Modood, Tariq. 2007. *Multiculturalism: A Civic Idea*. Cambridge: Polity.

Morgenstern, Oskar. 1971. 'Morgenstern's Account of Kurt Gödel's Naturalization', 13 September, personal document, Shelby White and Leon Levy Archives Center, Institute for Advanced Study, Princeton, NJ.

Murdoch, Iris. 1970. *The Sovereignty of Good*. London: Routledge and Kegan Paul.

———1997. 'The Sublime and the Beautiful Revisited'. In *Existentialists and Mystics: Writings on Philosophy and Literature*, edited by Peter Conradi. Harmondsworth: Penguin Books.
National Multicultural Advisory Council [NMAC], 1999. *Australian Multiculturalism for a New Century: Towards Inclusiveness*. Canberra: AGPS.
Nehamas, Alexander. 2010. 'The Good of Friendship'. *Proceedings of the Aristotelian Society* 110 (3): 267–294.
Oakeshott, Michael. 1977. *Rationalism and Other Essays*. London: Methuen.
Office of Multicultural Affairs [OMA]. 1989. *National Agenda for a Multicultural Australia*, Canberra: AGPS.
Olubas, Brigitta. 2007. 'Truth, Writing and National Belonging in *Romulus, My Father*'. *Australian Humanities Review* 43. Accessed 28 January 2014, http://www.australianhumanitiesreview.org/archive/Issue-December-2007/Olubas.html.
Orsuto, Donna Lynn. 2006. 'The Harmony of Love: "Idem velle atque idem nolle"'. In *The Way of Love: Reflections on Pope Benedict XVI's Encyclical*, Deus Caritas Est, edited by Livio Melina and Carl A. Anderson. San Francisco: Ignatius Press.
Plato. 1892. *Lysis, or Friendship*. In *The Dialogues of Plato*, vol. 1, translated by Benjamin Jowett. Oxford: Oxford University Press.
Podhoretz, Norman. 1999. *Ex-Friends: Falling Out with Allen Ginsberg, Lionel and Diana Trilling, Lillian Hellman, Hannah Arendt, and Norman Mailer*. New York: Free Press.
Potter, Dennis. 1988. *Christabel*. London: Faber and Faber.
Ratzinger, Joseph Cardinal. 2004. 'The End of Time'. In *The End of Time? The Provocation of Talking about God: Proceedings of a Meeting of Joseph Cardinal Ratzinger, Johann Baptist Metz, Jürgen Moltmann, and Eveline Goodman-Thau in Ahaus*, edited by Tiemo Rainer Peters and Claus Urban; English edition translated and edited by J. Matthew Ashley. Mahwah, NJ: Paulist Press.
———2005. *Homily Pro Eligendo Romano Pontifice*, addressed to the College of Cardinals, 18 April, Vatican Basilica. Accessed 8 October 2013, http://www.vatican.va/gpII/documents/homily-pro-eligendo-pontifice_20050418_en.html.
Rawls, John. 2001. *The Law of Peoples: With, The Idea of Public Reason Revisited*. Harvard: Harvard University Press.
Rogers, Robert. 1959. 'The Emperor's Displeasure – amicitiam renuntiare'. *Transactions and Proceedings of the American Philological Association* 90: 224–237.
Rosenberg, John D. 1961. *The Darkening Glass: A Portrait of Ruskin's Genius*, New York and London: Columbia University Press.
Ruskin, John. 1988. *Ruskin Today*, chosen and annotated by Kenneth Clark. Harmondsworth: Penguin.
Saint-Pierre, Charles Iréneé Castel de. [1713] 2009. *Projet Pour Rendre La Paix Perpetuelle en Europe*. Kessinger Publishing.
Sallust. [1921]. *De coniuratione Catilinae*. In *War with Catiline, War with Jugurtha, Selections from the Histories. Doubtful Works*, translated by J.C. Rolfe. Cambridge: Harvard University Press.
Scanlon, T.M. 2008. *Moral Dimensions: Permissibility, Meaning, Blame*, Cambridge MA: Belknap Press of Harvard University Press.

BIBLIOGRAPHY

Schmitt, Carl. 2003. *The Nomos of the Earth in the International Law of the Jus Publicum Europeaum*, New York, NY: Telos Press Publishing.

Schwartz, Daniel. 2007. *Aquinas on Friendship*. Oxford: Clarendon Press.

Scott, Evelyn. 2000. 'The Importance of Reconciliation for Multiculturalism'. Speech at the Multicultural Extravaganza Dinner, Logan Diggers Club, 7 October. Accessed 28 January 2014, www.austlii.edu.au/au/other/IndigLRes/car/2000/0710.html.

Sereny, Gitta. 1999. *Cries Unheard: The Story of Mary Bell*. London: Macmillan.

Shelley, Percy Bysshe. 1847. *The Complete Works of Percy Bysshe Shelley*, edited by Mrs. Shelley, Vol. 2. London: Edward Moxon.

Simone, Nina. 'Who Knows Where the Time Goes?'. Accessed 8 October 2013. Available from: http://www.youtube.com/watch?v=OXeh742_jak.

Simpson, Gerry. 2012. 'Atrocity, Law, Humanity'. In *Cambridge Companion to Human Rights Law*, edited by Conor Gearty and Costas Douzinas. Cambridge: Cambridge University Press, 114–133.

Singer, Peter. 1993. *Practical Ethics*, 2nd ed. Cambridge: Cambridge University Press.

Snyder, Gary. 1990. *The Practice of the Wild*. New York: North Point Press.

Soutphommasane, Tim. 2009. *Reclaiming Patriotism*. Melbourne: Cambridge University Press.

Taylor, Craig. 2012. *Moralism: A Study of a Vice*. Durham: Acumen.

Tolstoy, Leo. 2009. *The Death of Ivan Ilyich and Other Stories*, translated by Richard Pevear and Larissa Volokhonsky. London: Vintage.

Velleman, J. David. 2006. 'Love as a Moral Emotion'. In *Self to Self: Selected Essays*. Cambridge: Cambridge University Press.

Whitman, Walt, 1973. *Leaves of Grass*, edited by Sculley Bradley and Harold W. Blodgett, New York.

Wight, Martin. 1960. 'Why Is There No International Theory?'. *International Relations* 2: 35–48.

Williams, Rowan. 2008. 'Archbishop's Lecture – Civil and Religious Law in England: A Religious Perspective', lecture presented at the Royal Courts of Justice, 7 February: http://rowanwilliams.archbishopofcanterbury.org/articles.php/1137/archbishops-lecture-civil-and-religious-law-in-england-a-religious-perspective.

Wolf, Susan. 2011. 'Blame, Italian Style'. In *Reasons and Recognition: Essays on the Philosophy of T. M. Scanlon*, edited by R. Jay Wallace, Rahul Kumar and Samuel Freeman. Oxford: Oxford University Press.

Xingjian, Gao. 2006. *The Case for Literature*. Sydney: Fourth Estate.